MY EPICUREAN JOURNEY

Elegant and Inspirational Recipes for Life

by Harminder Singh Magon

◆ FriesenPress

Suite 300 - 990 Fort St
Victoria, BC, Canada, V8V 3K2
www.friesenpress.com

ISBN
978-1-4602-7451-4 (Hardcover)
978-1-4602-7452-1 (Paperback)
978-1-4602-7453-8 (eBook)

1. Cooking, Courses & Dishes

Distributed to the trade by The Ingram Book Company

DEDICATION

I AM DEDICATING THIS BOOK TO MY DEAR FATHER SARDAR KARTAR SINGH, ONE OF THE MOST GENTLE and an extremely humble soul who left us all at a very early age and secondly, my grandfather Baba Isher Singh Magon, rather a strict but, disciplined and a very principled man that I ever knew.

This dedication comes with all my love and gratitude, without their guidance and commitment to good culinary delights, this book would not have been possible.

These two giants and true foodie souls were the greatest inspiration for me who influenced me at a very early age to get me into the kitchen to cook and explore the wonderful world of exotic cuisines. It was only a natural progression that their wisdom and passion for food compelled me to author this book as a tribute and a legacy in their memory for our children and grandchildren to enjoy for decades to come. It is my earnest desire to see my family's younger generation to keep this tradition alive through their kitchens and share the fruits of their devotion with all around them.

I learnt from my parents that to become a master in any skill, it takes the total effort of your soul, mind and heart working together in harmony, just like the musicians in a concert creating magic. Similarly, a chef has to be the conductor who must have total control over all the ingredients, flavors and aromas to create a perfect harmony and symphony in his/her pots and pans.

My father often used to say that there are no secrets to successful cooking, never feel disappointed if you fail, re-set your goals and go after them with all your strength, determination and tenacity you can gather and at the end, your efforts will be well rewarded and take you places that will amaze you. And always remember that if you have made mistakes, even serious ones, there is always another chance for you to fix it. What we call failure is not the falling down, but the staying down. When you rise to excel in any task be completely committed and dedicated, but above all be willing to accept constructive criticism.

Dear dad the little time I spent with you in my early childhood, I learnt a lot from your cooking techniques, hints and tips. You shared the families heirloom recipes and I am so glad for what you did as I can keep them alive for our future generations to come. I am sure you are always watching me whenever I am cooking and keep a keen eye on me to ensure that I am not disappointing you. Thanks dad you will always be remembered.

Contents

Badami Jalpari
Raj Kachori
Greek-Style Appetizers
Grilled Vegetables
With Peanut Sauce
Malai Murgh Kebab
Mishkaki (Nyama Choma)
Chicken And Mushroom Parcels
Pakoras
Shahi Malai Tikkas
Chana Daal Wadas
Chicken Wings À La Mag
Dhebras
Thai Chili Chicken Wings
Chapli Kebabs
Fried Chicken In Pandanus Leaves
Island Crab Cakes
Bite-Sized Side Ribs
Fried Tofu With Peanut Sauce
Kenyan-Style Meat Samosas
Hakka Fish Pakoras
Paneer Tikkas
Vegetable Samosas
Sweet Corn Patties
Japanese-Style Chili Fried Jumbo Shrimp
Refreshing Fresh Fruit Chaat

Tillie Aloo Tikki
Ultimate Potato Wedges
Chicken Pakoras
Grilled Mogho
Homemade Spring Rolls
Rice Paper Shrimp Salad Rolls
Chicken Satay

Mag's Crab Bisque
Tom Yum Soup
Mulligatawny Soup
Seafood Chowder
With Baby Clams
Vegetarian Tom Yum Soup
Warm Corn Salsa
Khao Soi
Creamy Green Salad Dressing
Cranberry Salad Dressing
Vietnamese Pho
Spicy Snow Crab And Asparagus Soup
Pomegranate Salsa
Kachumbar
Mango Salsa
Fresh Garden Salad With Roasted Red Pepper Dressing
Cucumber Salad
Baby Spinach Salad With Mango Shavings
Spicy Chicken Salad
Caesar Salad
Mache Leaf Salad With Mango And A Wicked Dressing
Mache Leaf Salad With Mango, Mushrooms, And Radish
Quick Pickled Carrots

Coriander Chutney
Tamarind Chutney
Pudina Chutney
Hot Peri Peri Butter Sauce
Cucumber Raita
Thai Chili Sauce
Fresh Lemon-Ginger Chili Pickle
Mag's Extra-Hot Chili Oil
Horseradish Sauce

Malaysian Peanut Sauce

Mag's Garlic Sauce

Passion Fruit Sauce

Tangy Chili Seafood Sauce

Tartar Sauce

Thai Dipping Sauce

Park Road Tomato Sauce

Ultimate Meatless Pasta Sauce For Vegetarians

Homemade Sriracha Sauce

Thai Chicken Fried Rice

Jeera Rice

Ugali

Buddha's Biryani

Mag's Special Lamb Biryani

Wild Rice Pilaf With Pecans And Shiitake Mushrooms

Rice Pilaf With Peas

Phulka

Exotic Spicy Shrimp Pilaf

Mandazi

My Ultimate Paella

Tandoori Roti

Tandoori Naan

Zafrani Zarda

Handvo-Style Corn Bread

Lachedar Paratha

Poori

Drunkard's Noodles

Missi Roti

Gobi Paratha

Ultimate Pad Thai With Meat And Shrimp

Thai-Style Noodles

Spicy Hakka Noodles With Meat And Shrimp

Ambarsari-Style Fish Pakoras

Garlic Shrimp And Scallops In Spicy Sauce

Ambarsari Masala Fish

Pineapple Shrimp Curry

Jumbo Shrimp In A Light Spicy Cocunut Curry
Sauce With Squash And Yellow Zucchini

Mussels In Kaffir Lime And Lemongrass Sauce

Alaskan King Crab Legs In A Spicy Garlic-Gingercurried Glaze
Baked Pacific Salmon With Dill-Garlic Sauce
Coastal Fish Kofta Curry
Manchurian Chili Pepper Fish
Spicy Yellow Curry Coconut Mussels
Pan-Seared Ginger-Glazed Mahi-Mahi Steaks
Pan-Seared Tilapia
Pan-Seared Red Snapper In Spicy Orange Sauce
Penne Rigate In Mustard Mushroom Sauce With Shrimp
Seafood Medley In Mustard Mushroom Cream Sauce With Shrimp
Farfalle In Mustard Mushroom Sauce With Shrimp
Peri Peri Buttered Grilled Shrimp
Lobster In A Light Spicy Coconut Curry Sauce
Alaskan King Crab Legs In Black Bean Sauce
Spicy Black Pepper Crab In Garlic-Ginger Sauce
Mama Sarge's Bajan Fish And Chips
Lobster Thermidor
Shrimp Zanzibari
Poached Pacific Salmon With Dill And Pink Peppercorn Sauce

MEAT 143

Khumb Mattar Korma Curry With Cashews
Manchurian Tofu
Medley Of Sweet Baby Peppers With Mushrooms And Onions
Pav Bhaaji
Shahi Mattar Paneer Curry
Spiced Bhindi With Piaz
Stuffed Baby Eggplants, Sweet Peppers, And Lady's-Fingers
Ultimate Pep Curry
Toor Daal
Vegetarian Frittata

DESSERTS. 237

Badami Mango Kulfi
Gajrella
Paneer Barfi
Thai-Style Bananas With Ice Cream
Chiang Mai Pancakes
Motichoor Ke Ladoo
Shahi Kheer
Gulab Jamun
Tropical Fruit In Ginger Sauce
Mango Ice Cream Parfait
Tiramisu
Trifle
Viking Lychees
Sharife Ki Kulfi
Badami Halwa
Kesari Balushahis

INTRODUCTION

MY GRANDFATHER GREW UP IN PUNJAB IN NORTHERN INDIA, THE LAND OF FIVE RIVERS, WHOSE history has produced a colourful cultural palette; unique art forms, architecture, and music; and indeed some of the finest Asian cuisine. The people from this particular region of India love to eat, drink, and enjoy life.

As a young man, my grandfather had a passion for adventure and travel. In the early 1900s, this passion brought this young merchant to Nairobi, Kenya. By 1926, he was well established as one of the prominent businessmen in the country and later went on to raise a large family.

From my early childhood, I was introduced to the fine and refined tastes of Punjabi cuisine. Some of the delicacies that I enjoyed were centuries old and had originated during the Moghul era, from the early sixteenth century to the mid-1700s, when powerful Moghul warlords ruled northern India.

Every evening after a hard day's work in the family business, my grandfather and father looked forward to perfection in their evening meals. We grew up in a joint family, where my mother and my aunts were charged with preparing the food and had to face the daily challenges of meeting the high standards my grandfather set for his meals.

Another challenge lay in blending the native tastes of East Africa with the European cuisine of the day, without sacrificing the unique spices and sauces of the Punjab. So fusion cooking had been practiced for a long time in our household. The fact that my mother was born in Sumatra and had been raised in Bangkok, Thailand, added yet another flavourful dimension to our palates.

After completing high school, I went to India to further my studies. During my three years there, I experienced the authentic tastes of Indian foods from all over the country. It was an extraordinary experience in the culinary traditions that were as varied as that nation's fifteen different languages spoken in over 250 dialects.

I returned to Kenya with a wealth of new Indian culinary techniques, traditions, and ideas. However, my stay there was short-lived, as I decided to move yet again to another country, prompted in part by the same paternal kindling of travel and adventure that had brought my family to Kenya in the first place.

So, in the mid-1960s, I moved to Saskatoon, Saskatchewan, in central Canada where I quickly learned that I was ill-equipped for such a great culture shock. Bitter-cold winters on the prairies found me surviving on hamburgers, hot dogs, French fries, pizza, chop suey, and egg rolls. As a new immigrant to Canada, I was consuming a very unhealthy fast-food diet, because at that time, no restaurant offered the foods that I had grown up eating.

Soon I grew weary of bland burgers and started to cook my own meals using the skills I had learned in Kenya from my parents and from the cook in India who used to prepare food for me.

Surprisingly, it wasn't easy to find the ingredients that I needed for my kind of cooking, and I remember driving more than sixteen hours from Saskatoon to Vancouver just to stock up on my supply of Indian groceries. But I could hardly drive to the west coast of Canada every time I ran low on my cooking needs. I soon learned to improvise and to replicate the various flavours and tastes. I also learned how not to be discouraged when I could not find ingredients and would simply be bold and brave in using substitutes.

During my years in Saskatoon, my culinary expertise was further influenced by many different cultures, namely those of Europe and especially that of the French. This new abundance of cooking skills encouraged me to venture into a gourmet style of cooking rather than embrace the "curries in a hurry" type of dishes.

In the 1980s, I hosted a television show called Cook with Mag, (Mag being my nickname) featuring international cuisine with a twist using both authentic and fusion styles. My nickname had been given to me by my first-ever workplace manager in Saskatoon, and the show was a great success and was broadcast for more than nine years. l also taught Asian cooking classes at the Confederation Park Community Centre in Saskatoon.

While residing in Saskatoon, I also had the honor of cooking for some world-renowned celebrities. Among them were Pandit Ravi Shankar, the great sitar maestro; the late Ustad Alla Rakha and his son Ustad Zakir Hussain, both world-famous tabla players of the twentieth and twenty-first centuries; Pandit Jasraj; Ustad Vilayat Khan; Pandit Shivkumar Sharma; and the highly esteemed flutist Pandit Hariprasad Chaurasia. I also enjoyed cooking for Ghazal Kings Jagjit Singh and Ustad Ghulam Ali, as well as for dignitaries like the Honourable Balram Jakhar, the speaker of the upper house, Parliament of India, and Dr. Najma Heptulla, the speaker of the lower house and a future vice president of India.

I cooked for His Excellency, the late Sir Lionel Luckhoo, QC, Guyana's High Commissioner to the United Kingdom and an eminent criminal lawyer named in the Guinness Book of World Records; for Dr. Arnold Beckett, Anti-Doping Commissioner for the International Olympics Committee; and for several chief executive officers of prominent pharmaceutical companies in North America who visited Saskatoon.

Once again that paternal wanderlust struck. After twenty-three years as a long-range subdivision design planner with the City of Saskatoon, I moved to Ottawa in 1990 with my family to pursue a career in human rights. I decided to make my home in the national capital partly because it offered some of the finest restaurants and specialty food stores. Never again would I need to search for the special ingredients that I needed for my culinary delights. Every kind of epicurean flavour was to be had here. My inherited passion had achieved new heights.

Kenya may be famed for its pride in game reserves and safaris; however, its cuisine is less well known. Nyama choma and mboga na mchuzi are among its simple foods and are often accompanied by a staple diet that includes dishes such as ugali and sukuma wiki. Delicacies like kuku paka, samaki na viazi, mishkaki, lobster thermidor, scallops smothered in mango and ginger glaze, and oysters from Mombasa—these dishes have certainly influenced Indian and European cooking in East Africa.

In all these years away from Kenya, I have often been disappointed not to have found a restaurant or a cookbook that truly reflects the many cuisines that I have explored during my enchanting culinary journey. Often I have thought about how personally rewarding it would be for me to share these culinary experiences and maintain the legacy of my family's recipes.

Now I have realized that dream. I feel blessed and must admit that I have been truly inspired by my wife, Sona, who is a superlative cook. My son, nephews, nieces, and many friends have always been very supportive of my cuisine, given me the encouragement to create numerous delicacies, and have kept my passion alive and growing for decades. I am proud to offer this book for your cooking, reading, and eating pleasure. This collection of recipes is the first in a series around my personal culinary journey, and there will be more to come, for which specific topics are already cooking on the stove.

Above all, it is a great honor to share with you the legacy of my grandparents, parents, uncles, and aunts, who readily passed on to me the secrets and pleasures of exquisitely fine cuisine—their precious heirlooms.

THREE GOLDEN RULES IN COOKING

EVERY COOK'S GREATEST ASPIRATION IS TO ACHIEVE A PERFECT DISH AT THE END OF EVERY COOKING episode. Evidently such success results only when the dish meets the following three golden rules:

The food must look good.

The food must smell good.

The food must taste good.

In order to meet the above golden rules, the following factors must also be taken into account before embarking on preparing for any recipe:

CHOICE OF INGREDIENTS:

It is extremely important to always use fresh and seasonal ingredients for the best results. Equally important is to understand the properties and the characteristics of each ingredient—for example, its shelf life, its nutritional value, and any change of chemistry when the ingredient is exposed to temperature variations, etc.

When buying vegetables, they should be green, crisp, and young-looking. Never buy withered, over-grown, or brownish produce.

Similarly, when buying meat, it's crucial that you get specific cuts for different delicacies and that the meat is fresh with a firm texture, lean without excessive fat, and odour-free. Always avoid buying pinkish meat.

When buying poultry, particularly chicken, remember that the weight of the bird plays a significant role in the preparation of different recipes.

PROPORTIONS AND QUANTITIES:

It is a known fact that Indian cuisine is prepared by using approximation and one's experience rather than exact proportions and quantities. For this very reason, one should pay close attention to the usage of the right proportions and quantities for each of the ingredients used in a recipe.

For example, when cooking rice dishes, the proportion is always two parts of boiling water to one part of rice. Any deviation from this rule may result in raw or sticky rice.

Excessive use of chilies or strong spices in a dish may ruin it completely. Similarly, in any recipe that calls for yogurt, its excessive use would make it very sour and unappetizing. Always remember that spicy ingredients are supposed to enhance flavours, not kill them by being overpowering.

SEQUENCE OF COOKING:

The sequence of cooking is most crucial in creating perfect dishes. Never attempt to cut corners or take the easy way out. If the recipe calls for onions to be browned first, adding any whole or ground spices or tomatoes to the onions before they achieve the required colour would surely change the taste and flavour of the food for the worse.

Often cooks have a tendency in their haste to add all the ingredients into cold oil or butter at the same time. This results in a disaster, a dish that does not have any appeal for taste or flavour.

Another example is when marinating meat: If oil is added first before garlic and other seasonings, the oil acts as a sealant and restricts the meat from absorbing any flavours or seasonings. This results in the meat tasting bland. Marinating is a common practice in tenderizing meat; if the appropriate sequence is not followed, the meat may remain tough and chewy after cooking.

MY EPICUREAN JOURNEY

GLOSSARY OF SOUTH ASIAN CULINARY TERMS

Achar – Pickle

Adrak – Ginger root

Ajwain – Carom seeds

Akhrot – Walnuts

Aloo – Potato

Aloo bukhara – Dried plum

Aloo ki tikki – Potato cutlet

Amchoor – Dried sour mango powder

Anardana – Dried pomegranate seeds

Atta – Whole-wheat flour

Badam – Almonds

Badami – Dishes prepared with almonds or almond sauce

Badi elaichi – Black cardamom pods

Baingan – Eggplant

Bandh gobi – Cabbage

Bara jhinga – Jumbo shrimp/Lobster

Basmati – Fragrant long-grain rice from India or Pakistan

Besan – Ground chickpea flour/Gram flour

Bharwaan – Stuffed

Bhatura – Deep-fried bread made with all-purpose flour

Bhindi – Okra/Lady's-finger

Bhoona – Cooking technique combining braising and sautéing to a "dry" masala

Bhajia – Vegetable fritters, such as pakoras

Biryani – Layered rice dish with meat or vegetables

Boti kebab – Grilled marinated cubes of meat

Boondi – Tiny dumplings made from gram flour

Brinjal – Eggplant

Barfi – Fudge-like sweetmeat prepared with milk and nuts

Chai – Spicy Indian tea

Champan – Chops

Chana daal – Chickpeas hulled and split

Chana – Chickpeas

Chapati – Whole-wheat unleavened bread

Chaat – Spiced vegetables and fruits served as appetizers or light snacks

Chutney – Sweet and spicy sauce or relish

Chuara – Dry dates

Chawal – Rice

Cheeni – Granulated sugar

Choley – Chickpeas

Choti elaichi – Green cardamom pod

Dahin – Yogurt

Daal – Dry lentils

Dalchini – Cinnamon

Deggi mirch – Paprika from Kashmir

Dhaba – Roadside eatery common in India

Dhania – Coriander

Doodh – Milk

Dum – Method of sealed cooking

Elaichi – Cardamom

Gajar – Carrot

Garam masala – Mixture of ground aromatic spices

Ghee – Clarified butter

Gobi – Cauliflower

Gosht – Meat

Gulab jal – Rose water

Gulab jamun – Deep-fried milk balls soaked in sugar syrup

Haldi – Turmeric powder

Halwa – A rich, sweet fudge made with flour, semolina, nuts, and fruits

Hari mirch – Hot green chili peppers

Heeng/Hing – Asafoetida

Imli – Tamarind

Kale til – Black sesame seeds

Khajur – Date

Kesar/Zafran – Saffron

Jaggery – Unrefined cane sugar

Jaifal – Nutmeg

Javitri – Mace

Jeera – Cumin seeds

Jhinga – Shrimp

Kebab – Skewered meat cubes, fruits, or vegetables

Kadai – Wok

Kaddu – Pumpkin

Kaju – Cashews

Kala chana – Small black chickpeas

Kala jeera – Black cumin seeds

Kali mirch – Black peppercorns

Kalonji – Onion seeds

Kari patta – Curry leaves

Kasoori methi – Dried fenugreek leaves from Kasoor

Keema – Ground or minced meat

Kewda – Vetiver

Kheer – Indian rice pudding

Khus khus – White poppy seeds

Khoya – Milk cooked painstakingly until it is like fudge

Kishmish – Raisins

Kofta – Minced meat, fish, or vegetable balls

Korma – Rich braised curry made with yogurt

Kulcha – Leavened white-flour bread cooked in a tandoor

Kulfi – Rich Indian ice cream with nuts

Lachedar paratha – Layered pan-fried paratha

Lal mirch – Red chili pepper/Cayenne

Lasan – Garlic

Lassi – Sweet or savoury yogurt drink

Laung – Cloves

Machi – Fish

Magaz – Melon seeds

Makhani – Buttered and whisked with cream

Malai – Heavy cream

Masala – A blend of spices

Mattar – Peas

Mawa – Dried milk fudge, also known as khoya

Methi ka beej – Fenugreek seeds

Mirch – Pepper

Moghlai – Rich and spicy dishes from the era of the Moghuls

Moongphali – Peanuts

Moong daal – Green moong beans when whole, and yellow when hulled and split

Mulligatawny – Popular spicy Indian soup

Murgh – Chicken

Namak – Salt

Naan – Tear-shaped bread cooked in a tandoor

Narial – Coconut

Pakora – Vegetable, meat, or fish fritters

Palak – Spinach

Paneer – Fresh homemade Indian cottage cheese

Pani – Water

Papita – Pawpaw/Papaya

Papad/Papadum – Thin crackers made from spiced lentil dough

Paratha – Whole-wheat bread pan-fried with butter; can be flaky and stuffed

Phool gobi – Cauliflower

Phulka – Puffed-up whole-wheat leavened bread

Piaz – Onion

Pilau – Rice cooked in stock with meat or vegetables and nuts

Pista – Pistachio

Poori – Deep-fried leavened bread

Pudina – Mint

Rai – Mustard seeds

Rajma – Kidney beans

Russ – Soup, juice, or drippings

Rogan josh – Moghul-style lamb curry

Roti – Whole-wheat unleavened bread

Saag – Cooked spinach or greens

Safed jeera – White cumin seeds

Safed til – White sesame seeds

Samosa – Triangular pastry filled with spiced meat or vegetables

Sarson – Mustard greens

Saunf – Fennel

Seekh kebab – Spiced ground meat wrapped around skewers and grilled

Shalgam – Turnips

Shimla mirch – Green bell peppers

Sirka – Vinegar

Saunth – Sweet-and-sour chutney made with dried mangoes and sugar

Sooji – Semolina

Sukhi mirch – Dried red chili peppers

Tamatar – Tomato

Tamarind – Tart tropical fruit with sharp citrus flavour

Tandoor – Indian clay oven

Tandoori – Food BBQ'd in a tandoor

Tarka – Tempering and seasoning hot butter/oil with spices and onions

Tawa – Flat Indian griddle

Tej patta – Bay leaf

Thal – Large metal Indian platter

Thali – Metal dinner plate

Tikka – Cutlet

Varak – Edible thin silver or gold leaf used for garnishing festive foods

Vindaloo – Very hot meat curry dish originally from Goa and South India

CONVERSION GUIDE

KEY

fl oz = fluid ounce

gm = gram

kg = kilogram

lb = pound

lt = litre

ml = millilitre

qt = quart

oz = ounce

tbs = tablespoon

tsp = teaspoon

IMPERIAL WEIGHT	METRIC WEIGHT
½ oz	15 gm
1 oz	30 gm
2 oz	60 gm
3 oz	90 gm
4 oz (¼ lb)	125 gm
6 oz	185 gm
8 oz (½ lb)	250 gm
12 oz	375 gm
16 oz (1 lb)	500 gm
24 oz (1½ lb)	750 gm
32 oz (2 lb)	1000 gm (1 kg)
3 lb	1500 gm (1½ kg)
4 lb	2000 gm (2 kg)

IMPERIAL LIQUID MEASURES	CUP MEASURES	METRIC LIQUID MEASURES
1 fl oz		30 ml
2 fl oz	¼ cup	
3 fl oz		100 ml
4 fl oz (¼ pint US)	½ cup	
5 fl oz (¼ pint imp.)		150 ml
6 fl oz	¾ cup	
8 fl oz (½ pint US)	1 cup	250 ml
10 fl oz (½ pint imp.)	1¼ cups	
12 fl oz	1½ cups	
14 fl oz	1¾ cups	
16 fl oz (1 pint US)	2 cups	500 ml
20 fl oz (1 pint imp.)	2½ cups	
32 fl oz	4 cups	1 litre

OVEN TEMPERATURE CONVERSION GUIDE,			
Gas Mark	Celsius (°C)	Fahrenheit (°F)	Oven Heat
¼	100	200	Cool
½	120	250	Very slow
2	150	300	Slow
3	160	325	Moderately slow
4	180	350	Moderate
5	190	375	Moderately hot
6	200	400	Hot
8	230	450	Very hot

BASIC RECIPES

IT IS NO SECRET THAT SPICES, FRESHLY GROUND EACH DAY, ARE THE BASIS OF GOOD INDIAN COOKING. All spices have their own characteristics, and they are used in varying proportions to make the correct combination for a particular delicacy. The art and the magic lie in blending individual spices and herbs to create a plethora of dishes, each one distinctive and different. It is extremely important to know which spice or herb is most suited to a particular food. Once you understand this aspect of Indian cooking, you can create exotic dishes even when using something simple like potatoes.

Equally important to remember is that using the same combinations or the pre-packaged garam masala and curry powder can restrict your culinary adventures, as everything you cook will likely taste the same regardless of the different meat or vegetables you choose to use. Your creative ability to conjure up any new delicacy stagnates this way as well. For this very reason, there is absolutely no place in my kitchen for any packaged curry powder or garam masala that is easily available at most Indian stores.

You can make two kinds of basic masalas:

Wet masalas, which are in the form of a paste and are usually ground with water, vinegar, or oil.

Dry masalas, which are usually combinations of various spices used either whole or ground.

Most of the ingredients featured in my journey are readily available at most Indian stores and supermarkets. However, some can be made easily at home. The following are a few basic recipes:

PANEER:

In pot bring about 4 litres whole milk to a boil. Just as it starts to boil whisk in about 8 tbs lemon juice or vinegar. This will make milk curdle immediately. Remove pot from heat and strain curdled milk through muslin cloth, making sure that all moisture and whey are totally drained. By twisting muslin cloth, wrap paneer tightly inside and place a heavy weight or larger pot full of water on top of wrapped paneer for at least 3 hours. This will result in a nice block of paneer. Cut into desired number of pieces or cubes. Cubes can be lightly deep-fried and frozen for later use.

KHOYA:

In heavy-bottomed pot add 4 litres whole milk and bring to a boil. Reduce heat and cook, stirring occasionally until milk is reduced by half. Continue to cook and stir, scraping thickened milk from sides of pot until thick, paste-like consistency is formed. This will take approximately 2 hours or more. As it cools it will also solidify, and you may freeze it for future use.

GARAM MASALA:

Whereas Magon's special blend has sixteen different spices, this is a very basic recipe for garam masala. You may choose to use additional spices to enhance the flavours.

3 black cardamom pods
10 green cardamom pods
4 cloves
½ tsp black peppercorns
8 tsp cumin seeds
2 bay leaves
2 pieces cinnamon, about 2" long

Lightly roast above ingredients in shallow pan. Add roasted ingredients to blender and grind into fine or coarse powder. Store ground spice mixture in airtight jar and use as needed. It is always better to make smaller quantities of the masala, as it loses its flavour if stored for longer periods of time.

YOGURT:

Although commercially bought yogurt is readily available, it is fairly easy to make natural yogurt at home.

In pot, heat 2 litres whole milk to about 110°F, or until you can immerse your finger in milk for a few seconds without discomfort. Whisk about 4 tbs plain yogurt in 6 tbs warm milk and gently add to milk in pot. If you have yogurt culture you may use that instead of yogurt. Mix milk well, cover pot, wrap in towel, and place in draft-free space overnight or until yogurt is set. Refrigerate yogurt.

BROWN ONION PASTE:

Slice about 10 onions and stir-fry in oil until onions are golden brown.

Remove onions from pan and allow to cool. Grind cooled onions and store paste in airtight jar. You may wish to store some onions without grinding to use for rice delicacies.

GINGER PASTE:

Peel about 1 lb fresh ginger root, chop, and add to food processor. Pulsate until fine paste is formed. You may need to add a little water if necessary. Store paste in airtight container and refrigerate. Paste can be safely refrigerated for 1 month.

GARLIC PASTE:

Soak about 1 lb fresh garlic cloves in boiling water for about 30 minutes to loosen skin. Peel skin off, place cloves in food processor, and pulsate to form paste. Remove paste, store in airtight container, and refrigerate. Paste can be stored in refrigerator for at least 6 weeks.

RED CURRY PASTE:

10 small red chilies, dried, soaked in water
3 tbs shallots
1 tbs garlic paste
1 tsp galangal, chopped
2 tbs lemongrass, chopped
2 tsp kaffir lime leaves, chopped

2 tbs coriander leaves, chopped

10 black peppercorns

½ tsp roasted cumin seeds, ground

1 tsp shrimp paste

1 tsp salt

Add all ingredients to blender and grind into a paste. Store in jar and refrigerate. Shrimp paste is readily available at most Asian stores. If you wish to use fresh shrimp, just add 1 tsp soy sauce to paste.

GREEN CURRY PASTE:

12 finger hot green chili peppers

3 tbs shallots

1 tbs garlic paste

1 tsp galangal, chopped

2 tbs lemongrass, chopped

1 tsp kaffir lime leaves, chopped

1 tbs fresh coriander stems, chopped

1 tsp shrimp paste

1 tsp salt

Add all ingredients to blender and grind into a paste. Store in jar and refrigerate.

SWEET-AND-SOUR SAUCE:

In pot mix 1 cup ketchup, 1 cup white vinegar, 1 cup brown sugar, 1 tbs dark soy sauce, and 1 cup water. Mix all ingredients well and bring to a boil. Turn heat to medium and let sauce simmer for about 1 hour. Dissolve 1 tbs cornstarch in ¼ cup cold water and gently add to sauce. Bring sauce to a boil again, stirring constantly, and as soon as sauce starts to

thicken, turn heat off and use sauce as needed.

HOT SAUCE:

In pot add 1 cup white vinegar, 2 tbs hot red chili powder, ¼ tsp garlic paste, and ½ tsp salt. Mix all ingredients and bring to a boil. Turn heat to medium and simmer for about 15 minutes. Cool sauce and store in bottle. It makes an excellent Tabasco substitute.

MAG'S HOT CHILI OIL:

This is my signature chili sauce. In pot add ½ cup brown onion paste, 4 tbs fresh garlic paste, 1 cup crushed red chilies, 1 tbs salt, and 2 cups vegetable oil. Mix all ingredients well and cook on medium heat, stirring occasionally for about 1 hour. Cool chili oil and store in mason jar. You need not refrigerate this oil; it has a long shelf life.

WHITE WINE SAUCE:

In saucepan melt 2 tbs butter. Then add 2 tbs all-purpose flour and cook to form rue. Add 1 cup stock of your choice or 1 cup white wine and mix well. Slowly pour in 1 cup cream and stir gently until nice, smooth, thick sauce forms. Add salt and white pepper to taste. Mix and use in your favourite recipes.

CHANA DAAL WADAS

Wadas are basically
deep-fried lentil balls
and can be made
with practically any
kind of legume

Appetizers

Badami Jalpari

A RESTAURANT IN HALIFAX, NOVA SCOTIA, INSPIRED ME TO CREATE THIS RECIPE. I ENJOYED A PLAIN fillet of Pacific salmon crusted with pine nuts, pan-fried in butter, and served with some turned vegetables. Having found the fish somewhat bland for my taste, I decided to give it a little twist and add some zing to this recipe. So here is my variation, which should add some elegance to your next gathering of friends or family.

INGREDIENTS:

8 fish fillets (tilapia), cut into 2"x2"x1" pieces

Juice of 1 fresh lemon

1 tsp garlic paste

1 tsp ginger root paste

1 finger hot green chili pepper

2 tbs fresh coriander leaves, chopped

½ cup almond flakes

1 whole egg, beaten

4 tbs all-purpose flour

2 tbs cornstarch

Salt and pepper to taste

Vegetable oil for deep-frying

METHOD:

Squeeze juice of 1 lemon on fish, add salt and pepper, and mix well. Let fish marinate for about 30 minutes.

In grinder add chili pepper, garlic paste, ginger root paste, and coriander leaves. Pulsate mixture to a fine paste. Add paste to fish and mix well. Marinate for at least 3 hours at room temperature.

Add whole beaten egg, flour, and cornstarch to fish and mix well, ensuring that all fillets are evenly coated. In shallow dish spread almond flakes and gently dip each fillet in flakes individually to coat evenly. Carefully press flakes onto fillets to ensure that they bind well. Place fillets on flat sheet covered with wax paper. Do not place fillets on top of each other. Refrigerate fillets before frying (minimum 1 hour).

Heat oil in wok and fry fillets to a golden brown crispness. Do not overload wok with fillets when frying.

Serve fish piping hot with your favourite sauce or lemon wedges. You may use shrimp or any other fish fillet of your choice.

Raj Kachori

RAJ KACHORIS MAKE AN EXCELLENT EVENING SNACK, AND THIS VERSION IS VERY DIFFERENT FROM any other kachori you may have indulged in. My first ever experience enjoying this delicacy was in New Delhi, and believe you me it was nothing like what I had expected or tasted before.

Instead of the larger authentic raj kachoris, mine is a mini version made with gol gappe; thus, I call them sliders. The authentic raj kachori is a large, puffed-up poori. It is very crispy on the outside but soft inside, filled with several flavourful and delicious ingredients like soft pakodis, chanas, moong beans, potatoes, yogurt, and spices. It is topped with more whipped yogurt, sweet tamarind chutney, and chili or coriander chutney and finally garnished with finely chopped coriander and fine sev. Usually, one large kachori is enough for a filling snack; about eight of my mini kachoris are the equivalent.

To make this delicacy, there is hardly any cooking, only a tedious assembly. But these days no matter what part of the world you are in, every ingredient is available at most Indian grocery or food stores.

Brands like Haldiram's, Bikaneri, and Surti Foods, or any other that is available in your vicinity, make life easy! If you can prepare any of the items at home, however, I wholly recommend doing so.

INGREDIENTS:

32 gol gappe

1 cup potatoes, boiled and diced

1 cup plain chickpeas, cooked

1 cup besan boondi, soaked in warm water and squeezed

½ cup chat papdi mix

1 cup whipped yogurt

½ cup sweet-and-sour tamarind chutney

2 tbs hot coriander chutney

½ cup dhania, finely chopped

2 tbs green chilies, finely chopped

Good-quality chaat masala

½ cup fine sev

METHOD:

Arrange 4 quarter plates, place 4 gol gappe in middle, gently punch out holes in gol gappe, and fill each one with some potatoes, chickpeas, boondi, chaat papdi mix, and a hint of green chutney. Next, punch holes in all of remaining gol gappe, fill with same ingredients, and place them neatly on plate. Please note to stuff gol gappe with each ingredient and not overfill with just one.

Place 3 filled gol gappe on each of 4 gol gappe on plate, and then place 1 gol gappe on top of the three. Now you should have a pyramid on each plate. Garnish each plate with hot chili, coriander, and a sprinkle of chaat masala to taste. Finally, with spoon gently drizzle whipped yogurt on all gol gappe and then drizzle tamarind chutney on top. Just before serving, garnish each plate with the star of this kachori—the fine sev.

Greek-Style Appetizers

HERE WE HAVE ANOTHER SIMPLE, GREAT PICK-UP PARTY APPETIZER THAT MY GREEK NEIGHBOURS used to serve every time I went for a drink of Ouzo at their place.

Makes 24 appetizers.

INGREDIENTS:

3 tbs olive oil

½ tsp oregano

2 cloves garlic, crushed

3 English muffins, split into 6 halves

6 tomato slices

1 tbs red onion, minced

1 tbs black olives, sliced

2/3 cup feta cheese

METHOD:

Pre-heat oven to broil. Heat olive oil in saucepan.

Remove pan from heat and add garlic and oregano. Allow mixture to cool for 10 minutes. Strain mixture and save flavoured oil.

Place muffin halves on cookie sheet. Brush them with flavoured oil. Top each muffin with 1 tomato slice, onion, and olives. Sprinkle with cheese. Place muffins under broiler until cheese has melted (about 3 minutes). Cut each muffin into 4 wedges.

A dash of hot sauce or chili flakes on top of muffins adds a nice bite to these appetizers. Serve them warm.

Grilled Vegetables With Peanut Sauce

THIS IS AN EXCITING APPETIZER FOR VEGETARIANS. LEFTOVERS MAKE EXCELLENT WRAP SANDWICHES.

INGREDIENTS:

3 6"- to 8"-long Japanese eggplants, cut into 1" pieces

18 small white button mushrooms

12 metal or wooden skewers

Marinade:

1 tsp red curry paste

4 tbs light soy sauce

2 tbs lemon juice

8 tbs peanut oil

For peanut sauce see Malaysian Peanut Sauce recipe (page 76).

METHOD:

In bowl mix all marinade ingredients well. Add eggplant and mushrooms to marinade and mix well. Allow vegetables to marinate for 1 hour.

In the meantime, if using wooden skewers soak them in water for about 10 minutes. Thread eggplant and mushrooms alternately onto skewers, about 3 pieces each.

Grill vegetables over hot charcoal or place on greased cookie sheet and broil in pre-heated oven, frequently brushing vegetables with leftover marinade and turning skewers until nicely grilled. Serve hot with peanut sauce.

Malai Murgh Kebab

THIS IS ANOTHER VARIATION OF CHICKEN TIKKA THAT MAKES AN EXCELLENT COCKTAIL SNACK OR accompaniment to a main course. A good friend of mine who now lives in Delhi calls this delicacy "Afghan Kebabs," as he learned this recipe from an Afghan friend.

Punjabi cuisine has traditionally emphasized robust food, prepared with the simplest ingredients and basic techniques. Punjabis have hardly had any inhibitions or taboos regarding eating meat. Game has always been considered celebratory and tonic.

Geographically, Punjab on either side of the border was situated at the crossroads of the Silk Route. This allowed Punjabis from both countries to practice diverse culinary methods. The close proximity of the Punjab to central Asia, Persia, and Afghanistan also gave Punjabis premier access to the best of fresh and dried fruits, spices, and nuts.

A famous BBQ dhaba in Amritsar, Barawwahn Da Dhaba, has kept the glow of those ancient embers alive. In playing my part to do the same, I am delighted to share this delicacy with you.

INGREDIENTS:

1 kg boneless chicken breast, cut into 1" cubes

3 tbs garlic paste

3 tbs ginger paste

1 tsp white pepper

Salt to taste

¼ cup mild white cheddar, finely grated, or paneer

2 tbs fresh coriander leaves, finely chopped

1 tbs fine corn flour

1 whole egg, beaten

6 finger hot green chilies, finely chopped

½ tsp mace powder

½ tsp nutmeg powder

½ cup full cream

¼ cup clarified butter for basting

1 lemon

METHOD:

In small mixing bowl add garlic and ginger pastes, white pepper, and salt. Mix well and rub mixture onto chicken pieces. Let marinate for 1 hour.

In separate bowl beat egg together with cheese, corn flour, chilies, mace, nutmeg, and cream. Add only chicken without marinade and mix well. Cover bowl and set aside for at least 3 hours.

Thread chicken pieces onto skewers, leaving some space between each piece, and roast on charcoal grill for about 5 minutes, turning skewers to ensure even cooking. Or you may cook kebabs in pre-heated oven at 300°F for about 7 minutes. Remove skewers from heat and hang them for a few minutes to let excess moisture drip off.

Finally, brush clarified butter on kebabs and roast again for a few minutes, until meat is golden brown on all sides. Squeeze fresh lemon juice on kebabs and serve them piping hot.

Mishkaki (Nyama Choma)

MISHKAKI VENDORS ARE USUALLY FOUND ALONG ROADSIDES AROUND THE COASTAL TOWNS IN KENYA. Just like the chip wagons in Ontario, snack and fruit vendors in India, and roadside satay stalls in Thailand, the mishkaki BBQ stands in Kenya enjoy good business with travellers driving through the coastal communities. My first experience indulging in this delicacy was a brutal one, as I dared to eat the hottest batch, which was almost suicidal. I did not realize that the peppers used in this preparation are the peri peri peppers. This particular pepper is fairly hot and should be used carefully. Over the years, I have learned to endure the heat of these peppers, but if you are using them, exercise caution.

INGREDIENTS:

1 kg sirloin tip of beef or lamb, cubed

1 tbs ginger paste

1 tbs garlic paste

2 tbs peri peri pepper powder

2 tbs peanut oil 1 tbs tomato paste

2 tbs white vinegar

Salt and freshly ground black pepper to taste

2 tbs fresh coriander leaves, chopped

1 small onion, finely sliced into rings

1 fresh lemon

METHOD:

To mixing bowl add cubed meat. In smaller bowl add ginger and garlic pastes, peri peri powder or chili powder, peanut oil, tomato paste, vinegar, and salt and pepper and mix well. Add marinade to meat and mix well. Allow meat to marinate for at least 12 hours. For better results, marinate overnight.

Thread cubes on metal skewer and cook to perfection on charcoal BBQ or in pre-heated oven at 450°F.

Garnish cooked meat with onion rings, coriander leaves, and lemon juice. You may also wish to garnish with hot green chilies if you like heat.

Chicken And Mushroom Parcels

WHAT A WONDERFUL WAY TO START OFF AN ASIAN MEAL WITH THESE SUCCULENT, CRISPY STARTERS. The following is a recipe that has these nibbles filled with mushrooms and chicken. However, the filling can range from simple vegetables to exotic seafood and other meats, or a combination of them all. The potential is limitless.

INGREDIENTS:

½ lb boneless chicken meat

1 cup white mushrooms, washed, pat-dried, and finely chopped

1 tsp garlic paste

2 stems green onion, finely chopped

1 tbs light soy sauce

1 tbs fresh coriander leaves, chopped

1 tsp ginger root, finely chopped

1 finger hot green chili, finely chopped

Salt and pepper to taste

50 wonton wrappers

Oil for deep-frying

METHOD:

Put chicken in blender and coarsely blend for about 20 seconds. Put chicken into mixing bowl, add remaining ingredients, and mix together well.

Heat 2 tbs vegetable oil in shallow pan, add chicken mixture, and stir-fry for about 8 minutes, breaking all the lumps and browning mixture. Remove mixture from pan, place in bowl, and allow to cool for 15 minutes.

If using frozen wrappers, thaw them in fridge overnight. Place about 4 wrappers at a time on damp towel and leave remaining wrappers covered in a lightly moist towel. Dampen edges of wrappers with water using a brush or your fingertips. Place 1 tsp of mixture in middle of wrapper, gently lift wrapper, and make a pouch by pressing edges together and twisting wrapper lightly at

the top to seal. The parcel should look like a wonton. Repeat process with remaining wrappers until mixture is used up.

Heat enough oil in wok to fry about 10 parcels at a time. Fry parcels for about 3 minutes until golden brown. Remove parcels from wok using slotted spoon and drain on paper towel. Keep parcels warm while frying remaining parcels.

Arrange fried parcels on warmed-up platter and serve immediately, with your favourite sweet or chili sauce. Try adding spoon full of hot chili sauce to 1 cup plum sauce. You may wish to add additional sauce to suit your preference.

Pakoras

PAKORAS ARE A POPULAR AND BELOVED DELICACY FROM THE INDIAN SUBCONTINENT AND ARE usually complemented with tamarind chutney and other sauces. South Asians across the globe enjoy pakoras, or bhajjia, regularly.

In Canada this is a perfect snack for any blustery winter day and is enjoyed with sweet-and-sour or spicy tamarind sauce or mint chutney; a hot cup of chai served alongside makes for a memorable afternoon tea break.

Growing up in Kenya my favourite snack used to be the pakoras my mom made with all kinds of vegetables, or a plate of the famous "Maru's Bhajjia" served with a special tamarind sauce. These were simple crispy potato fritters coated with special seasoning and chickpea flour and then deep-fried to perfection. Eating this bhajjia became a ritual for the Desi community in Kenya, and enjoying pakoras used to be a must for every visitor to Nairobi. Maru's Café was one of the earlier establishments where one could enjoy this delicacy in the comfort of one's car. Now Maru's Bhajjia has become very popular in London, England, taking Londoners by storm.

Pakoras are prepared by taking any number of ingredients, such as onion, eggplant, potato, spinach, paneer, cauliflower, zucchini, chili pepper, and/or sometimes fish and chicken, seasoning them, dipping them in a batter of gram flour, and then deep-frying them. The most popular kinds are pakoras that include all of the abovementioned finely cut vegetables, and are then mixed in a seasoned spicy chickpea flour batter and deep-fried.

Several decades ago I remember enjoying the best-ever cauliflower and eggplant pakoras at a small snack shop in Lakkar Bazaar, in lower Shimla, India. The secret was the mustard oil used for frying this snack; it was the first time I had ever tried anything fried in mustard oil. It was awesome—the taste and flavours were full of goodness—and a truly memorable experience.

I am sharing my recipe for the vegetable pakoras that are fried individually. Any vegetable of your choice may be used and seasonings can be adjusted to your liking.

INGREDIENTS:

1 head fresh cauliflower, cut into florets

2 small eggplants, sliced ¼" thick

5 medium-sized red potatoes, peeled, washed, and sliced 1/8" thick

6 finger hot green chilies, slit lengthwise

1 onion, peeled and sliced into ¼"-thick rings

Oil for deep-frying

SEASONING:

2 tbs salt

2 tbs red chili powder

1 tbs ajwain

1 tsp garam masala

1 tbs garlic powder

2 tbs coriander, finely chopped

BATTER:

1½ cups besan

Salt to taste

½ tsp sugar

1 tsp turmeric powder

1 tsp fine garlic paste

1 tsp garam masala

3 tbs lemon juice

1 tsp baking powder

Cool water as required

METHOD:

In small mixing bowl add all ingredients for seasoning and mix well.

In another mixing bowl add each vegetable separately and sprinkle seasoning on vegetables. Arrange them individually on large plate and set aside for at least 1 hour before frying.

Next, prepare batter by sifting chickpea flour in mixing bowl. Add salt, sugar, turmeric powder, garlic paste, garam masala, lemon juice, and baking powder. Mix all ingredients thoroughly, adding a little water at a time, and keep whisking to make a thick, runny batter. Ensure that there are no lumps in batter and that it is silky smooth.

Once batter is ready, heat oil in wok. Depending upon your preference you may want to use mustard oil for tastier pakoras. As soon as oil is ready for frying add cauliflower into batter without any liquid. Gently pick up each floret, shake off excess batter, and drop into hot oil. Do not overcrowd wok, keep turning cauliflower with slotted spoon, and fry it to a nice, crisp, golden brown finish. Once done, drain and remove pakoras from wok and place onto paper towel. Repeat process until all vegetables have been fried separately.

Arrange pakoras on serving platter and serve hot with tamarind chutney or any other chutney or sauce of your choice.

Shahi Malai Tikkas

THIS IS AN EXCELLENT NON-VEGETARIAN APPETIZER OR CAN BE SERVED AS AN ACCOMPANIMENT TO A vegetarian lentil and rice meal.

INGREDIENTS:

1 lb mutton, ground hind leg meat

4 slices white bread, crust removed, soaked in milk for 5 minutes

2 finger hot green chilies, finely chopped

1 tbs fresh coriander leaves, finely chopped

1 tsp garlic paste

1 tsp ginger paste

1 tbs fresh mint leaves, finely chopped

1 tsp chili powder

1 tsp garam masala

½ tsp turmeric powder

2 small onions, finely chopped

2 whole eggs, beaten

Salt to taste

1 cup all-purpose flour, sifted

2 small onions, cut into rings

1 lemon, cut into 8 wedges

Vegetable oil to deep-fry

METHOD:

In shallow frying pan add ground meat with garlic and ginger pastes, stir well, and cook for about ½ hour. Then add chilies, chili powder, garam masala, turmeric, onions, and salt and cook for another 3 minutes. Turn heat off and mix in bread slices. When mixture is fully cooled, add mint and coriander, and knead mixture well with moist hands. Divide meat into 16 equal portions and shape each piece into small flattened oval-shaped kebabs.

Heat oil in wok. Dip each kebab in flour with one hand, and then using other hand dip kebabs in beaten egg. Gently drop kebabs into heated oil and fry until golden brown.

Remove with slotted spoon, drain excess oil, and place on paper towel. Arrange kebabs on serving platter and garnish with onion rings and lemon wedges. Serve hot or warm. These kebabs can be pan-fried as well in a non-stick pan.

Chana Daal Wadas

WADAS ARE BASICALLY DEEP-FRIED LENTIL BALLS AND CAN BE MADE WITH PRACTICALLY ANY KIND of legume. Throughout India and elsewhere they are one of the most popular snacks. Chor Bazaar—"Thieves Market"—is very famous for these savoury snacks; street vendors fry these balls and serve them hot with coconut chutney. This recipe comes from the coastal city of Mombasa in Kenya and is my favourite.

INGREDIENTS:

3 cups chana daal

2 onions, finely chopped

6 finger hot green chilies, finely chopped

½ medium tomato, crushed

10 curry leaves

Salt and pepper to taste

Oil for deep-frying

METHOD:

Wash and rinse daal thoroughly, soak in cool water for about 4 hours, and then grind to a coarse paste by adding a little water as needed. Transfer ground paste into mixing bowl and add chopped onions, green chilies, curry leaves, tomatoes, and salt and pepper and mix well. Let mixture rest for about 1 hour before frying wadas.

In the meantime heat oil in wok. As soon as oil heats up start forming balls using a teaspoon. Take a heap of mixture, place between your moistened palms, and gently roll mixture into desired round or oval shape. If you find that wada mixture is not binding well due to excessive moisture you may add some besan to stiffen it for easy handling.

Deep-fry wadas on medium heat until crisp and golden brown. Serve hot with your favourite chutney or sauce. Coconut chutney goes great with this snack.

Wadas can be frozen and then warmed in convection oven for best results. Microwave warming is not recommended, as it will make them chewy.

Chicken Wings À La Mag

THESE CHICKEN WINGS ARE A MUST AT EVERY MAGON GATHERING. IN THIS PREPARATION EAST TAKES over West in both taste and flavour—a truly finger-licking good experience.

INGREDIENTS:

2 lb chicken wings, cleaned and cut

Marinade:

2 tbs garlic paste

2 tbs ginger root paste

1 bunch green onions, finely chopped

4 finger hot green chilies, finely chopped

3 tbs dark soy sauce

1 tbs cornstarch

2 tbs Mag's hot chili sauce (red chili with garlic and shallots in oil)

2 tbs hoisin sauce

2 tbs cooking oil

Salt to taste (please taste marinade for salt, as soy sauce may have enough)

Garnish:

2 sprigs fresh green onion

2 tbs fresh coriander leaves, chopped

1 fresh lemon

2 finger hot green chilies, chopped for additional heat (optional)

METHOD:

In large mixing bowl add all ingredients for marinade and mix well. Add chicken wings to marinade and mix thoroughly. Allow chicken wings to marinate for at least 3 to 4 hours at room temperature.

Preheat oven to 375°F. Spread chicken wings on cookie sheet and place it on middle shelf of oven. Bake wings for about 20 minutes or until fully cooked. Just before pulling chicken out of oven, turn on broiler to give wings a crisper, golden-brown look.

Serve piping hot as an appetizer. Garnish with mixture of coriander, green onions, and chili peppers. Squeeze juice of fresh lemon over wings and enjoy. Make lots, as they don't last long.

Dhebras

THIS AWESOME GUJARATI SNACK IS A HEALTHY DELICACY PACKED WITH IRON AND FIBRE AND MADE with fresh fenugreek leaves and millet. It ends up being so scrumptious that no matter how much you make, a full platter will be devoured in no time. So please take my advice and prepare more than you think is needed.

Usually dhebras are served with curds, pickles, and chutneys of choice. They are best enjoyed at breakfast or as an afternoon snack with a cup of hot chai. Although dhebras are cooked on a tawa like rotis or poronthis, deep-frying this snack makes it even better, so once in a while forget your health-watch slogans and indulge a little.

Growing up in Kenya amongst Gujarati neighbours was like a celebration every day, as we were introduced and treated to many different kinds of snacks and foods. However, dhebras have to be my all-time favourite savoury-hot snack with a little hint of sweetness.

I remember in Kenya, Gujarati women, especially grandmothers, loved to bake and make all kinds of goodies to serve to all those living around them. It was always heartwarming and satisfying to watch these lovely women put smiles on the faces of children with the food they had cooked with love. I always made an entry at the right moment to share a piece of that love. This recipe comes straight from the heart of one of those grandmothers

INGREDIENTS:

1½ cups bajra flour (millet)

1 cup corn flour

1 cup besan

1 tbs hot oil

½ cup sour yogurt

4 hot green chilies, ground

¼ tsp asafoetida

1 tbs garlic paste

1 tbs ginger paste

1 tbs red chili powder

1 cup fresh methi, chopped

4 tbs sesame seeds

1 tbs sugar

1 fresh lemon

Salt to taste

Vegetable oil for frying

METHOD:

In large mixing bowl add bajra, corn, and besan flours and mix well. Make a well in centre of mixed flour with fingers and add hot oil, green chilies, asafoetida, garlic and ginger pastes, red chili powder, chopped methi, salt, and sesame seeds. Squeeze juice of 1 lemon over mixture, gently mix all ingredients, slowly add whipped yogurt, and blend to make semi-soft dough. You may need a little extra yogurt for dough if it is too dry. Once dough is mixed well, taste for seasonings and make any adjustments. Cover mixing bowl and allow dough to ferment for a few hours.

When ready to fry dhebras, heat vegetable oil in wok. Next, with fingers place some dough on palm and flatten to make small patty. Gently slide patty into hot oil. Fry about 6 patties at a time and do not overcrowd wok.

Fry dhebras for few minutes and as soon as they start to puff a little, gently turn them over and fry until evenly browned. Remove dhebras with slotted spoon and place on paper towels. Repeat process until all dough is used. Serve hot or warm with pickles or chutney. If not serving immediately, store in airtight container once dhebras are totally cool. They can be safely stored for a few days—unless a dhebra monster is on the loose.

Thai Chili Chicken Wings

EVERY YEAR IN NORTH AMERICA, MANY SPORTS FANS COUNT DOWN TO THE SUPER BOWL, WHICH FOR football enthusiasts traditionally also means nibbling on chicken wings and sipping chilled beverages. Aside from serving regular buffalo wings, you might want to try out something different this year, and I have just the recipe for you.

This is a recipe that I adapted. These flavourful, spicy wings are somewhat similar to traditional wings but have many more exotic spices and a distinct Asian flair from ingredients like lemongrass and Thai curry paste. The heat comes from Sriracha Thai hot sauce and Chinese hot chili oil paste. This recipe turns out amazingly well, even without smothering this delicacy in hot sauce and serving with blue cheese dip and celery or carrot sticks. This has to be one of the best finger foods at any party. Please make sure to have loads of these babies at your next gathering, because you are bound to run out of them fast.

INGREDIENTS:

24 whole chicken wings, with excess skin trimmed off and discarded

Cut and discard the wing tips. Separate each wing from the little drumstick and you should have 48 pieces.

MARINADE:

4 tbs soy sauce

4 tbs Sriracha chili sauce

2 tbs hot chili oil paste

1 tbs Thai red curry paste

2 tbs fine garlic paste

1 tbs ginger paste

1 tbs lemongrass powder

1 cup buttermilk

½ cup all-purpose flour

2 tbs cornstarch

Salt to taste

Coarse black pepper, freshly ground

Vegetable oil for deep-frying

GARNISH:

1 small onion, halved and thinly sliced

1 green bell pepper, washed, cleaned, and cut into small chunks

Fresh coriander, chopped

METHOD:

In mixing bowl combine all marinade ingredients to form smooth batter and then add chicken wings. Mix well. Let chicken wings marinate for a few hours.

In wok heat oil to 350°F. Once oil is hot, pick up chicken wings one at a time, shaking off any excess batter, and gently drop into wok. Do not overcrowd wok and fry wings until golden brown and crisp. Remove wings from oil, drain, and place onto paper towel. Just before serving add a little oil to clean wok and heat. Next, add onions, peppers, and 2 tbs of leftover marinade and toss mixture well. Immediately add fried wings and toss well. Finally, garnish with fresh coriander and serve piping hot with or without your favourite sauce.

Chapli Kebabs

THIS RECIPE WAS PASSED ON TO MY DEAR DAD BY MY GRANDFATHER, AND THEN ON TO ME. THESE famous kebabs hail from the northwest frontier of Pakistan and are a favourite of the people of Peshawar. They are favourites at Magon gatherings both in Canada and Kenya too.

These delicacies are named for the process by which they are prepared: the kebab mixture is placed in the centre of the palm, rolled to form a smooth ball, and then flattened by carefully pressing firmly with the palm directly onto a hot pan.

INGREDIENTS:

2 kg mutton or beef, coarsely ground

4 eggs, scrambled

1 tbs garlic paste

½ cup pomegranate seeds, crushed

½ cup pomegranate seeds or ½ cup coriander seeds, whole

4 to 6 finger hot green chilies

4 medium firm tomatoes, finely diced

½ cup fresh coriander, finely chopped

2 large onions, finely chopped and squeezed to drain juice

½ cup corn flour

1 tbs black pepper, coarsely ground

Salt and red chili powder to taste

Clarified butter or oil for frying

METHOD:

In large bowl add ground meat. Keep adding above ingredients in the order they appear and mix gently. Once all ingredients are mixed well make a small ball of mixture and test-cook it for taste and any adjustment of spices.

Once you are satisfied, heat oil or butter in large shallow pan or tawa with a lip. Peshawaris like to use banaspati for this delicacy. Once oil is hot take handful of mixture into centre of palm, roll to form smooth ball, and then flatten ball, carefully pressing firmly with palm directly onto hot pan. CAUTION: Be very careful when doing this, as both oil and pan are hot. Your flattened kebabs should be about ¼" to ½" in thickness.

Using flat spatula, shallow pan-fry kebabs on both sides until cooked to a fine, crisp finish. Continue process until all mixture is used.

Serve kebabs piping hot with salad, onion rings, and wedges of fresh lemon. Tandoori roti or naan goes great with this delicacy. I personally enjoy these kebabs with steamed, good-quality basmati rice.

Fried Chicken In Pandanus Leaves

STREET VENDORS ALL OVER THAILAND SELL THIS SNACK AT THEIR ROADSIDE STALLS. THE PANDANUS leaf is very similar to the banana leaf and may be available at any Thai grocery store. Banana leaf can be used as a substitute. However, it's the fragrance of the pandanus leaf that makes this recipe so unique and flavourful. If all else fails then you may resort to good old tin foil.

INGREDIENTS:

1 lb boneless chicken, 1" cubed (approximately 30 pieces)

½ tsp black pepper, freshly ground

2 tsp garlic paste

2 tsp brown sugar

2 tbs light soy sauce

1 tbs sesame oil

30 pandanus leaves

Cooking oil for deep-frying

METHOD:

In mixing bowl add chicken pieces along with pepper, garlic, brown sugar, soy sauce, and sesame oil. Mix well and allow chicken to marinate for at least 1 hour.

Neatly wrap each chicken piece in pandanus leaf to form a triangular package and secure with banana fibre.

Heat oil in wok, gently slide parcels into hot oil, and fry on medium heat for about 10 minutes. Do not overcrowd wok. Remove with slotted spoon, making sure that all oil is drained, and place fried parcels on absorbent paper to soak up any more oil.

Serve hot with chili dipping sauce of your choice. Remove chicken pieces from pandanus wrappers before dipping in sauce.

Island Crab Cakes

IN THIS RECIPE, I HAVE ATTEMPTED TO REPLICATE THE CAKES THAT WE ENJOYED IMMENSELY AT A resort in Barbados. The cakes were served with a hot mango salsa. And now that I've perfected the recipe, my son and my better half claim that Dad's cakes have turned out even better.

INGREDIENTS:

16 oz crabmeat

4 oz potatoes, cooked and mashed

1 tsp Dijon mustard

2 tbs mayonnaise

1 finger hot chili pepper, finely chopped

1 tsp ginger root, ground

1 tbs fresh coriander leaves, finely chopped

Salt and freshly ground black pepper to taste

1 egg white, beaten

½ cup flour for dusting

Oil for frying

METHOD:

In mixing bowl combine crabmeat with mashed potatoes, mustard, mayonnaise, chili pepper, ground ginger root, coriander, and salt and pepper. Add egg white and mix well. For best results, chill mixture for at least 30 minutes to allow flavours to blend as well as to help crab cake mixture bind.

After mixture has chilled well, wet hands lightly and divide mixture into 8 portions. Shape each portion into a patty between palms, lightly dust patties with flour, and place onto wax paper.

Heat oil in frying pan and fry crab cakes for a few minutes on each side until cakes turn golden brown.

Serve hot crab cakes on bed of shredded lettuce with side of mango salsa or your favourite salad. You may wish to garnish them with fresh lime or lemon wedges and fresh coriander leaves.

Bite-Sized Side Ribs

FOR THOSE OF YOU WHO ARE NOT AWARE THAT MY NICKNAME HAS BEEN "MAG" SINCE THE DAYS OF my television cooking show Cook with Mag, this delicacy was one of my signature dishes that my fans loved most.

INGREDIENTS:

2 lb side ribs (have butcher cut them to bite-sized pieces)

MARINADE:

2 tbs garlic, crushed

2 tbs ginger root, crushed

¼ cup white vinegar

1 bunch green onions, finely chopped

1 tbs fresh lime rind, finely chopped

2 tbs fresh coriander stems, chopped

2 stalks fresh lemongrass, cut and mashed into 2" pieces

6 hot green chilies, finely chopped

1 tbs dark soy sauce

1 tbs cornstarch

2 tbs hot chili sauce

2 tbs cooking oil

Salt to taste (please taste marinade for salt, as soy sauce may have enough)

GARNISH:

2 sprigs fresh green onion, chopped

2 tbs coriander, freshly chopped

1 cup fresh pineapple or mango cubes

1 fresh lemon

Green chilies, chopped (optional in case you want ribs to be hot)

METHOD:

Mix all ingredients for marinade well.

Pat-dry ribs and put them in large bowl. Pour marinade over ribs and mix well. Allow ribs to marinate for at least 2 hours at room temperature before cooking.

In large pot, add marinated ribs and cook for about 5 minutes on high heat, constantly stirring to avoid any

scorching. Turn heat to medium and cover pan to steam-cook ribs for another 6 to 8 minutes, stirring a few times. Remove ribs from stove. If pan has too much juice, separate ribs and cook juice until reduced to a thick sauce. Remove all lemongrass stalks from sauce, place ribs back into pot, and mix well. You may refrigerate ribs until ready to serve.

Fried Tofu With Peanut Sauce

THIS IS ANOTHER EXCITING, HEALTHY APPETIZER FOR VEGETARIANS THAT CAN ADD A TOUCH OF class to your table at your next gathering. Your guests can help themselves with cocktail forks or fancy sticks.

INGREDIENTS:

1 lb firm plain tofu (bean curd)

5 tbs all-purpose flour

2 whole eggs

4 tbs milk

½ tsp baking powder

½ tsp chili powder

Oil for deep-frying

For peanut sauce see the Malaysian Peanut Sauce recipe (page 76). Please note that for making this recipe vegetarian you may wish to omit the fish sauce and substitute it with some soy sauce.

METHOD:

Cut tofu into 1" triangles and keep aside. For batter sift flour into bowl and gently whisk in beaten eggs and milk. Stir in baking powder and chili powder and mix well to form a nice, creamy batter.

Heat oil in wok, dip tofu triangles in batter, and deep-fry until golden brown. Remove and drain fried tofu and place onto paper towel. Arrange tofu on platter with bowl of peanut sauce.

Kenyan-Style Meat Samosas

SAMOSAS ARE A DEEP-FRIED PASTRY SNACK THAT ORIGINATED IN INDIA AND EAST ASIA. THEY HAVE also become an African favourite, especially in East Africa and South African countries, due to the influx of Indian immigrants there. I would say this snack's popularity is quickly spreading all over the globe! If you have never tried one before, you are in for a treat. These savoury pastry snacks are quite addictive.

Kenyan samosas are unique, as their pastry is thinner and crispier than that of the traditional Indian samosas. The meat filling can be made from ground beef, lamb, goat, or pork. In Kenya, we grew up on samosas filled with ground goat meat. A family friend used to make the best meat samosas at his restaurant, and the following recipe is closest to the snack that he used to make.

INGREDIENTS:

1 kg goat meat, minced

1 tbs garlic paste

3 tbs ginger root, finely chopped

5 finger hot green chilies, finely chopped

1 tsp red chili powder

1 tbs cumin seeds

Salt to taste

½ tsp cinnamon powder

¼ tsp cardamom powder

1 pinch clove powder

1 cup onions, finely diced

¼ cup fresh coriander leaves, finely chopped

1 large lemon

2 oz samosa wrappers (if frozen thaw before filling)

4 tbs all-purpose flour, mixed in water to make paste

Vegetable oil for deep-frying

METHOD:

In shallow pan cook minced meat with 1 cup water on medium heat. Break any lumps and then add garlic paste, ginger root, green chilies, chili powder, and cumin seeds. Mix all ingredients and stirring occasionally continue to cook until meat is cooked and all moisture has evaporated. Turn heat off and add diced onions, and cinnamon, clove, and cardamom powders. Mix all ingredients and allow mixture to cool. Finally, add coriander leaves, squeeze juice of 1 lemon onto mixture, and set aside until ready to stuff pastry.

Place samosa wrapper onto palm and fold one edge of pastry to form cone. Fill pocket of cone with meat filling. Fold down top of pastry wrapper and neatly seal all open sides with flour paste. You should end up with a neatly secured triangular meat-stuffed pastry. Place stuffed samosas on lightly floured cookie sheet until ready to fry.

In wok heat oil and gently slide samosas into hot oil. Do not overcrowd wok. Fry over medium heat until golden brown. Drain samosas and arrange on serving platter. Serve hot.

These crispy meat samosas are best served with small wedges of lime. Chutneys do not do justice to the meat filling, hence the lime. However, there is no set convention; if you like chutney, go ahead and enjoy your samosas with it.

Hakka Fish Pakoras

THIS IS A SUCCULENT, SPICY DEEP-FRIED FISH FRITTER PREPARED WITH AN ASIAN FLAIR.

INGREDIENTS:

1 lb fresh cod, chopped into ¼" pieces

1 large onion, finely chopped

2 finger hot green chilies, finely chopped

1 tbs fresh ginger root, finely chopped

1 tsp fresh garlic paste

¼ cup coriander, finely chopped

½ tsp ajwain, rubbed between palms (optional)

1 tbs light soy sauce

1 cup besan, sifted

Salt and pepper to taste

Oil for deep-frying

METHOD:

In mixing bowl add all ingredients except besan. Mix well and then add besan, salt, and pepper. Batter should be fairly thick and not runny. If runny, add more besan.

In wok heat oil and as soon as oil is hot start making small balls with batter mixture, gently dropping them into hot oil. Make sure oil is not too hot, otherwise balls will brown on outside and inside will remain uncooked. Once pakoras are in oil you may turn heat down and fry them slowly until golden brown. This way pakoras will be crispy on outside and fully cooked and soft inside.

Place pakoras onto paper towel and then onto serving platter. Serve with sweet chili sauce or pickled carrots and daikon.

You may use bits of boneless chicken or chopped shrimp for this recipe instead of fish. If you are using chicken then season, pan-fry, and cool it before adding to batter.

Paneer Tikkas

FOR A LONG TIME I HAD BEEN COOKING MOSTLY NON-VEGETARIAN SNACKS AND APPETIZERS UNTIL MY nieces complained and wanted something exotic for vegetarians. Soon I started to experiment with paneer, one of the most popular foods amongst vegetarians. I dedicate the following recipe to all of my vegetarian fans.

INGREDIENTS:

2 lb fresh paneer, cut into 2"x2"x1" pieces

2 tsp ajwain, roughly ground

1 tsp cumin seeds, roughly ground

1 tbs garam masala

½ tsp turmeric powder

½ tsp ginger paste

2 finger hot green chili peppers, ground

½ tsp garlic paste

½ tsp rubbed Kasoori methi

Salt and pepper to taste

BATTER:

1 egg or 1 tbs cornstarch

3 tbs besan

½ cup cream

Vegetable oil for deep-frying

METHOD:

In mixing bowl, sprinkle ajwain, cumin, garam masala, turmeric powder, ginger, chili peppers, garlic, and Kasoori methi onto cut-up paneer and mix well without breaking paneer pieces. Add salt and pepper and set aside for 1 hour.

In the meantime prepare batter by whisking egg along with gram flour and cream. If not using egg then add cornstarch. Mix batter well and pour over paneer, ensuring every piece is covered. Let sit for 1 hour before cooking.

If you do not wish to deep-fry then arrange paneer on skewers, leaving space between each piece, and either cook in pre-heated oven at 300°F or grill over charcoal BBQ.

If deep-frying, heat oil in wok. Gently drop paneer pieces into hot oil and fry until golden brown. Do not overcrowd fryer for best results. Serve hot with your favourite chutney or sauce. Non-vegetarians also love this cocktail snack. Make plenty to go around.

Vegetable Samosas

SAMOSAS ARE NOW GLOBALLY A FAVOURITE SNACK, AND CAN BE STUFFED WITH A VARIETY OF FILLings, such as minced meat, mixed vegetables, cheese, or spiced lentils.

The pastry from the subcontinent differs from the one I grew up on in Kenya and other parts of Africa. The Indian version is usually made from scratch with dough that results in a thicker, more tender and flaky pastry compared to the African variation, which is thin and crisp like wontons or spring roll wrappers.

The Kohinoor Restaurant in Kenya was very famous for its vegetarian samosas and used to supply this snack to almost all the schools in Nairobi when I was growing up there. I remember lining up for the hot samosas to stave off my hunger until mealtime. Kohinoor samosas had a unique flavour from a hint of cinnamon, turmeric, and sugar. The filling also had no pomegranate seeds, but did have shredded cabbage, corn, and freshly squeezed lemon juice and was stuffed into a thin, crispy wrapping.

Due to the mass influx of immigrants to Canada from East Africa, many entrepreneurs have made the task of preparing samosas easier by producing samosa wrappers that can be found in the freezer sections of most Indian grocery stores.

INGREDIENTS:

PASTRY:

1 lb all-purpose flour, sifted

½ tsp salt

4 tbs margarine or vegetable oil

Flour for dusting

FILLING:

5 cups potatoes, ¼" diced

½ cup green peas, fresh or frozen

1 medium onion, diced

1 tbs cumin seeds

3 tbs ginger root, chopped

1 tsp red chili powder

6 green chilies, finely chopped

2 tbs pomegranate seeds, dried

1/3 cup coriander leaves, finely chopped

Salt to taste

5 tbs vegetable oil

Vegetable oil for deep-frying

METHOD:

In shallow dish mix salt and flour, make a bay in middle of flour heap, add oil, and mix gradually. Once oil is fully mixed with flour add about 6 tbs water to flour and start kneading gently to form into dough that is not too hard. Cover dough with moist cloth and set aside for about ½ hour.

For filling, immerse diced potatoes into bowl of water. This helps keep potatoes from discolouring. In the meantime boil green peas until tender, drain, and set aside.

In shallow saucepan heat vegetable oil. Add cumin seeds and as soon as cumin starts to crackle, add onions and sauté for 1 minute. Add drained potatoes, ginger, chili powder, chopped chilies, pomegranate seeds, coriander leaves, and salt. Mix well and stir-fry for about 5 minutes. Add peas, mix well, and cook until all moisture has evaporated and mixture is dry. Let mixture cool before filling.

Uncover dough, divide into 6 equal balls, and keep them covered. Place a ball on lightly floured surface and flatten with rolling pin into disc about 8" in diameter. Cut disc into 2 half-moons. Place 1 half-moon flat onto palm with its straight edge along the forefinger. Now dip other forefinger in water and moisten edges. Align edges of pastry to make cone. Stuff cone with filling and seal open end by pinching pastry firmly. You may need to moisten pastry to firmly seal samosa and form into a triangle. Place stuffed samosas onto floured cookie sheet until ready to fry.

In wok, heat oil and deep-fry samosa on medium heat until golden brown. Do not overcrowd wok with samosas. While frying gently turn samosas to evenly brown.

Arrange samosas on serving platter and serve hot with tamarind, mint, or coriander chutney.

Sweet Corn Patties

THESE PATTIES MAKE A DELICIOUS ADDITION TO ANY BUFFET TABLE. FAIRLY SIMPLE AND EASY TO make, they can be served with any relish or chutney. Mango salsa or pomegranate salsa makes them even tastier.

INGREDIENTS:

1 can (11 oz) sweet corn, drained

1 medium onion, finely chopped

1 tsp fresh garlic paste

1 tbs fresh ginger root, finely chopped

1 tbs fresh coriander leaves, finely chopped

1 tsp red chili powder

1 potato, boiled and finely grated

½ tsp black pepper, coarsely ground

4 tbs all-purpose flour

½ tsp baking powder

1 large egg, beaten

Salt to taste

Vegetable oil for pan-frying

METHOD:

In mixing bowl add drained sweet corn and mash well. Then add remaining ingredients except cooking oil and mix batter well. Heat oil in frying pan and gently drop about 2 tbs batter onto hot oil without crowding. Cook for about 4 to 5 minutes on each side until batter is golden brown and firm.

Particular attention should be paid when turning patties; if turned too soon, chances are they may break up.

Remove patties gently and place onto paper towel. Arrange on serving platter and garnish with thinly sliced spring onions.

Please note that batter can be prepared well ahead of time and refrigerated for at least a couple of days.

Serve hot with your favourite sauce or salsa.

Pre-heat oven to 400°F. Spread ribs evenly on cookie sheet and place onto middle shelf of oven.

Cook ribs until they start to sizzle and turn brown. Just before pulling ribs out, turn broiler on to give ribs that nice golden brown and crisp look. Be careful that ribs do not overcook and burn while broiling.

Pull ribs out of oven and spread onto serving platter. Garnish with green onions, chopped coriander, and chopped chilies if you like them hot.

Lastly, squeeze juice of 1 fresh lemon over ribs, then place cubed fruit all over ribs. Serve ribs piping hot as an appetizer.

Japanese-Style Chili Fried Jumbo Shrimp

JUMBO TIGER SHRIMP ARE FRIED IN A BEER BATTER AND SERVED WITH A CREAMY CHILI SAUCE IN this recipe. This is a crunchy and succulent delicacy from Tokyo, Japan.

INGREDIENTS:

1 cup all-purpose flour, sifted

1 tbs cornstarch

1 tsp salt

1 tsp baking powder

1 tsp black pepper, coarsely ground

¾ cup beer, any brand

½ cup milk

2 eggs

2 lb jumbo tiger shrimp, shelled, deveined, with tails on

2 qt vegetable oil for frying

Chili flakes for final garnish

SAUCE:

½ cup Japanese mayonnaise

½ tsp garlic paste

1 tsp chili flakes, finely ground

1 tbs fresh lime juice

METHOD:

In small mixing bowl add all ingredients for sauce and mix well. Cover and refrigerate.

In large bowl, add flour, cornstarch, salt, pepper, and baking powder and mix well. Next, add beer, milk, and eggs. Blend all ingredients to make a fine batter.

Add cleaned and pat-dried shrimp into batter and coat well. Let shrimp stand for about 15 minutes.

Heat oil in wok to 375°F. Gently drop battered shrimp into hot oil one at a time and do not overcrowd wok. Fry shrimp until golden brown. Fry all shrimp in batches and make sure to maintain temperature of oil.

Plate 4 to 5 shrimp on small serving plates, tails up. Smother sauce on top of shrimp and just before serving sprinkle with chili flakes.

Refreshing Fresh Fruit Chaat

MANY WOULD ARGUE THAT MOST CHAATS ORIGINATED IN SOME PARTS OF UTTAR PRADESH IN INDIA, but they are now eaten all across the country. There are many different kinds of chaats, and this snack is considered one of the most popular street foods in India. While the original chaat—a mixture of boiled potato pieces, fried rice flakes, puffs, crisp fried <u>dahi wadas</u> made of gram or chickpeas and lentils, and tangy-savoury spices—has always been a favourite, other popular varieties include <u>aloo tikkis</u> or <u>samosas</u> garnished with onion, coriander, hot spices, a dash of curd, and even chickpeas.

Ready-made chaat masalas are easily available at most Indian grocery stores nowadays, but hardcore chaat connoisseurs prefer to make their own blends. The most crucial ingredient in making a tasty chaat is the chaat masala, a special blend typically consisting of <u>amchoor</u>, <u>cumin</u>, <u>kala namak</u> (rock salt), <u>coriander</u> seeds, dried <u>ginger</u>, <u>salt</u>, <u>black pepper</u>, and <u>red chili peppers</u>. These ingredients are ground and all chaats are seasoned and garnished with a sprinkle of this magic masala before serving. Whipped yogurt, fine sevs, lime or lemon juice, tamarind sauce, coriander, and mint chutneys are also key components that make or break a good, delicious chaat.

Chaats are usually considered healthy snacks, and even healthier are fresh fruit chaats—in moderation, of course. The following is my chaat, a healthy, refreshing, tangy, and spicy fruit salad that can be enjoyed anytime. To personalize this dish, you may also use other fresh fruits of your choice.

INGREDIENTS:

2 large crispy apples

1 banana

1 firm mango

3 small guavas

1 lime

¼ cup passion fruit juice

Chaat masala of your choice, to taste

METHOD:

Gently wash all fruits. Cut apples into quarters and deseed wedges. Cut wedges into ½" pieces and add to mixing bowl. Peel banana, discard skin, cut banana into ½" pieces, and add to mixing bowl. Next, peel mango, cut around pit, cube mango, and add to bowl. Now cut guavas into quarters, cut quarters into halves, add to bowl, and gently mix all fruit. Squeeze lime juice over mixed fruit and add passion fruit juice. Finally, sprinkle chaat masala to taste, gently toss salad well, and serve.

Tillie Aloo Tikki

THESE ARE DEEP-FRIED SESAME SEED-COATED POTATO CUTLET DELIGHTS.

INGREDIENTS:

1 kg potatoes, boiled

1 tsp garam masala

1 tsp red chili powder

Salt to taste

3 tsp green chilies, finely chopped

1 tbs fresh coriander leaves, finely chopped

1 tbs fresh ginger root, finely chopped

3 tbs fine bread crumbs

2 tsp corn flour

½ cup sesame seeds

Oil for frying

METHOD:

Peel cooled boiled potatoes and mash in mixing bowl. Add all remaining ingredients except sesame seeds and oil to bowl and thoroughly mix. Divide mixture into 16 equal portions and shape each into a flat, round cutlet.

Put sesame seeds into shallow dish and coat each cutlet with them, gently pressing seeds to cutlets.

Heat oil in wok and deep-fry cutlets until golden brown. Remove and drain any excess fat. Arrange neatly on serving platter and serve hot with your favourite relish or chutney. Mint chutney or coriander chutney is recommended.

Ultimate Potato Wedges

POTATO WEDGES ARE A VARIATION OF FRENCH FRIES. THEY ARE OFTEN LARGE, PEELED OR UNPEELED, and may be oven-baked or fried with all kinds of herbs, seasonings, and cheese.

Over the years I have tried many different varieties of potato wedges and after much trial and error have finally nailed my own signature recipe, using a special spice mixture that I have created called "Mag's Magic Blend."

The best kind of potato for this recipe is the russet, or Idaho potato. Truly a wonder potato, the russet is long and large with a thick, rough skin. It is high in starch, with a flesh that's snowy white and very dry. Russets are great for baking, making French fries, and making mashed potatoes, as they are soft, light, and absorbent. They're also delicious baked into creamy cheese sauces.

INGREDIENTS:

6 medium-sized russet potatoes

2 to 3 tbs Mag's Magic Blend

Salt and black pepper to taste

Olive oil or coconut oil if oven-baking

Vegetable oil for deep-frying

MAG'S MAGIC BLEND:

1 tbs coriander seeds, coarsely ground

1 tsp ajwain, coarsely ground

1 tsp mustard seeds, toasted and coarsely ground

1 tbs cumin, toasted and ground

1 tbs homemade garam masala

½ tsp green cardamom powder

½ tsp nutmeg powder

½ tsp cinnamon powder

1 tbs amchoor

2 tbs pomegranate seeds, ground

1 tbs saunf

1 tbs garlic powder

1 tbs ginger powder

2 tbs dehydrated onion flakes, ground

1 tsp Kasoori methi, powdered

1 tbs turmeric powder

1 tbs deggi mirch

Salt and pepper to taste

METHOD:

In large bowl gently mix well all ingredients for Mag's Magic Blend. Taste and make any necessary adjustments. Store in airtight container and use as required. Omit or add any ingredient to your liking; similarly, increase or decrease quantities to your preference. It is always best to make a small batch initially to achieve right blend of spices. Once required flavour has been achieved you may wish to make larger batch. Always store in airtight container.

Please note that blend may also be used for stuffing vegetables like bhindis, baingans, whole aloos, or karelas. When planning to stuff veggies, add oil and tomato paste to magic blend and mix well.

For wedges, scrub potatoes clean and get rid of any gnarly bits. Cut each potato in half lengthwise, then cut each half lengthwise again for 4 equally sized wedges. Add to pan of boiling water and parboil for 6 to 8 minutes. Drain in colander and leave to steam-dry for a couple of minutes.

If oven-baking gently place drained wedges into mixing bowl and splash enough olive oil or coconut oil to coat. Sprinkle magic blend all over wedges. Line sheet pan with foil and place potato wedges, skin side up, onto it. Toss meticulously to coat potatoes evenly down on foil. Be sure to space evenly to cook uniformly. Place potatoes into pre-heated oven at 400°F and bake for 30 minutes, or until golden brown, crusty edged, and cooked through. Serve immediately, sprinkled with salt and pepper if desired.

If frying heat oil in wok and fry drained potato wedges until golden brown. Gently transfer fried wedges with slotted spoon into mixing bowl and immediately sprinkle with magic blend, tossing meticulously to coat evenly. Finally, sprinkle salt and pepper to taste and serve hot.

Chicken Pakoras

THESE CHICKEN PAKORAS ARE A MUST TO TRY; I HAD THEM AT A DHABA JUST OUTSIDE THE HOLY CITY of Amritsar in the Punjab. They make an excellent appetizer with cocktails or a great snack with afternoon tea.

INGREDIENTS:

1 lb boneless chicken breast, cut into 2"x1" strips

1 tsp red chili powder

½ tsp turmeric powder

½ medium onion, finely sliced

½ tsp ajwain

½ tsp garlic paste

Salt to taste

1 tbs white vinegar

1 whole egg, beaten

½ cup besan

Cooking oil for deep-frying

METHOD:

In mixing bowl add chicken strips along with chili powder, turmeric powder, ajwain, garlic paste, sliced onions, vinegar, and salt. Mix all ingredients well and marinate for at least 1 hour before frying.

In separate bowl beat 1 whole egg and add only chicken without marinade. Coat chicken well with egg. In plastic bag add sifted besan and then add chicken. Shake bag so chicken gets coated well with besan. You may have to add a little more besan to ensure that chicken pieces are fully coated.

Heat oil in wok. Gently drop chicken pieces into hot oil. Fry pakoras until golden brown. Serve hot with your favourite chutney.

Shrimp can be substituted for chicken, and vegetarians may wish to use zucchini, eggplant, or yam sticks.

Grilled Mogho

MOGHO IS A LONG, TUBEROUS, STARCHY ROOT THAT GROWS ABOUT TWO INCHES AROUND AND EIGHT inches long. The root has a brown fibrous skin and snowy-white interior flesh. Because it bruises easily, it's often sold covered in a protective wax coating. Other names for mogho are cassava, yucca, manioc, mandioca, yucca root, casabe, and tapioca. The texture is similar to that of sweet potatoes but has a fairly bland taste and no sweetness. However, mogho is a lot healthier than potatoes and sweet potatoes.

Growing up in Kenya, I would enjoy this favourite street food on my way to school. Vendors would grill peeled and cut mogho, smother a mixture of salt and red chilies on top, and then squeeze fresh lemon juice over it to enhance the flavour and taste.

INGREDIENTS:

1 kg yucca root
¼ cup salt

¼ cup red chili powder
2 fresh lemons

METHOD:

Carefully peel yucca and cut each root lengthwise into 4 pieces. Soak in cold water. (If you are planning to fry yucca, cut into thick home fries.)

In both cases parboil yucca for a few minutes, but do not overcook. Immediately remove cut pieces with slotted spoon and let them cool.

Fire up gas or charcoal grill. Place cooled yucca pieces on grill and make sure to turn them to get charred grill marks on pieces. Remove pieces from grill and place onto serving platter.

Next, in small bowl mix salt and chili pepper. With sharp knife carefully cut lengthwise slits in grilled yucca and fill with salt-chili mix, sprinkling it all over. Squeeze fresh lemon juice all over and serve hot.

Homemade Spring Rolls

THAI SPRING ROLLS USUALLY HAVE MEAT IN THEM COMPARED TO THE CHINESE SPRING ROLLS THAT are usually vegetarian. However, Thai rolls can be vegetarian as well—just skip the meat and substitute it with finely sliced cabbage, bamboo shoots, bean sprouts, and julienned firm tofu. This particular recipe is my family's favourite.

Makes about 30 mini rolls or 15 large rolls.

INGREDIENTS:

1 tbs light soy sauce

4 shiitake mushrooms, dried

50 gm bean thread vermicelli

½ tsp fresh garlic, chopped

1 bunch green onions, chopped

100 gm fresh bean sprouts, chopped

1 medium carrot, grated

1 cup cabbage, finely sliced

1 tbs coriander leaves, finely chopped

50 gm bamboo shoots, chopped

1 finger hot chili pepper, thinly sliced

1 pkg frozen spring roll wrappers (depending on the size you want to make)

Vegetable oil for deep-frying

METHOD:

Remove spring roll wrappers from package and keep them covered in moist kitchen towel to thaw at room temperature.

Soak shiitake mushrooms in hot water for about 10 minutes, and in separate dish soak bean thread vermicelli in hot water for about 15 minutes.

Drain vermicelli, cut into 1½" lengths, and place into large mixing bowl. Similarly, drain mushrooms, cut off and discard stems, finely chop caps, and add to bowl. Next, add remaining vegetables to bowl and thoroughly mix all ingredients. Lightly heat large wok or frying pan and quickly sauté mixture for a few minutes. Add soy sauce and mix well. Do not overcook mixture. Filling may be refrigerated for later use.

When ready to fill rolls, make sure that wrappers are fully thawed. If you have larger wraps and you wish to make smaller rolls, simply cut them into quarters, separate, and keep covered in damp cloth.

Place each wrapper on clean surface and put spoon full of filling closer to one corner of wrapper. Fold that corner over filling. Then fold two sides over filling and roll wrapper toward unfolded corner. Make sure you moisten this last corner for wrapper to stick and stay intact while frying. Also ensure that filled wrappers are placed on wax paper and covered with moist cloth to avoid drying out before frying.

Heat cooking oil in deep fryer or wok. When oil is medium to high heat, gently slip rolls in, about 4 to 5 at a time (do not overcrowd fryer), and fry until golden brown. Transfer fried rolls onto paper towel in order to absorb any excess oil.

Arrange rolls on sheets of lettuce on serving platter and serve hot with your favourite hot sauce or plum sauce. Usually, Thai sweet chili sauce goes great with these rolls.

Rice Paper Shrimp Salad Rolls

THESE UNCOOKED SALAD ROLLS ARE A REFRESHING CHANGE AND HEALTHIER THAN THE DEEP-FRIED spring rolls. Nutritious fillings including shrimp, BBQ'd meat, fresh vegetables, and aromatic herbs, such as fresh mint, are wrapped in delicate rice paper sheets and served cold with traditional Vietnamese dipping sauces. These rolls can be prepared up to five hours ahead of serving and chilled in the fridge, covered with plastic wrap or a clean, dampened kitchen towel to keep them moist. The sky is the limit when it comes to options for fillings—let your imagination run wild.

INGREDIENTS:

2 oz rice vermicelli noodles

2 tbs rice vinegar

1 tbs sugar

1 tsp garlic paste

1 cup cabbage, finely shredded

1 carrot, peeled and grated

1 tbs cilantro, finely chopped

1 tbs soy sauce

2 sprigs green onion, finely sliced

24 medium-sized shrimp, shelled, deveined, pre-cooked, and butterfly cut

1 cucumber, julienned

1 bunch fresh mint

16 sheets of 8" rice paper

METHOD:

Soak rice noodles in boiling water for 5 minutes. While noodles are soaking, in separate bowl combine rice vinegar, sugar, soy sauce, and garlic paste. Mix well to dissolve sugar. Rinse noodles with cold water, drain well, and then cut noodles about 3" long. Place drained noodles in mixing bowl and add cabbage, carrots, cilantro, and green onions. Pour prepared dressing over mixture and mix well.

In shallow dish add warm water. Soak 1 sheet of rice paper for about 15 to 20 seconds, remove, and drain well. Gently place softened rice paper sheet on top of clean, dry kitchen towel and place 2 tbs of vegetable and noodle mixture toward lower edge of rice paper. Next, place julienned cucumber and a few fresh mint leaves on top of mixture. Finally, place on top 2 to 3 pre-cooked cut shrimp. Now neatly fold bottom edge of rice paper over filling. Then fold in sides of rice paper. Roll up rice paper roll to form a neatly packed cylinder (like a fat cigar). Repeat above process for 16 rolls, or enough to serve 8 as an appetizer. Make sure to cover all rolls with moist cloth or plastic wrap.

Serve 2 of these rolls per person as an appetizer with spicy peanut sauce or your favourite dipping sauce.

Chicken Satay

WHEN I FIRST EXPERIENCED THIS APPETIZER FROM THE ORIENT, I WAS REMINDED OF MISHKAKIS from Kenya. Both dishes share a similar concept but the meat used is different and there is a lot of variation in the seasoning. This dish turns out perfectly when prepared on a BBQ and will be a hit at your next gathering.

Makes about 24 skewers.

INGREDIENTS:

500 gm boneless chicken breast

½ small onion, chopped

1 clove garlic

¾ cup coconut milk

½ cup crunchy peanut butter

2 tbs Thai sweet chili sauce

1 finger hot pepper, finely chopped (optional)

2 tbs brown sugar

1 tsp lemongrass, powdered or finely chopped

1 tbs nam pla (fish sauce)

6" bamboo skewers (soaked in water)

Peanut oil for basting

METHOD:

Slice chicken into 2 cm–wide strips and place in bowl. Soak skewers in cold water prior to threading the meat. This will prevent skewers from burning while cooking.

Place remaining ingredients in food processor. Pulsate to a smooth paste. Use some of paste to marinate sliced chicken and thread it onto lightly oiled skewers. Place skewers in flat dish, cover, and let marinate for a few hours, turning skewers a few times.

In the meantime add remaining paste to saucepan with some water and heat for a few minutes to make a nice, creamy sauce. Additional heat may be added to suit your taste.

Just before grilling skewers, brush them lightly with peanut oil and grill over a charcoal or gas BBQ. Turn them occasionally during cooking process. Serve skewers piping hot with creamy peanut sauce.

SIMPLE DESI SALAD

Soups And Salads

Mag's Crab Bisque

THE FIRST TIME I ENJOYED THIS HEARTY SOUP WAS IN BALTIMORE, MARYLAND, AND I HAVE MANAGED to replicate this exotic soup to share with you. This creamy seafood soup makes an excellent starter course for a fine dining experience.

Serves 6.

INGREDIENTS:

½ lb crabmeat, lump

2 cups clam juice, bottled

2 cups water

1 cup white wine

1 medium onion, roughly diced

2 stalks celery, roughly diced

2 whole cloves garlic, peeled

1 tbs coriander leaves, chopped

1 cup cream

1 tsp tomato paste

Salt and white pepper to taste

METHOD:

Combine clam juice, water, wine, onion, celery, and garlic in large soup pot. Slowly bring mixture to a boil. Reduce heat and simmer for 30 minutes. Strain mixture and return liquid to pot. Whisk in cream and tomato paste. Add remaining ingredients and stir well. Simmer another 25 minutes. Add salt and pepper and serve warm.

Tom Yum Soup

SEVERAL YEARS AGO MY SON TRAVELLED TO BANGKOK FOR A HOLIDAY. UPON HIS RETURN HE RAVED about Thai food and in particular the Tom Yum soup. He posed a challenge to me to prepare a soup that would be comparable to the one he had enjoyed in Thailand. Until then, I had never ventured to cook this soup; twice I tried, but not to his satisfaction. The same year, I had the opportunity to visit Bangkok for the first time and was curious to visit the diner where my son had enjoyed this fascinating soup and taste it for myself. Upon taking my first sip, I was speechless—yes, it was indeed very delicious—and thoroughly enjoyed the soup while attempting to discern its possible ingredients. Having tried the soup at a few other venues, I was confident that I had figured out the perfect recipe.

Upon my return home, I prepared my version of Tom Yum soup for my son and his friends and waited for their verdict. I passed with flying colours—they affirmed that my soup was better than what they had had in Bangkok! It is now my pleasure to share this recipe with you.

INGREDIENTS:

6 cups chicken stock

2 cups shrimp shells

3 stalks fresh lemongrass, mashed

1 tsp garlic paste

4 kaffir lime leaves, veins removed

1 tbs shrimp paste

2 tbs red curry paste

4 fresh green chilies, chopped

¼ cup fresh coriander stems, finely chopped

½ tbs nam pla (fish sauce)

¼ cup fresh lime juice

1 tsp palm sugar

1 tbs fresh ginger root, finely julienned

12 whole cherry tomatoes

6 small grape-sized Thai eggplants

12 small mushrooms, halved

12 jumbo shrimp, shelled and deveined

¼ cup coriander leaves, finely chopped

4 limes, quartered

METHOD:

In large saucepan heat stock with shrimp shells. Add lemongrass stalks, garlic paste, kaffir lime leaves, shrimp paste, curry paste, green chilies, and fish sauce. Mix all ingredients and bring to a boil. Turn heat to medium and simmer stock partially covered for about 30 minutes.

Strain stock into clean pot and place on stove at low heat. Now add lime juice, sugar, ginger, mushrooms, cherry tomatoes, and shrimp. Bring soup to a quick boil and turn heat off. Let sit for a few minutes before serving. Taste soup and make any necessary adjustments.

Plate soup individually and garnish with fresh coriander leaves. Ensure each bowl has two shrimp, mushrooms, cherry tomatoes, and eggplants. Serve quartered lime with each soup bowl.

Mulligatawny Soup

DECADES AGO I HAD THE OPPORTUNITY TO ENJOY THIS DELICIOUS SOUP AT A FANCY INDIAN RESTAU-rant in London. My first impression of the soup was that the chef had used leftover daal, pureed it, and then spiked it with some chilies, spices, and leftover finely chopped tandoori chicken.

My research revealed that this soup has its roots in the British Raj period in India and that it is a chicken-vegetable soup delicately flavoured with Indian spices. The name Mulligatawny comes from two Indian words meaning "peppery water" and "curry powder," the latter of which is the key ingredient that gives this incredible soup its unique flavour and colour.

Of course, being a foodie I had the yearning to prepare this soup and in my initial attempt used my own leftover daal and chicken. The result was a total disaster, but I went right back to the drawing board, as I was not going to give up. Here is my recipe that I think you will love.

INGREDIENTS:

10 cups chicken stock

1 boneless and skinless chicken breast, cubed small

1 chicken giblet, finely chopped

¼ cup butter

1 cup moong daal beans, washed

1 tsp garlic paste

1 tbs ginger paste

4 hot green chilies, finely chopped

1 large onion, finely chopped

2 stalks celery, finely chopped

1 large carrot, finely diced

1 tbs Madras curry powder

1 tsp cumin seeds, roasted and lightly rubbed

½ cup coconut milk

½ cup whipped plain yogurt

2 tbs fresh lemon juice

Salt and pepper to taste

Coriander for garnish, freshly chopped

METHOD:

Melt butter in large pot over medium-high heat. Add chicken and giblets and sauté until lightly browned on all sides and cooked through.

Remove cooked chicken and giblets and keep aside. Add celery, onion, carrot, chilies, and garlic and ginger pastes to pot and mix well. Add a few cups of stock to pot and cook over low heat, stirring constantly, until vegetables are tender.

Next, add curry powder and roasted cumin and mix well. Add moong beans and remaining stock to pot.

Bring mixture to a boil, turn heat down, and let soup simmer until moong daal is fully cooked. Add cooked soup to blender and puree to a smooth, silky finish before pouring back into pot.

Gradually add yogurt and coconut milk to pot and stir well. Finally, add cooked chicken and giblets, lemon juice, and salt and pepper. Bring soup to a boil and simmer for about 10 more minutes. Serve hot, individually garnished with fresh coriander.

Seafood Chowder With Baby Clams

AUTHENTIC CHOWDER IS A MATTER OF DEBATE BETWEEN NEW ENGLANDERS AND THOSE FARTHER down the East Coast. New Englanders say that milk must be used, while New Yorkers and Philadelphians maintain that chowder cannot be authentic unless the stock is made from fish and contains tomatoes. In other parts of the country, the subject is academic, and both are acceptable.

Chowder is a name given to any seafood or vegetable stew, often cooked with milk or cream and mostly eaten with saltine crackers or bread. Chowder can be milky or fairly thick and creamy. Over the years I have had the opportunity to try several chowders all over the States and the Canadian Maritimes. The following chowder recipe is my favourite. My inspiration hails from a restaurant in Halifax, Nova Scotia, and this delicacy has no tomatoes, just the goodness of fresh seafood. Of course, I have given it a little twist with a hint of ginger root, and instead of cayenne pepper a green chili provides the heat.

INGREDIENTS:

½ cup dry white wine (optional)

3 tbs butter

2 stalks celery, thinly sliced

1 onion, finely chopped

Sea salt and black pepper to taste

1 finger hot green chili, finely chopped

½ tsp garlic paste

2 tbs all-purpose flour

1½ cups milk

1½ cups fish stock

1 can baby clams, with juice

1 medium potato, washed, peeled, and cubed small

½ cup small mushrooms, sliced

12 oz haddock fillets or other firm-fleshed fish, cut into small cubes

12 oz fresh bay scallops

12 oz baby shrimp

1 tsp fresh ginger root, finely julienned

2 cups 10% cream

¼ cup fresh parsley, chopped

Calculate

METHOD:

In Dutch oven, melt butter over medium heat; fry celery and onions, and add sea salt and freshly ground black pepper. Add garlic and chopped chilies and stir occasionally, until softened, about 5 minutes. Stir in flour and cook for 1 minute. Next, add wine, clams with juice, milk, and fish stock and gently stir in potatoes and mushrooms. Mix well and bring mixture to a boil. Reduce heat and let mixture simmer covered, and continue to gently stir occasionally, until potatoes are tender, about 10 minutes. As soon as potatoes are cooked, gently add haddock, scallops, shrimp, and ginger. Stir well and bring chowder to a boil. Reduce heat and simmer for 5 minutes, stirring in cream and parsley. Stir until heated through for another few minutes.

Serve chowder piping hot with garlic bread or plain buttered baguette.

Vegetarian Tom Yum Soup

A TRIED-AND-TRUE CLASSIC. PLEASE NOTE THAT THE ORIGINAL SOUP IS MADE WITH FRESH SHRIMP and the soup stock is made with fish heads and shrimp shells. My vegetarian friends and family members had been missing out on enjoying this goodness, so I came up with a vegetarian version of this world-renowned dish, which even non-vegetarians love.

INGREDIENTS:

8 cups vegetable stock

2 stalks fresh lemongrass, mashed

1 tbs garlic paste

1 tsp galangal, finely chopped

1 tsp ginger, finely chopped

4 kaffir lime leaves, veins removed

2 tbs Thai red curry paste

4 fresh green chilies, chopped

¼ cup fresh coriander stems, finely chopped

¼ cup fresh lime juice

1 tsp palm sugar

6 small grape-sized Thai eggplants, halved

1 tbs fresh ginger root, finely julienned

12 whole cherry tomatoes

6 white mushrooms, halved

½ cup shimeji mushrooms

¼ green bell pepper, quartered

¼ red bell pepper, quartered

METHOD:

In large saucepan heat vegetable stock with mashed lemongrass, garlic paste, kaffir lime leaves, galangal, ginger root, red curry paste, green chilies, and coriander stems. Mix all ingredients plus palm sugar and bring to a boil. Turn heat to medium and simmer stock partially covered for about 30 minutes.

After 30 minutes strain stock into clean pot and place on stove at low heat. Add Thai eggplants and lime juice to pot. Next, add mushrooms, cherry tomatoes, bell peppers, and ginger root. Bring soup to a quick boil and turn heat off. Let sit for a few minutes before serving. Taste soup and make any necessary adjustments.

Plate hot soup individually and garnish with fresh coriander leaves. Ensure that each bowl has mushrooms, bell peppers, cherry tomatoes, and eggplants. Serve quartered lime with each soup bowl. Have some chili sauce on hand just in case you like it hotter.

¼ cup coriander leaves, finely chopped

3 limes, quartered

Warm Corn Salsa

THIS WARM CORN SALSA IS AN EXCELLENT ACCOMPANIMENT TO ANY KIND OF PAN-FRIED OR BAKED fish. It can also be served as a salad. Prepared a day ahead, it stays good in the fridge.

INGREDIENTS:

2 cups corn kernels, fresh or canned

2 large firm field tomatoes

1 large red onion

2 bunches green onions

2 finger hot green chilies

1 large pomegranate

3 lemons

1 lime

½ cup fresh coriander leaves, washed and chopped

Salt and pepper to taste

1 tbs granulated sugar

METHOD:

In large mixing bowl add corn kernels; if using fresh kernels boil them and cook until slightly tender. Keep warm. Wash tomatoes, dice to same size as corn, and place into mixing bowl. Peel onion, dice, and add to bowl. Wash green onions, chop off and discard roots, finely cut onions including green stems, and add to bowl. Mix well. Slice finger hot chili lengthwise, finely chop, and add to bowl.

Cut pomegranate in half and gently beat each half on skin with wooden spatula, ensuring that cut side of fruit is facing bowl so seeds can easily fall in. Mix all ingredients in bowl.

Next, squeeze juice of lemons and lime into bowl, ensuring that all seeds are discarded. Now add coriander and sugar, and season salsa with salt and pepper. Mix all ingredients well, cover bowl with saran wrap, and refrigerate for at least 4 hours before serving. Just before serving salsa heat up corn and add to mixture. If you want cool salsa do not heat up corn.

Before serving, taste salsa and make any seasoning adjustments. For more heat you may add more chopped chilies.

Khao Soi

MY FIRST EXPERIENCE WITH KHAO SOI WAS IN CHIANG MAI DURING A VISIT TO THAILAND. THIS delicacy did not have chicken, but pork curry with coconut milk. It also had some soft egg noodles at the bottom and was garnished with crispy noodles, coriander, fried chili, and lime.

This was an amazing dish and I recall joking about its name. Khao = Eat. Soi = Sleep. Thus, Khao soi = Eat and sleep.

Below is my recipe for this authentic Thai delicacy.

INGREDIENTS:

2 lb chicken, cut into medium-sized pieces (boneless and skinless optional)

2 tbs red Thai curry paste

2 tbs vegetable oil

2 cups coconut milk

½ tsp turmeric powder

½ tsp cardamom powder (optional)

1 to 1½ cup(s) chicken stock

1 tsp palm sugar

Dash of light fish sauce to taste (usually very salty)

ADDITIONAL INGREDIENTS:

Cooking oil

1 pkg Asian egg noodles (about 3 cups uncooked)

4 sprigs green onions, finely sliced

½ cup Chinese pickled mustard greens, rinsed and sliced

6 large shrimp, shelled, deveined, and lightly pan-fried

1 cup fresh bean sprouts

2 limes, sliced

4 red chilies, dried

½ cup fresh cilantro, chopped

METHOD:

In large pot heat oil and add red curry paste, curry powder, and turmeric and cook, stirring for a few minutes until curry paste releases its aroma. Make sure not to burn paste.

Add 1 cup coconut milk, stir to blend, and let milk come back to a boil. Let bubble for a few minutes over high heat, stirring constantly until oil separates from coconut milk mixture. Add second cup coconut milk, stir well, and again allow oil to separate.

Next, add chicken pieces to pot, with 1 cup chicken stock, and mix well. Bring mixture to a boil, then turn heat down to simmer. Simmer mixture, occasionally stirring until chicken is cooked.

Finally, add a few dashes of fish sauce, remaining chicken stock, and coconut milk. Stir well, taste, and make any necessary changes to seasonings.

NOODLES:

Take 1 cup egg noodles and fluff them until strands are separated. Heat oil in large wok and when oil is fairly hot quickly fry noodles, in small quantities at a time, flipping both sides to achieve an even golden brown finish. Set aside crispy fried noodles on paper towel to absorb any excess oil. Once noodles are fried quickly fry dried chilies, ensuring not to burn, and set aside.

For remaining egg noodles, rinse with cold water to rid of any excess starch, drain, and add to pot of boiling water for 1 minute. Do not overcook. Stir noodles to avoid any sticking. Quickly drain noodles and set aside.

SERVING AND GARNISHING:

Place boiled noodles in large soup bowls and top with piping-hot chicken curry soup and pan-fried shrimp. Garnish with crispy fried noodles and a fried chili. Finally, add green onions, freshly chopped cilantro, and bean sprouts. Squeeze fresh lime juice over curry before digging in.

Suggestions: You may add other veggies of your choice, like baby Thai eggplant and mushrooms. For additional lime taste add a few kaffir lime leaves to chicken curry. Lastly, once chicken curry soup is done you may skim and discard any excessive fat from surface.

Creamy Green Salad Dressing

THIS TYPE OF SALAD DRESSING HAS BEEN VERY POPULAR IN CALIFORNIA AND GOES GREAT WITH
leafy salads or can be used as a vegetable dip.

Makes about 2 cups of dressing.

INGREDIENTS:

1 cup mayonnaise

2/3 cup sour cream

1/3 cup parsley, chopped

2 tbs chives, chopped

2½ tsp tarragon

2 tsp lemon juice

2 tsp anchovy paste (optional)

Salt and pepper to taste

METHOD:

Place all ingredients in food processor. Pulsate until well blended. Refrigerate dressing and use as needed.

Cranberry Salad Dressing

THIS IS A FRESH AND VERSATILE DRESSING FOR SALADS.

Yields about 2 cups.

INGREDIENTS:

1 cup cranberries, fresh or frozen

2 tsp honey

1/3 cup red wine vinegar

½ cup olive oil

½ tsp ginger paste

Salt and pepper to taste

METHOD:

Cook cranberries in small amount of water until tender. Add honey, oil, vinegar, and ginger paste. Pureé mixture in blender or food processor, adding water or orange juice to achieve desired consistency. Use as dressing, sauce, or dip. Store in airtight salad dressing jar.

Vietnamese Pho

PHO IS A VERY POPULAR SOUP SERVED IN A LARGE BOWL WITH WHITE RICE VERMICELLI OR EGG noodles and thin slices of beef. Variations of this delicacy feature tripe, meatballs, chicken, BBQ pork, and seafood like shrimp, calamari, fish cakes, and fish balls.

The broth for this dish is traditionally simmered with beef bones, oxtail, flank steak, charred onion, charred ginger root, and various spices. For a more intense flavour, meaty bones may be used.

Chicken bones also work well and produce a rich broth. The broth takes several hours to make. Seasonings may include cinnamon, star anise, roasted ginger, roasted onion, black cardamom, coriander seeds, fennel seeds, and cloves. The spices are often wrapped in cheesecloth or a soaking bag to prevent them from floating all over the pot. For chicken pho, only the meat and bones of the chicken are used in place of beef and beef bones, but the spices remain the same.

Ginger and onion are carefully roasted over an open fire for a few minutes before adding them to the stock. This helps to bring out their full flavour. All the impurities that float to the top while cooking are carefully skimmed off; this is key to a clear broth. Salt is usually added toward the end.

When serving this pho, cooked warm noodles of choice are placed in a bowl with the meat or seafood and the hot broth is poured all over. Finally, fried onions, chili peppers, cilantro, lime, bean sprouts, and Thai basil are added as garnish.

Spicy Snow Crab And Asparagus Soup

THE FIRST TIME I ENJOYED THIS HEARTY SOUP WAS IN BALTIMORE, MARYLAND. ALTHOUGH YOU MAY find this soup on many Chinese menus, this delicious seafood dish makes an excellent starter course for any fine dining experience.

INGREDIENTS:

1 tbs butter
½ lb snow crab meat
½ lb fresh asparagus, cut into ¾" pieces
3 cups clam juice, bottled, or light fish stock
2 cups water

1 cup white wine
1 medium shallot, finely chopped
1 stalk celery, finely diced
1 tbs coriander leaves, chopped
Salt and white pepper to taste

METHOD:

In large soup pot add butter and heat. Add shallots and celery to pot and sauté for a few minutes. Next, add clam juice, water, and wine and stir well.

As soon as mixture comes to a boil add cut-up asparagus. Reduce heat and simmer for 30 minutes. Just before serving add crabmeat and fresh coriander along with salt and pepper.

Serve piping hot in individual soup bowls. A dash of chili sauce takes this soup to a higher level.

Pomegranate Salsa

THIS FRUIT IS COMMON IN SOUTH AMERICA, THE MEDITERRANEAN, AND SOUTHEAST ASIA. RECENTLY, it was introduced to the North American palate and like a wildfire chefs have featured pomegranate in many of their delightful recipes. This salsa is refreshing, wonderfully sharp, and flavourful. It makes an excellent accompaniment to grilled fish and meat.

INGREDIENTS:

1 large ripe pomegranate's seeds

1 medium onion, finely chopped

¼ cup fresh lime juice

1 tsp lemon rind, finely grated

1 tbs olive oil

2 finger hot green chilies, finely chopped

½ cup fresh cilantro leaves, chopped

½ cup fresh mint leaves, chopped

½ tsp black pepper, coarsely ground

1 tsp granulated sugar

Salt to taste

METHOD:

Cut pomegranate into 2 halves. Holding fruit with cut side above large bowl, beat skin gently to allow seeds to separate from fruit and fall into bowl. Remove and discard any skin particles that may have fallen along with seeds.

Mix all remaining ingredients with pomegranate seeds, cover bowl, and refrigerate for at least 1 hour before serving.

Kachumbar

KACHUMBAR IS A VERY COMMON INDIAN AND AFRICAN TOSSED SALAD WITHOUT ANY SALAD LEAVES. Kachumbar is often served with biryanis, BBQs, and main meals or as a garnish with many delicacies.

INGREDIENTS:

1 lb red onions, finely diced

½ lb firm fresh tomatoes, finely diced

4 finger hot green chilies, finely chopped

3 tbs fresh coriander leaves, chopped

1 large fresh lemon

Salt and pepper to taste

½ lb cucumber, peeled and diced (optional)

METHOD:

In mixing bowl add onions, tomatoes, and chilies and mix well. Add washed coriander leaves into bowl and squeeze juice of lemon carefully onto salad, ensuring that seeds do not drop in.

Salad may be chilled prior to adding seasonings. Add salt and pepper just before serving; otherwise kachumbar will have too much liquid, as salt will draw fluids from onions and tomatoes. Onions will lose crunch as well.

Mango Salsa

THIS MANGO SALSA IS AN EXCELLENT ACCOMPANIMENT TO ANY KIND OF PAN-FRIED, BAKED, OR BBQ'D fish. It can also be served as a salad. Prepared a day ahead, it stays good in the fridge.

INGREDIENTS:

4 firm sweet mangoes

2 large firm field tomatoes

1 large red onion

2 bunches green onions

2 finger hot green chilies

1 large pomegranate

3 lemons

1 lime

½ cup fresh coriander leaves, washed and chopped

2 tbs fresh ginger root, julienned

Salt and pepper to taste

1 tbs granulated sugar

METHOD:

Peel mangoes, dice them small, and add to large mixing bowl. Wash tomatoes, dice them the same size as mangoes, and mix with mangoes. Peel onion, dice, and add to bowl. Wash green onions, chop off and discard roots, finely cut onions including stems, add to bowl, and mix well.

Slice finger hot chilies lengthwise, finely chop, and add to bowl.

Cut pomegranate into 2 halves and gently beat each half on skin with wooden spatula, ensuring that cut side of fruit is facing bowl. Seeds will easily fall into bowl. Finely chop peeled ginger root, add to bowl, and mix all ingredients in bowl. Next, squeeze juice of lemons and lime into bowl, ensuring that all seeds are discarded.

Now add coriander, add sugar, and season salsa with salt and pepper. Mix all ingredients well, cover bowl with saran wrap, and refrigerate for at least 4 hours before serving. Before serving, taste salsa and make any seasoning adjustments. For more heat add more chopped chilies.

Fresh Garden Salad With Roasted Red Pepper Dressing

THIS HAS TO BE ONE OF THE BEST GARDEN SALADS YOU CAN SERVE AT YOUR NEXT SUMMER BBQ OR brunch get-together.

INGREDIENTS:

1 large red pepper

1 large green pepper

1 head romaine lettuce

1 head Boston lettuce

1 small head radicchio

1 small head purple cabbage

1 medium red onion

2 large carrots

2 small zucchinis

1 cup cherry tomatoes

½ lb white mushrooms

¼ lb shiitake mushrooms

¼ lb snow peas

¼ lb portobello mushrooms

½ lb tender asparagus

¼ lb fresh bean sprouts

1 small pkg baby spinach

DRESSING:

1 large red pepper, finely diced into ¼" cubes

(Place cubes on cookie sheet and roast in oven at 500°F for about 10 minutes. Be sure not to burn peppers. Cool in dish.)

¼ cup white vinegar

¼ cup balsamic vinegar

¼ cup virgin olive oil

1 tbs garlic paste

2 tbs Parmesan cheese, grated

1 tsp Dijon mustard

1 tbs Hellmann's mayonnaise

1 tsp Tabasco sauce

2 tbs fresh basil, chopped

Salt and freshly ground black pepper to taste

1 tbs palm sugar (optional)

METHOD:

Wash and clean all ingredients for salad. Cut vegetables to your liking and place into large salad bowl. Break greens with hands and add to bowl. Slice red cabbage and add to bowl. Remove and discard heads of bean sprouts and add to bowl. Add whole cherry tomatoes. Toss all ingredients well with roasted red peppers.

In dressing jar add all dressing ingredients and stir well. Pour dressing over salad just before serving and toss well. Dressing can be made several hours before serving salad.

Cucumber Salad

THIS IS A REFRESHING SALAD FOR YOUR NEXT THAI DINNER OR WITH ANY GRILLED FISH.

INGREDIENTS:

2 tbs peanut oil

2 tbs peanuts, shelled and blanched

1 large English cucumber, peeled

2 red Thai chilies, thinly sliced

1 green Thai chill, thinly sliced

1 shallot, finely chopped

1 tbs lime rind, finely chopped

2 tbs fresh lime juice

2 tsp nam pla (fish sauce)

1 tsp palm sugar, crushed

15 shrimp, dried and finely chopped

METHOD:

In small pan heat peanut oil and add peanuts. Cook for a few minutes until peanuts are lightly browned. Remove peanuts and cool on absorbent paper towel.

Cut peeled cucumber lengthwise and using teaspoon scoop out seeds and discard. Cucumber pieces should look like canoes. Slice cucumbers about 1/8" thick to look like crescents and place in bowl.

In small bowl mix remaining ingredients well except shrimp. Pour this dressing over cucumbers and mix well. Garnish salad with chopped toasted peanuts and sprinkle chopped shrimp.

Baby Spinach Salad With Mango Shavings

SPINACH IS BELIEVED TO HAVE ORIGINATED IN ANCIENT PERSIA. ARAB TRADERS CARRIED IT INTO India, and then the plant was introduced to ancient China, where it was known as "Persian vegetable." The earliest available record of the spinach plant was recorded in Chinese, stating it was brought to China via Nepal (probably around AD 647).

Spinach is a wonderful vegetable with high nutritional value and is extremely rich in antioxidants, especially when fresh, steamed, or quickly boiled. It is a rich source of vitamins A, B2, B6, C, E, and K, as well as magnesium, manganese, folate, betaine, iron, calcium, potassium, folic acid, copper, protein, phosphorus, zinc, niacin, selenium, and omega-3 fatty acids.

This has to be my most popular spinach salad creation. I created it for my two foodie friends Rocky Mohan and Atul Sikand, who both love spinach salads. The sweet and savoury combination of mango strips, ripe cherry tomatoes, and small morsels of lightly peppered boiled eggs make this salad sensational. There is very little oil in the simple dressing, but you won't miss it.

INGREDIENTS:

8 cups fresh baby spinach leaves, washed and spin-dried

3 hard-boiled eggs, quartered

12 cherry tomatoes, washed

2 firm sweet mangoes, peeled and thinly shaved

DRESSING:

½ cup pulp-free orange juice

1 tbs honey

Pinch salt

1 tbs olive oil

Coarse black pepper, freshly ground

METHOD:

Mix all dressing ingredients gently in measuring cup except pepper.

In large mixing bowl add spinach, pour in dressing, and mix well. Distribute spinach equally on 4 individual salad plates and randomly drop strips of mango on top of each plate. Next, place 3 cherry tomatoes, well spread,

on each plate. Lastly, place 3 quartered eggs on each plate between tomatoes. Grind fresh pepper onto salad and serve.

You may also wish to garnish this succulent salad with toasted almond flakes or any other nut of your choice.

Spicy Chicken Salad

THIS SALAD MAKES A WONDERFUL SIMPLE ENTRÉE DISH OR EXCELLENT SANDWICHES FOR PICNICS and family get-togethers.

Yields 6 individual salads or 12 sandwiches.

INGREDIENTS:

1 whole chicken, cleaned (2½ to 3 lb)

½ tsp white pepper

1 tsp salt

1 bay leaf

½ oz ginger root, finely chopped

½ tsp garlic, crushed

10 black peppercorns

1 finger hot pepper

DRESSING:

½ cup mayonnaise

½ tsp Dijon mustard

¼ cup celery, diced

¼ cup onion, finely chopped

1 tsp Tabasco

METHOD:

Place chicken in large soup pot and add all ingredients for stock. Cover chicken with lukewarm water and cover pot. Bring water to a quick boil, reduce heat, and let chicken simmer for 1 hour or until tender. Remove chicken from pot and let cool. Strain stock and save for other recipes. Carefully remove skin of chicken and discard. Debone chicken, dice meat, and place into mixing bowl. Toss in celery, and add mayonnaise, mustard, chopped onion, and Tabasco. Mix salad well. You may wish to add mayonnaise a little at a time until desired texture is achieved. Chill salad before serving.

Caesar Salad

THIS IS A FAVOURITE RECIPE THAT GOES GREAT WITH GRILLED MEAT AND PASTA DISHES.

INGREDIENTS:

1 head romaine lettuce

½ cup garlic croutons

1 tbs fresh bacon bits

1 hard-boiled egg

DRESSING:

1 whole egg

¼ cup olive oil

1 tbs balsamic vinegar

1 tbs white vinegar

1 tbs fresh lemon juice

1 tsp anchovy paste

2 cloves garlic, crushed

2 tbs Dijon mustard

2 tbs dry mustard powder

2 tbs Hellmann's mayonnaise

Salt and freshly ground black pepper to taste

METHOD:

Pulsate all dressing ingredients in blender at medium-low speed for a few minutes. Store dressing in jar and refrigerate.

Break washed lettuce with hands and add to large salad bowl. Just before serving add dressing and toss salad.

Garnish with garlic croutons, bacon bits, and sliced hard-boiled egg.

Suggestions: Vegetarians can skip anchovy paste, bacon bits, and hard-boiled egg. For tasty croutons use home-made leftover garlic bread.

Mache Leaf Salad With Mango And A Wicked Dressing

IN CANADA WE ARE BLESSED TO HAVE WONDERFUL SUMMERS, THE PERFECT TIME TO ENJOY REFRESH-ing, healthy salads. Thanks goes to a farmer in California and American salad eaters, who have embraced mache lettuce.

Mache is also called lamb's lettuce, and has been cultivated in France since the seventeenth century. But in California's Salinas Valley, the tiny, dark green plant with the sweet, nutty flavour has recently made its American commercial debut.

Mache is now available in hundreds of stores across North America. With the introduction of it we are seeing a trend toward a sweeter, gentler kind of lettuce and a departure from bitter greens like radicchio and arugula.

When I discovered this new baby spinach–like salad green, I started creating different recipe combinations and complementary dressings to enjoy this sweet and nutty wonder leaf. Once again I am very pleased to share another symphony of colours and succulent tastes with you all.

INGREDIENTS:

4 cups washed mache leaf salad greens

½ cup red radishes, halved and sliced

1 large ripe mango, pitted, peeled, and julienned

¾ cup cherry tomatoes, washed and halved

½ lime, cut in half and thinly sliced

DRESSING:

1 tsp ginger marmalade

1 tsp habanero pepper jelly

¼ cup orange juice

1 tbs balsamic vinegar

1 tbs olive oil

Juice of 1 lime

Salt to taste

METHOD:

In salad bowl gently toss all salad ingredients. For dressing, mix all dressing ingredients in dressing jar and whisk well. Individually plate mixed salad and pour dressing onto salad per your liking. Finally, add freshly ground black pepper and serve.

Mache Leaf Salad With Mango, Mushrooms, And Radish

TWO DECADES AGO SEVERAL AMERICAN CHEFS RETURNED FROM FRANCE WITH SEEDS FOR BABY lettuce, and soon spring mix salad was born in the United States. Today, you can find the tender little leaves in bags and bins in nearly every grocery store. Since then, Americans have experienced a romance with radicchio, arugula, and frisée, a member of the chicory family with a frizzy texture as well as a deliciously bitter edge. These days, thanks to a farmer in California, American salad eaters have turned over a new leaf and embraced mache lettuce.

Recently, I spotted mache leaf lettuce at a local grocery store in Ottawa. At first I thought this was a younger variety of spinach, but soon discovered it was a new leaf salad. I had to try it, so I bought a pack and as soon as I tasted it, the sweetness and nuttiness blew my mind. Immediately, the culinary wheels started to turn and I created a new simple but succulent salad that is worthy of sharing with you all.

INGREDIENTS:

4 cups washed mache leaf salad greens

1 cup small white mushrooms, quartered

½ cup red radish, julienned

½ cup sweet red peppers, diced

1 ripe mango, peeled and cubed

DRESSING:

1 tsp fresh ginger root paste

¼ cup mango juice

¼ cup orange juice

Juice of 1 lime

Salt to taste

METHOD:

In salad bowl toss all salad ingredients. For dressing, mix all dressing ingredients in dressing jar and shake well.

Pour dressing onto salad per your liking, add freshly ground black pepper, and serve.

Quick Pickled Carrots

THESE DELECTABLE DELIGHTS ARE CARROT STICKS IN A HOT AND SWEET-AND-SOUR GLAZE.

INGREDIENTS:

2 cups carrot sticks, cut into ¼" pieces

1 hot green chili, sliced

1 tbs coriander, finely chopped

1 tbs chili sauce

1 tsp light soy sauce

1 tbs brown sugar

2 tbs white vinegar

Salt and pepper to taste

METHOD:

In mixing bowl combine all ingredients and refrigerate for a few hours. Serve with your favourite savoury snacks, like pakoras, tikkis, or samosas.

CAULIFLOWER AND TURNIP PICKLE

Chutneys,
Condiments,
And Sauces

Coriander Chutney

THIS FAIRLY SIMPLE TO MAKE CHUTNEY IS A MUST IN EVERY KITCHEN, AS IT HAS MANY USES.

INGREDIENTS:

10 sprigs spring onions, including green tops, chopped

3 cups firmly packed coriander leaves, including stems, cleaned and chopped

2 cloves garlic, peeled and crushed

1 tsp salt

1 tbs brown sugar

1 tbs garam masala

¼ cup fresh lemon juice

¼ cup prepared tamarind

METHOD:

Place all ingredients in blender or food processor and puree to a smooth consistency. Scrape sides during blending process if necessary.

Taste chutney and fine-tune by adjusting salt, lemon juice, or tamarind. If you wish to make it hotter add some red chili powder or green chilies.

Jar chutney and enjoy with your favourite snack. Mason jars work really well for storing. Chutney will stay good for months in fridge.

Tamarind Chutney

TAMARIND CHUTNEY IS ONE OF THE MOST COMMONLY USED CHUTNEYS IN SOUTH ASIAN HOMES around the globe. This chutney can be served practically with any snack. Plain tamarind sauce can be used in several Thai and Indian recipes.

INGREDIENTS:

1 lb packaged tamarind

6 cups water

1 cup sugar

1 tsp ginger powder

1 tsp cumin seed powder, toasted

1 tsp chili powder

Salt to taste

METHOD:

Bring water to a boil in saucepan and add tamarind. Turn heat off, cover pot, and allow tamarind to soak for at least 6 hours.

Using hands rub tamarind in water to dissolve and separate seeds. Discard seeds and any stems. Blend and strain sauce into glass bowl and add sugar, cumin, ginger, salt, and pepper. Mix well. Taste sauce and make any necessary adjustments.

Store chutney in mason jars and refrigerate. This chutney can be safely refrigerated for 2 months and can also be frozen for long-term storage.

Chopped onions, green chilies, grated carrots, chopped coriander leaves, finely chopped ginger root, and chopped pitted dates can be added to make chutney exotic. It makes an excellent accompaniment to vegetarian meals and yogurt delicacies.

Pudina Chutney

A HOT AND TANGY FRESH MINT RELISH THAT WILL TICKLE THE TASTE BUDS.

INGREDIENTS:

3 tbs anardana, soaked in warm water

1 cup fresh mint leaves

1 cup fresh coriander leaves

3 finger hot green chilies

1 clove garlic, chopped

½ medium onion, chopped

2 tbs raw mango, chopped

½ medium tomato, chopped

1 tsp sugar

1 tsp red chili powder

Salt to taste

METHOD:

Drain pomegranate seeds, add to blender or food processor, and crush finely. Clean, wash, and chop mint, coriander, and chilies and add to blender. Now add all remaining ingredients and blend into a coarse paste. Taste chutney and make any necessary adjustments. If you prefer chutney a little tart you may add juice from half a lemon.

Store chutney in jar and refrigerate. Pudina chutney can be stored in fridge for a few months.

Serve chutney with your favourite pakoras and snacks, or as a condiment with any meal. This chutney goes great with any daal or roti.

Hot Peri Peri Butter Sauce

THIS IS AN EXCELLENT SIMPLE SAUCE, TRADITIONALLY SERVED WITH ALL KINDS OF SHELLED SEAFOOD. Since it is a dipping sauce, it should be served in small individual serving dishes heated by small tea light candles.

I tried a similar version of this recipe in Malaga, Spain. It had a hint of anchovy paste and white wine and was used in the preparation of steamed mussels. It was simply divine.

INGREDIENTS:

½ cup unsalted butter

Juice of 1 lemon

¼ tsp lemon rind

8 peri peri peppers, ground

¼ tsp garlic paste

METHOD:

In small saucepan melt butter on medium heat and add remaining ingredients. Cook for a few minutes, stirring sauce. Remove from heat and butter is ready to be served.

Cucumber Raita

A DELICIOUS AND REFRESHING ACCOMPANIMENT, YOGURT IS COMMONLY SERVED WITH BOTH VEG-etarian and non-vegetarian Indian meals. Some believe that it puts the fire out when indulging in hot and spicy cuisine. This may be true, but yogurt also helps with digestion and to diminish any aftereffects such as heartburn from eating heavily spiced foods.

Raitas are made in many different ways. The one with cucumber is the most popular and easy to make. However, one may also add diced boiled potatoes, fried okras, steamed grated squash, pineapple tidbits, and boondi.

INGREDIENTS:

2 cups yogurt

½ cup cucumber, seeded and grated

1 tbs onion, finely chopped

1 tsp fresh mint, finely chopped

1 tsp fresh coriander leaves, finely chopped

1 finger hot green chili, finely chopped

Salt to taste

½ tsp black pepper, freshly ground

¼ tsp red chili powder

1 tsp cumin seeds, roasted

METHOD:

In serving bowl add yogurt and whisk. Mix in grated cucumber, onion, mint, coriander, chili, and salt. Stir all ingredients well. Garnish with black pepper and red chili powder. Finally, rub roasted cumin seeds between palms and sprinkle all over yogurt mixture. Cover with plastic wrap and refrigerate until ready to serve.

Thai Chili Sauce

THIS SAUCE IS AN EXCELLENT ACCOMPANIMENT AS A CONDIMENT TO ANY THAI MEAL. IT WILL GIVE any Asian meal that extra fiery touch.

INGREDIENTS:

½ lb Thai green chilies, washed, stems removed, and finely chopped

1 tbs ginger root, finely chopped

1 tsp garlic paste

½ cup light soy sauce

2 tbs nam pla (fish sauce)

2 tbs fresh coriander stems, finely chopped

1 tsp brown sugar

METHOD:

In mason jar mix all ingredients and store in refrigera-tor. Sauce is immediately ready to use. However, it tastes much better after storing in fridge for a day or two, and can be safely refrigerated for at least 1 month.

Fresh Lemon-Ginger Chili Pickle

THIS IS A VERY SIMPLE HOMEMADE PICKLE RECIPE PREPARED WITH FRESH GINGER ROOT, CHILIES, and juicy lemons. If you follow the instructions carefully this pickle has a good shelf life. Usually, it turns out to be so delicious that this preparation goes fast, as it can be used with practically every Desi meal.

INGREDIENTS:

16 fresh juicy lemons, washed and pat-dried

2 lbs fresh ginger

1 lb fresh green chilies, stems removed, washed, and pat-dried

½ cup salt

1 tbs turmeric powder

1 tbs ajwain

METHOD:

Cut 12 lemons into quarters, slice them about ¼" thick, and discard any seeds. Place cut lemon in large, clean, dry pan. Next, peel ginger root neatly and slice into manageable-sized pieces. Add to lemons. With sharp knife carefully slit all chilies and add to mixing pan. Sprinkle ajwain over cut-up ingredients and gently mix. Next, add salt and mix well.

In cup squeeze juice of remaining 4 lemons and discard seeds. Add turmeric powder to lemon juice and mix well. Next, pour mixture all over pickle and mix well.

Into large sterilized jar with tight lid, gently pour pickle and close lid. Shake jar well and store in a bright place. Continue to shake jar occasionally for 2 to 3 days so skin of lemons starts to soften. This pickle will take another 5 to 6 days before lemon skin loses bitterness and pickle becomes edible.

Please always use dry, clean spoon to take pickle out of jar. No refrigeration needed.

Mag's Extra-Hot Chili Oil

CHILI OIL IS A CONDIMENT MADE FROM VEGETABLE OIL OR ANY OTHER OIL OF CHOICE THAT HAS BEEN infused with chili peppers and other ingredients. This oil is commonly used in Chinese cooking, and is particularly popular in Sichuan, Manchurian, and Hakka cuisines. It is often used as a dip for BBQ'd meat, noodles, and dim sum delicacies. I love using it in pho and spring rolls by mixing it with plum sauce.

I have tried chili oil in many Asian restaurants, but never found one that was hot enough to tickle my taste buds. Thus, I decided to prepare my own special beyond extra-hot chili oil; my version has no room for sugar or any sweetener. Please exercise caution when making this wickedly hot oil. Make sure your kitchen is well ventilated or prepare it outdoors. You may use any oil of your choice for this recipe.

Once the oil is ready and jarred, the solids typically settle to the bottom of the container in which it is stored. While using chili oil in your cooking or dining, you may choose how much of the solids to use or simply flavour the food with only the oil.

INGREDIENTS:

½ lb habanero peppers

½ lb Thai hot red peppers

½ lb Thai green chilies

½ lb Scotch bonnet peppers

1 cup dry red chili flakes, crushed

¼ cup Sichuan peppercorns, coarsely ground

4 cups onions, finely chopped

½ cup garlic paste

½ cup tomato paste

1 tbs turmeric

3 cups light vegetable oil

½ cup white vinegar, boiled

3 tbs salt, or to taste

METHOD:

In large saucepan heat about ½ cup oil and sauté chopped onions until almost brown. Next, add garlic and cook for a few minutes. Then add turmeric, dry chili flakes, and Sichuan peppers and mix well, making sure onions do not burn and continuing to stir. Add tomato paste and salt. Mix well to ensure tomato paste blends with onion mixture.

In the meantime, wash all peppers and remove and discard stems. Once all peppers are washed and cleaned, pat dry using paper towel. Cut peppers small, place into blender, and puree to a fine paste. Avoid sniffing peppers and do not rub eyes. Add chili paste to pot with onions and mix well. Next, add boiled vinegar to mixture, stir well, and gradually add remaining oil. Stir oil into mixture, bring to a gentle boil, then immediately turn heat down and let oil simmer for at least 15 minutes. Turn heat down and let cool.

When chili oil has cooled, pour into small airtight mason jars and store until needed.

CAUTION:

When handling these peppers make sure to wear disposable gloves. Using a nose and mouth mask would also be a good safety measure.

Horseradish Sauce

THIS SAUCE CAN BE SERVED WITH ROAST BEEF OR PRIME RIB. IT ALSO GOES WELL WITH BEEF SANDwiches and can even be served as a veggie dip.

Makes about 1 cup sauce.

INGREDIENTS:

1 cup sour cream

2 tbs mayonnaise

2 tbs prepared horseradish

Salt and white pepper to taste

Mix all ingredients well. Chill sauce before serving.

Malaysian Peanut Sauce

PEANUT SAUCE IS COMMONLY USED TO ACCOMPANY CHINESE, MALAYSIAN, THAI, AND VIETNAMESE snacks, such as dumplings, rice paper salad rolls, or satays. Every country has its own recipe for this popular sauce. I have tried to integrate ingredients from all over in my recipe to enhance your dining pleasure.

INGREDIENTS:

1 medium onion, peeled and coarsely chopped

1 tbs ginger root, chopped

1 tsp galangal, chopped

1 lemongrass stalk, without hard outer layer, chopped

4 whole red chilies, dried and crushed

2 tbs nam pla (fish sauce)

3 tbs peanut oil

½ cup plain tamarind sauce

½ cup water

3 tbs brown sugar

1 cup crunchy peanut butter

METHOD:

In food processor add onion, ginger root, galangal, lemongrass, and nam pla. Process ingredients to form smooth paste.

In saucepan heat peanut oil, add paste, and sauté, stirring and scraping until paste has nicely browned.

Add tamarind sauce and water to pot and stir well. Bring to a boil, then turn heat down to medium and simmer for 10 minutes.

Now add crunchy peanut butter and sugar and simmer until sauce slightly thickens.

Serve sauce warm with your favourite snack.

Mag's Garlic Sauce

THIS IS A FAIRLY EASY RECIPE AND THE SAUCE HAS POTENTIAL FOR SEVERAL DIFFERENT USES.

INGREDIENTS:

½ cup mayonnaise

½ cup sour cream

1 cup hung yogurt

2 tbs fresh lemon juice

1 tbs fresh garlic paste

½ tsp hot sauce or chili sauce

Salt and pepper to taste

METHOD:

In mixing bowl add all ingredients except salt and pepper. You may want to add more or omit hot sauce depending on preference. Mix well, into velvet-like sauce. Add salt and pepper and mix again. Store in jar and refrigerate. It has a long fridge life.

Use sauce as desired. It has lots of uses so be certain to make enough to keep on hand. Try as a dip, in pita sandwiches, and with grilled meat. I have used it as a dressing for my Caesar salad and it worked extremely well. It also takes deviled eggs to a different dimension, and its marriage with tuna for sandwiches is exceptional. I leave the rest to your imagination.

Passion Fruit Sauce

THIS EXOTIC SAUCE IS FAIRLY SIMPLE AND EASY TO MAKE. IT SERVES AS AN EXCELLENT TOPPING FOR plain ice cream, fruit salads, cakes, flans, or cheesecakes. Passion fruit sauce is very fragrant and slightly tart. In Kenya several cocktails use this sauce to impart an exotic taste, a colourful visual experience, and an added texture from the edible seeds of the fruit.

INGREDIENTS:

10 ripe passion fruits, cut in half

½ cup water

1 tsp cornstarch

5 tbs granulated sugar

½ tsp lime rind, finely grated

1 cup orange juice, freshly squeezed and strained

2 tbs chilled butter, cut into small pieces

METHOD:

In small cup add 2 tbs orange juice, dissolve cornstarch, and keep aside.

Add remaining orange juice, sugar, and lime rind to saucepan and bring to a boil. Turn heat down and let mixture simmer until reduced by half.

Scoop passion fruit pulp and seeds into pot with ½ cup water and bring to a boil again. Add cornstarch mixture to pot, stir well, and cook for 1 minute until sauce thickens slightly. Remove pot from heat and whisk in butter pieces a few at a time.

The sauce is then ready to be used. It is served best when warm and can be refrigerated for at least 1 week. Warm it when needed.

Tangy Chili Seafood Sauce

THIS IS AN EXCELLENT SAUCE TO GO WITH YOUR STEAMED SHRIMP, CRAB, OR MUSSELS. I HAVE OFTEN served this sauce with BBQ'd or grilled meat and vegetable fritters.

INGREDIENTS:

2 cups tomato ketchup

2 tbs Worcestershire sauce

5 tbs prepared horseradish

2 tbs. Tabasco

METHOD:

In jar add all ingredients and mix well. Sauce is ready to be served. It is best to store it in fridge before using with your favourite seafood or any other delicacy.

Tartar Sauce

THIS IS A FAIRLY SIMPLE RECIPE FOR MAKING HOMEMADE TARTAR SAUCE.

Makes 1¼ cups sauce.

INGREDIENTS:

1 cup mayonnaise or salad dressing

¼ cup dill pickle or drained sweet dill pickle relish, finely chopped

1 tbs green onion, finely chopped

1 tbs fresh parsley, finely chopped

1 tbs pimiento, finely diced

1 tsp lemon juice

METHOD:

In small mixing bowl stir together mayonnaise or salad dressing, pickle, onion, parsley, pimiento, and lemon juice. Cover and chill for at least 2 hours. Store in jar. It can be refrigerated up to 2 weeks.

Serve with fried fish or any seafood meal.

Thai Dipping Sauce

THIS IS AN IDEAL DIPPING SAUCE FOR ALL DEEP-FRIED, STEAMED, OR BBQ'D THAI SNACKS. IT ALSO works wonders when poured over sizzling-hot BBQ'd meat, poultry, or fish.

INGREDIENTS:

½ cup rice vinegar

½ cup white vinegar

3 tbs dark soy sauce

3 tbs nam pla (fish sauce)

6 Thai red chilies, finely chopped

2 tbs brown sugar

2 tsp ginger root, finely chopped

½ tsp garlic paste

2 kaffir lime leaves, centre vein removed, finely shredded

1 stalk fresh lemongrass, hard outer layer removed, finely chopped

METHOD:

Mix all ingredients in jar and refrigerate. Sauce is ready to use in a few hours and can be stored in fridge for at least 1 month.

Park Road Tomato Sauce

THIS IS A DELICIOUS TOMATO SAUCE CREATED BY MAGON YOUNGSTERS FROM OUR PARK ROAD RESI-dence in Nairobi, Kenya.

I grew up in a house in Nairobi that was located on a corner, right across from the Park Road Primary School and Technical High School. Many of the recipes that I feature originated from the kitchen in this house. While many of the recipes that I showcase here were passed on to me by my ancestors, this is a delicacy that Magon youngsters can take full credit for.

I remember one Saturday morning some of my cousins and I decided to cook curried vegetable for lunch. We proceeded to make the basic sauce with some fresh ingredients following the methods our elders had introduced in our kitchen. The aroma was superb and as our hunger pangs kept growing none of us could resist tasting the sauce that we had created. Wow! It was so delicious that we ended up finishing all of it with sliced bread and licking the pot clean. Thus, a new sauce emerged that has been so popular that even today after five decades every member of the Magon clan craves this very simple yet tasty delicacy. Over the years we have hardly made any changes and the sauce still tastes the same as when we created it in our youth. We enjoy this sauce with parathas, pooris, and often some fresh white bread.

INGREDIENTS:

10 medium fresh tomatoes, diced

3 medium onions, sliced

1 tbs garlic paste

2 tbs fresh ginger root, chopped

4 finger hot green chilies

1 tsp turmeric

1 tsp garam masala, homemade

1 tsp cumin seeds

1 tbs butter

2 tbs fresh coriander leaves, chopped

1 tbs ginger root, julienned

Cooking oil or butter

Salt and pepper to taste

METHOD:

Note: This sauce should always be made with fresh ingredients. Also ensure that the sequence of the recipe is followed accurately.

In saucepan heat just enough oil to sauté onions. When oil is hot add sliced onions and sauté until almost golden brown. Add garlic paste and ginger. Stir-fry for a few minutes, then add turmeric, green chilies, and garam masala. Stir mixture well and add tomatoes, blending thoroughly. Add salt and pepper and cook for about 15 to 20 minutes, until fat starts to separate. Then rub cumin seeds between palms, add to sauce, and mix well. Taste for seasoning and make any necessary adjustments. Just before serving add some extra butter to sauce. As soon as it melts in, transfer sauce to serving dish and garnish with fresh coriander leaves and julienned ginger root. Serve sauce hot.

Lachedar parathas or pooris are excellent accompaniments to this sauce and make a great breakfast or lunch. This dish will also really enhance pastas.

Ultimate Meatless Pasta Sauce For Vegetarians

IN CANADA DURING THE COLD WINTER MONTHS, THE CONSUMPTION OF COMFORTING PASTA INCREASES all over the country. Along with pasta come along various rich, cheesy, and creamy sauces laced with loads of buttery goodness. However, several fresh garden vegetables and a generous sprinkling of herbs and spices can also liven up pasta sauces. I have come up with an ultimate savoury vegetarian sauce to top any pasta dish with Parmesan cheese and I guarantee that you'll never miss the meat. My vegetarian nieces and nephews inspired me to create this succulent sauce. It is a healthy and heart-friendly preparation that has a long list of applications in your kitchen.

INGREDIENTS:

¼ cup vegetable cooking oil

1 large Spanish onion, chopped

1 tbs garlic paste

2 green chilies, chopped

2 tbs fresh ginger root, chopped

1 large eggplant, finely diced

2 sticks celery, finely diced

1 large carrot, diced

1 large potato, washed, peeled, and diced

1 cup zucchini, diced

1 cup portobello mushrooms, diced

1 cup shimeji mushrooms, chopped

½ cup green onions, chopped

6 cups ripe tomatoes, chopped

2 tbs tomato paste

¼ cup fresh basil, chopped

1 tbs oregano, dried

Salt to taste

½ cup grated Parmesan cheese

Cherry tomatoes, halved

Green onions, chopped

Fresh basil leaves

Chili flakes

METHOD:

In large pot heat oil and add onions, garlic, chilies, and ginger root. Mix well and sauté mixture for a few minutes. Next, add eggplant, celery, carrot, potato, zucchini, mushrooms, and green onions. Mix all ingredients gently, and add salt and chopped tomatoes. Mix well and add oregano and chopped basil.

Cover pot and let sauce cook on medium heat for 1 hour or so, making sure to stir sauce occasionally. After 1 hour add tomato paste and half of Parmesan cheese, taste sauce, and make any adjustments. Simmer sauce for another 30 minutes. Let sauce sit for a few hours before serving. Just before serving reheat sauce and plate in large serving bowl. Garnish with coriander, remaining Parmesan cheese, and chili flakes. Finally, decorate with halved cherry tomatoes.

This sauce freezes well and can be used later for several pasta dishes. Serve on spaghetti, linguini, or any pasta of choice. I tried it on pizza and lasagne and the results were outstanding.

Homemade Sriracha Sauce

SRIRACHA CHILI SAUCE IS FREQUENTLY USED IN THAILAND FOR DIPPING, PARTICULARLY SEAFOOD. IN Vietnamese cuisine this sauce is used as one of the condiments for pho and fried noodles. Interestingly, people use plum sauce for egg rolls but I love this chili sauce with my egg or spring rolls. It is also great on sandwiches and hot dogs. The following is a simple recipe to make this wonderful sauce at home.

INGREDIENTS:

- 1½ lbs red jalapeño peppers, stems snipped off
- 6 cloves garlic, peeled
- 4 tbs light brown sugar
- 1 tbs kosher salt
- ½ cup distilled white vinegar

METHOD:

Add peppers, garlic, sugar, and salt into food processor and pulsate until chilies are finely chopped; make sure to carefully scrape sides of bowl as necessary. Transfer mixture to clean jar, cover, and let sit at room temperature.

Check jar each day for fermentation, when little bubbles start forming at bottom of jar in about 3 to 5 days, and stir contents daily. Let fermentation continue for few days until chilies are no longer rising in volume.

Transfer chilies to blender, add white vinegar, and puree until completely smooth, for 1 to 3 minutes. Strain pureed mixture into saucepan, using rubber spatula to push through as much pulp as possible; only seeded and larger chili pieces should remain in strainer and be discarded.

Bring mixture to a boil, reduce heat, and simmer 5 to 10 minutes until sauce slightly thickens and clings to spoon. Transfer to airtight container and store in refrigerator for up to 6 months.

SPICED WHOLE OKRA WITH GROUND LAMB

Typically, naan is served hot and brushed with ghee or butter.
It can be used to scoop other foods, or stuffed with a filling

Rice, Breads, And Noodles

Thai Chicken Fried Rice

THIS IS A VERY FLAVOURFUL RICE DISH ADAPTED FROM CHINESE FRIED RICE DISHES, BUT WITH A slight twist. The secret lies in the magic ingredients: the fish sauce, garlic, and hot pepper. Any kind of meat or seafood can be used for this recipe.

INGREDIENTS:

3 cups long-grain rice, cooked

3 tbs cooking oil

250 gm skinless chicken, diced up small

1 medium onion, finely sliced

½ tsp garlic, minced

1 tbs nam pla (fish sauce)

1 tbs light soy sauce

1 tsp hot chili sauce

150 gm fresh bean sprouts, washed and drained

Green onion sprig, shredded, for garnish

METHOD:

In wok heat oil, add chicken, garlic, and hot sauce, and cook until chicken is done. Remove chicken and keep aside. Add onions to hot wok along with bean sprouts and stir-fry until onions soften a bit. You may need to add a little more cooking oil at this stage. Immediately, add cooked rice and chicken to wok. Add nam pla and soy sauce and stir-fry on high heat until rice is thoroughly heated through. Taste and adjust for seasoning.

Serve rice in platter and garnish with shredded green onion. This is an excellent accompaniment to your Asian feast.

Jeera Rice

THIS SIMPLE BUT DELICIOUS DISH IS BASMATI RICE COOKED WITH CUMIN SEEDS. PEAS, CUMIN, CARdamom, cloves, cinnamon sticks, and black peppercorns can also be added to make a rice pilaf. Similarly, chopped vegetables can be added to make a vegetable pilaf.

INGREDIENTS:

1 cup basmati rice

1 tsp cumin seeds

1 tsp salt

3 tbs clarified butter

2 cups warm water

METHOD:

Wash rice and soak in boiling hot water for at least 15 minutes. In shallow saucepan heat butter and add cumin seeds. As soon as cumin seeds start to cook, drain rice and add to pan. Stir well and add salt. Now add warm water and bring rice to a boil, stirring gently.

Cover pan, turn heat to medium, and let rice cook until all water is absorbed and rice is fluffy. Serve piping hot with your favourite vegetarian or non-vegetarian dish.

Ugali

I GREW UP ON CHAPATIS AND RICE AS STAPLE FOODS, BUT WHAT ALWAYS AMAZED ME WAS THE cornmeal mush Kenyan Africans used to cook called ugali. Before I was introduced to pastas, injera, and couscous, I experienced ugali with a meat stew. There is a technique to eating ugali: you start by pulling off a small ball with your fingers, indent the ball with your thumb, and use it to scoop up the accompanying gravy, curry, meat, or vegetables.

Ugali is one of the easiest foods to cook and can be presented fashion-style with flair. The recipe I am sharing with you comes from one of our support staff in Nairobi.

INGREDIENTS:

2 cups white cornmeal, finely ground

4 cups water

2 tsp salt

METHOD:

In heavy-bottomed saucepan add water and salt and bring to a boil. Slowly stir in cornmeal. Turn heat to medium-low and continue stirring and mashing any lumps until mush pulls away from sides of pot and starts to become thick and cake-like. It should take about 10

minutes for cornmeal to become cake-like. Immediately, invert ugali onto serving plate. You may wish to cool it a bit before digging in. Serve ugali with your favourite curries or stews. Wetting your hand with water helps to shape ugali ball before eating.

Buddha's Biryani

A VEGETARIAN DELIGHT, THIS IS BEST MADE WITH BASMATI RICE. ALWAYS BUY THE BEST QUALITY OF rice and remember that aged basmati rice yields the best flavour.

INGREDIENTS:

STEP 1

2 cups basmati rice

4 cups warm water

6 tbs clarified butter

½ tsp cumin seeds

6 black peppercorns

4 small sticks cinnamon

2 bay leaves

6 green cardamom pods, crushed

2 black cardamom pods

6 cloves

½ tsp turmeric

1 tsp red chili pepper powder

½ tsp garam masala

1 tbs ginger root, julienned

1 medium onion, sliced

2 finger hot green chilies, chopped

Salt to taste

STEP 2

½ cup peas

¼ cup carrots, julienned

10 small white mushrooms, cleaned and quartered

1 medium potato, diced

¼ cup green beans

½ cup cauliflower florets

½ cup green pepper, diced

½ cup fresh tomato, diced

METHOD:

Thoroughly wash rice and soak in hot water for 1 hour. In heavy-bottomed pot heat clarified butter and all ingredients from Step 1 except rice and water. Continue to sauté mixture until onions are caramelized. Next, add all ingredients from Step 2 and cook for about 5 minutes, stirring occasionally.

Add drained rice and stir well. Cook for 1 minute, then add 4 cups warm water. Taste liquid and make any necessary adjustments. Bring mixture to a boil, cover pot, and reduce heat to medium. Cook rice until all water is absorbed and rice is cooked. Gently stir rice to fluff it and serve piping hot with mint chutney, raita, or kachumbar. This rice delicacy tastes even better when reheated the next day.

Mag's Special Lamb Biryani

IT TOOK ME ALMOST A DECADE TO PERFECT THIS DELICACY, A TRADITIONAL RICE PREPARATION WITH meat for special occasions. The first time I ever had this dish was en route to India by sea from Kenya to Mumbai. My recipe is a lot different from what I ate on the ship, but I have been told that my version is comparable to that of the master chefs of Hyderabad who created the original. I hope you enjoy!

INGREDIENTS:

STEP 1

1 kg lamb, boneless and cubed

1 tbs ginger root, finely chopped

1 tbs garlic paste

1 cup plain yogurt

Salt to taste

3 finger hot green peppers, finely chopped

2 tbs lemon juice

STEP 2

2 medium onions, sliced

4 small cinnamon sticks

6 green cardamom pods, crushed

1 black cardamom pod, crushed

6 peppercorns

½ tsp cumin seeds

½ tsp garam masala

½ tsp turmeric powder

1 cup fresh tomatoes, diced

2 tbs tomato paste

½ cup clarified butter

STEP 3

2 cups basmati rice

4 cups warm water

1 tsp salt

¼ tsp saffron

2 tbs butter

STEP 4

6 tbs fried onions

2 tbs fresh coriander leaves, chopped

METHOD:

In large mixing bowl add meat and all ingredients from Step 1. Mix well and allow meat to marinate for at least 6 hours in refrigerator, stirring occasionally.

In saucepan heat clarified butter and add all ingredients from Step 2, except tomato paste and tomatoes. Sauté mixture until onions caramelize, then add tomatoes and mix well. Cook another few minutes and add lamb. Cook on medium-high heat until almost done but firm and most liquid has reduced. Cover pot and set aside.

For Step 3, wash rice in warm water, soak at least 30 minutes in hot water, and drain. In pot bring 4 cups warm water to a boil and add drained soaked rice. Add salt, butter, and saffron. Mix well and bring rice to a boil. Reduce heat to medium, cover pot, and cook rice until almost done and fluffy.

In large ovenproof serving dish spread half of rice on bottom and gently spread cooked lamb all over bottom layer of rice. Now with remainder of rice make another layer on top of meat, covering it completely. Cover and seal serving dish with tin foil. Just before serving place dish in 350°F pre-heated oven and heat rice thoroughly.

For Step 4, carefully remove rice from oven, remove foil, and garnish with fried onions and coriander.

Serve this succulent biryani with kachumbar and plain yogurt.

Chicken, goat, or beef can be substituted for lamb. Please ensure that no matter what meat you use, it is not overdone and retains firmness though fully cooked. A whole skinless chicken with bones cut into small pieces gives added flavour to this dish. I have often cooked this delicacy with baby back pork ribs and lamb chops and the results have always been amazing.

Wild Rice Pilaf With Pecans And Shiitake Mushrooms

THIS IS AN EXCELLENT FULL-FLAVOURED SIDE DISH TO GO WITH YOUR FAVOURITE SEAFOOD OR BEEF entrée. I tasted wild rice for the first time when I was visiting a friend in La Ronge in northern Saskatchewan. Some of the finest wild rice comes from this area. Wild rice tastes better when cooked with any long-grain or brown rice and vegetables and nuts.

INGREDIENTS:

2 tbs olive oil

2 tbs clarified butter

1 medium onion, diced

¼ cup celery, diced

1 medium carrot, peeled and diced

½ cup pecans, toasted

½ cup wild rice

1 cup long-grain rice

1 cup shiitake mushrooms, fresh or dried, sliced

3 cups chicken or beef broth

Salt and pepper to taste

METHOD:

Wash and soak both rices in hot water for about ½ hour. Heat oil and butter in large skillet (with lid and that can go into oven). Add onion, celery, and carrots. Sauté vegetables on medium to high heat until just soft. If using dry shiitake mushrooms, soak them first in hot water until soft, then remove stems, rinse well, and slice. Wipe fresh mushrooms clean with lightly damp cloth and slice. Now add mushrooms and pecans to skillet along with drained rice. Stir-fry rice for a few minutes, then add broth and bring to a boil, stirring frequently. Add salt and pepper and cover pot with lid. Place into pre-heated oven at 350°F. Cook rice for about 50 minutes until fluffy and tender.

Garnish with toasted pecans and serve hot in platter with your favourite fish or beef main course.

Rice Pilaf With Peas

THIS IS A VERY POPULAR FRAGRANT BASMATI RICE PREPARATION LOVED BY ALL—BOTH VEGETARIANS and non-vegetarians. When cooked with butter it tastes even better.

INGREDIENTS:

1 cup basmati rice

1 tsp cumin seeds

1 tbs onion, finely chopped

4 whole cloves

2 green cardamom pods, bruised

1 stick cinnamon

6 black peppercorns

1 bay leaf

¼ cup frozen green peas

1 tsp salt to taste

3 tbs clarified butter

2 cups warm water

Crispy fried onion slices for garnish

METHOD:

Wash rice and soak in boiling hot water for at least 15 minutes. In shallow saucepan heat butter and add cumin seeds, cloves, cardamom, cinnamon, peppercorns, and bay leaf and sauté for a few minutes. Then add onions and peas. As soon as onions start to sweat, drain rice, add to pan, stir well, and add salt. Now add warm water and bring rice to a boil, stirring gently.

Cover pan and turn heat to medium. Let rice cook until all water has absorbed and rice is fluffy. Garnish cooked pilaf with crispy fried onions. Serve piping hot with your favourite vegetarian or non-vegetarian dish.

Phulka

JUST LIKE THE TANDOORI ROTI, PHULKAS, ROTIS, OR CHAPATIS ARE GENERALLY CONSUMED AT EVERY meal by Indians and Pakistanis all over the world. This is one of the most commonly eaten breads with any curried dish.

INGREDIENTS:

5 cups atta

½ tsp salt

½ cup atta for dusting

1 tbs clarified butter

METHOD:

In shallow dish sift atta with salt. With fist, make a little dip in centre of flour and pour in about 1 cup water. Gradually, start mixing flour and knead to make soft dough. You may have to add a little more water. When dough is ready cover with moist cloth and keep aside for about 30 minutes. Divide dough into 12 equal portions.

Make balls, lightly dust them with atta, and flatten with rolling pin into round discs about 6" in diameter. Cook both sides of phulkas lightly for about 1 minute each on heated tawa. Then phulka is puffed over an open charcoal fire or electric range using a rack over the heating element. Lightly butter to enhance flavour.

Exotic Spicy Shrimp Pilaf

THIS IS A MOUTHWATERING DELICACY OF SPICY SHRIMP COOKED WITH RICE.

INGREDIENTS FOR SHRIMP:

1 lb uncooked jumbo shrimp, peeled, deveined, with tails on

1 tsp crushed hot chili pepper or chili sauce

2 tbs clarified butter

1 tbs garlic paste

1 tbs fresh ginger root, julienned

1 medium firm tomato, diced

1 tbs butter

Salt and freshly ground black pepper to taste

METHOD:

Heat frying pan and add butter. As soon as butter heats up, add chilies and garlic paste, and stir-fry for 1 minute on high heat. Make sure garlic does not get too brown. Immediately add shrimp and ginger root. Stir-fry piously until shrimp start to cook and change colour. Quickly add tomatoes and stir-fry for another minute or so. This whole process should not take more than 6 to 8 minutes, otherwise shrimp may get tough.

Set cooked shrimp aside as you cook rice.

INGREDIENTS FOR RICE:

1 cup basmati rice

1 tsp cumin seeds

1 tbs onion, finely chopped

4 whole cloves

2 green cardamom pods, bruised

1 stick cinnamon

6 black peppercorns

1 bay leaf

1 tsp salt to taste

3 tbs clarified butter

2 cups warm water

1 tbs fresh coriander leaves, chopped

2 sprigs green onions, finely chopped

Fresh mint for garnish

1 lemon

METHOD:

Wash rice and soak in boiling hot water for at least 15 minutes. In shallow saucepan heat butter and add cumin seeds, cloves, cardamom, cinnamon, peppercorns, and bay leaf and sauté for a few minutes. Add onions. As soon as onions start to sweat, drain rice and add to pan. Stir well and add salt. Now add warm water and bring rice to a boil, stirring gently.

Cover pan and turn heat to medium, letting rice cook until water has almost absorbed and rice turns fluffy. At this stage gently add cooked shrimp into pot with rice and stir well. Cover pot and let cook for a few minutes on medium heat. Turn heat off and keep rice covered for at least 30 minutes. Just before serving garnish rice with coriander, mint, green chilies, and green onions.

Mandazi

MANDAZI IS A SIMPLE AND POPULAR FRIED BUN EATEN IN KENYA AND ITS SURROUNDING COUNTRIES. Often substituted for bread, it is eaten as a snack or for breakfast with hot tea, and is great for dipping in saucy delicacies.

INGREDIENTS:

4 cups all-purpose flour

2 cups warm water

2 tsp baking powder

½ cup granulated sugar

2 tbs butter or margarine

Pinch of salt

Oil for deep-frying

(If you would like your mandazi a little spicier, add about ¼ tsp of any of the following: cardamom powder, ginger, cinnamon, or allspice. If using any of these spices you may also wish to include 1 whole egg, slightly beaten, along with ¼ cup warm milk.)

METHOD:

In large mixing bowl combine flour, baking powder, sugar, and salt. Gradually add water and butter to flour mixture and knead into a dough. Dough should be smooth and elastic, which may take about 15 minutes of kneading. Cover dough with moist cloth and set aside for about 1 hour for dough to rise.

Make small dough balls between palms and place onto cookie sheet. You may roll or press balls into desired

shapes, place onto cookie sheet, and let them rise again for a second time.

Heat oil in wok or fryer to 300°F. Deep-fry dough balls in hot oil, turning a few times until golden brown. Do not overload fryer; you should fry just enough to ensure that balls float freely in oil and do not squish each other.

After frying, drain on paper towel and serve hot or cold. Mandazi can also be enjoyed with your favourite fruit preserve or any condiment.

My Ultimate Paella

EVERY COUNTRY HAS A DISH THAT BONDS ITS PEOPLE OR SOMETIMES DIVIDES THEM. IN SPAIN, PARticularly in the Valencia region, such a dish is paella, which has become popular and famous all over the world.

Paella is the generic name for over two hundred rice dishes across Spain. There are numerous paella recipes and the ingredients paella can incorporate are endless; with its international popularity, it is almost impossible to define exactly what this dish may contain. There may be as many variations of paella as there are cooks, and interestingly, every cook claims that his or her recipe is the best and most authentic.

Originally, paella was farm laborers' food, cooked by workers over a wood fire for their lunchtime meals. The preparation included rice and whatever else was available in the fields and countryside. The ingredients could include tomatoes, onions, beans, and even snails. Sometimes duck, rabbit, or chicken was added for special occasions, plus a touch of saffron for extra colour and flavour. It is no surprise that various types of seafood crept into the dish over the generations, with the Valencia region of Spain being coastal. To this day a "true" Paella Valenciana has no seafood but a mixture of chicken, rabbit, and snails, with green and white beans.

Many women still do the cooking in Spain, but making paella is usually left to men, much like BBQ's across the globe. This delicacy is traditionally eaten directly from the same pan in which it is cooked and each person uses his or her own wooden spoon.

Over the years I have learned how to make paella by following my intuition based on the paellas I have eaten in Spain and a few other countries. However, the foodie in me is always looking for authentic sources. This led me to come up with the following five basic but extremely important principles to cooking a good paella, which I learned from seasoned paella cooks: the rice, the pan, the distribution of heat, the sofrito, and the liquid.

- Spanish rice is rounded and short, it absorbs liquid well, and it stays relatively firm during cooking. The most used variety of Spanish rice is bomba. Arborio is an acceptable substitute; long-grain varieties are not.
- A genuine paella pan is round and wide, is shallow and has splayed sides, and is made of blue steel. It has two looped handles and may dip slightly in the middle so the oil can pool there for the preliminary sautéing. The shape of the pan, which is called either a paella or paellera, helps to ensure that the rice cooks evenly in a thin layer. If you do not have a paella pan, you may use a skillet but not a cast-iron pan. Remember, paella pans do not come with lids, as this delicacy must be prepared uncovered.

- Sofrito is a basic sauce, prepared with tomatoes, garlic, oil, salt, thyme, rosemary, bay leaf, and onions. This usually forms the base of many traditional Spanish dishes. It is very similar to the Indian curry sauce. This sauce refrigerates well for a week and can be frozen up to six months.
- Using a good heating source and a paella pan help to ensure even distribution of heat during the cooking process.
- For cooking the rice in paella, the liquid used other than water can be fish, chicken, or vegetable stock. Also make sure to use good-quality Spanish saffron.

A little bit of background and history of paella helps one understand and appreciate the origin of this gem from Spain. The following is my recipe, which I sincerely hope you enjoy.

INGREDIENTS:

4 tbs virgin olive oil

250 gm chorizo sausages, thickly sliced

250 gm chicken breast, skinned, boneless, and cut up small

250 gm squid, cleaned and finely sliced into rings

1 onion, finely diced

6 cloves garlic, peeled and roughly chopped

½ tsp thyme or oregano

1 green pepper, deseeded and roughly chopped

1 red pepper, deseeded and roughly chopped

1 cup tomatoes, finely pureed

1 small bunch fresh flat-leaf parsley leaves, picked, washed, and chopped coriander stalks, finely chopped

Sea salt to taste

Black pepper, freshly ground

1 tsp Spanish smoked paprika

1 healthy pinch Spanish saffron

200 gm fresh clams, scrubbed clean and debearded

200 gm fresh mussels, scrubbed clean and debearded

350 gm paella rice

1 lt chicken stock

12 large shrimp, with or without tails

12 medium fresh scallops

1 fresh lemon, cut into 8 wedges

2 sprigs green onion, finely sliced

METHOD:

In large paella pan over medium heat add olive oil, sliced chorizo, and chicken breast. Stir-fry mixture for about 8 minutes, stirring occasionally, and as soon as sausage begins to release fat and change colour add chopped peppers, garlic, onion, and parsley stalks along with salt and pepper, oregano or thyme, paprika, and saffron. Gently add pureed tomatoes, mix well, and cook for another 8 minutes.

Next, add rice to mixture and stir well to ensure rice is coated in sauce. Gently add chicken stock and stir well. Check seasoning and make any necessary adjustments. Bring mixture to a boil, then turn down to medium to low heat, add scallops, and stir constantly for about 15 minutes. To make sure that every grain of rice gets the same amount of tender, loving care, occasionally stir from outside of pan into middle so you get a pile of rice in middle of pan. Make sure it is not sticking to bottom of pan. Next, flatten pile with spoon and repeat process.

After 15 minutes rice should be almost cooked. Add sliced squid, mussels, clams, and shrimp. You may want to add an extra splash of stock, if rice looks a bit dry. Gently keep stirring, and as clams and mussels start to open and prawns begin to turn pink, discard any clams or mussels that don't open. Stir in chopped parsley and garnish with finely sliced green onions and lemon wedges before serving. You may serve a crispy salad with light dressing as an accompaniment.

CHICKEN RICE PULLAO

Tandoori Roti

THIS IS A VERY COMMON WHOLE-WHEAT FLOUR BREAD THAT NORTH INDIANS CONSUME AT EVERY meal. For optimal results, this roti is best made in a tandoor. However, when made in an oven on a pizza stone the results are equally good.

INGREDIENTS:

5 cups atta
½ tsp salt

½ cup atta for dusting
1 tbs clarified butter

METHOD:

In shallow dish sift atta with salt. With fist, make a little dip in centre of flour and pour in about 1 cup water. Gradually, start mixing flour and knead to make soft dough. You may have to add a little more water. When dough is ready cover with moist cloth and keep aside for about 30 minutes. Then divide dough into 10 equal portions. Make balls, lightly dust them with atta, and cover for a few minutes before cooking.

When ready to cook, pre-heat oven to 375°F. Flatten each ball between palms to make round discs approximately 6" in diameter. Place rotis onto greased baking tray and bake in oven for 5 to 6 minutes. If cooking in tandoor, place rotis onto cushioned pad, stick them inside hot tandoor, and bake about 2 minutes.

Rotis are best served immediately after removing from oven or tandoor. Before serving, you may wish to lightly brush them with butter.

Tandoori Naan

THE MOST FAMILIAR AND READILY AVAILABLE VARIETIES OF NAAN IN WESTERN COUNTRIES ARE THE South Asian kinds. In Iran, where the word originated, naan does not carry any special significance, as it is merely the everyday word for any kind of bread. Naan in other parts of South Asia usually refer to a specific kind of thick flatbread (another well-known kind of flatbread is chapati). Generally, it resembles pita and, like pita bread, is usually leavened with yeast or with bread starter (leavened naan dough left over from a previous batch); unleavened dough (similar to that used for roti) is also utilized. Naan is cooked in a tandoor, from which tandoori cooking takes its name. This distinguishes it from roti, which is usually cooked on a flat or slightly concave iron griddle called a tawa. Modern recipes sometimes substitute baking powder for the yeast. Milk or yogurt may also be used to impart distinct tastes to the naan. Milk used instead of water will, as it does for ordinary bread, yield softer dough. Also, when bread starter (which contains both yeast and lactobacilli) is used, the milk may undergo modest lactic fermentation.

Typically, naan is served hot and brushed with ghee or butter. It can be used to scoop other foods, or stuffed with a filling. For example, keema naan is stuffed with a minced meat mixture (usually lamb, mutton, or goat meat). Another variation is Peshawari naan. Peshawari naan and Kashmiri naan are filled with a mixture of nuts and raisins. In Pakistan, the most famous naan variety is the roghani naan, which is sprinkled with sesame seeds. Kulcha is another type. Amritsari naan, also called Amritsari kulcha, is stuffed with mashed potatoes, onion, and lots of spices. Possible seasonings in the naan dough include cumin and nigella seeds. The Pakistani dish of balti, popular in Birmingham, England, is usually eaten with naan, and this has given rise to the huge karack, or table naan, easy to share amongst large groups.

INGREDIENTS:

2 tsp active yeast

4 tsp sugar

2 cups all-purpose flour, plus additional for rolling

2 cups self-rising flour

1 tbs salt

6 tbs heaped plain yogurt

4 tbs melted butter

Melted butter for brushing finished naans

METHOD:

In cup dissolve yeast and 3 tsp sugar with 1½ cups warm water. Let sit until frothy, about 10 minutes.

Meanwhile, in large mixing bowl sift both flours, salt, and remaining 1 tsp sugar and mix well.

Once yeast is frothy, add yogurt and melted butter to bowl with dry ingredients and stir gently to mix everything. It will feel like there isn't enough flour at first, but keep going until it transforms into soft, slightly sticky, and pliable dough. As soon as dough is mixed well and comes together, stop kneading. Cover dough with plastic wrap or damp tea towel and let sit in a warm, draft-free place for 2 to 4 hours. The dough will be extremely soft and sticky—this is good!

When you're ready to roll, have 2 bowls: one with extra flour and the other with cooking oil. Divide dough into 10 to 12 equal portions and gently form into balls. Use oil to massage balls—this keeps them from sticking—and let oiled balls sit for 1 hour or so in a warm place.

Using rolling pin and flour to dust board, roll each piece of dough into teardrop or oval shape, narrower at the top than at the bottom. Each should be 8" to 9" long, 4" wide at its widest point, and about ¼" thick. Once you've formed the general shape, you can also pick each up by one end and wiggle it; the dough's own weight will stretch it out a little. Repeat this method with rest of dough.

Warm large cast-iron skillet over high heat until nearly smoking, or use pizza stone in oven pre-heated to 500°F and turn broiler on before placing rolled naan onto stone.

If cooking on skillet, flip naan after about 1 minute. They should be blistered and somewhat dark brown. Naan cooked on pizza stone should puff up and have golden brown finish.

Carefully remove naan from skillet or stone, and brush tops of naan with melted butter. Place cooked and buttered naan in tea towel–lined dish. Repeat process to cook all naan. Serve piping hot with your favourite meat or vegetarian curries, or BBQ'd meat and salads of your choice.

ROTI

Zafrani Zarda

ZARDA IS A TRADITIONAL SWEET RICE DELICACY WITH DRIED FRUITS AND NUTS. THIS PREPARATION is especially common in North India amongst Punjabis. Often it is served at festive occasions instead of desserts. Every household has its own recipe and foodies often boast about their creations.

I recall when we were living in Kenya, our Muslim friends and neighbours used to make amazing zarda and bring it over during the Eid Festival. To this day I believe my aunt, Foofi Jaan, used to make the best version. I am pleased to share the following recipe that I think comes pretty close to what she used to make.

INGREDIENTS:

1 lb basmati rice, soaked in warm water

½ lb sugar

¼ tsp yellow food colouring

3 tbs clarified butter

10 whole almonds, skin off

10 pistachios

10 cashews

6 fine slices coconut

2 small sticks cinnamon

6 green cardamom pods, slightly bruised

6 cloves

12 black peppercorns

¼ tsp good-quality saffron

METHOD:

In large pot almost half full of water, add food colouring, half of cloves and half of cardamom, cinnamon sticks, peppercorns, and drained rice. Bring mixture to a boil and cook until rice is almost done. Drain cooked rice and set aside in colander placed over pot.

Next, in large pan add clarified butter and fry remaining cloves and cardamom pods on low heat. Add rice, sugar, and saffron. Mix well, cover, and gently stir-fry mixture for about 5 minutes on low heat. Next, add almonds, pistachios, cashews, and coconut slices. Gently stir zarda and allow rice to heat through. Remove pan from heat and serve warm. If you are not using saffron, a little kewda essence may be used.

Handvo-Style Corn Bread

THIS DELICIOUS BREAD RECIPE HAS BEEN ADAPTED FROM THE POPULAR GUJARATI SNACK HANDVO.

INGREDIENTS:

1 cup milk

¼ cup clarified butter

2 large eggs (optional)

1¼ cups yellow cornmeal

1 cup all-purpose flour

1 tbs sugar

1 tbs baking powder

½ tsp salt

1 tsp garam masala

½ cup fresh corn kernels

1 medium onion, finely diced

1 tbs ginger root, finely chopped

1 tsp garlic paste

3 green chilies, finely chopped

¼ cup coriander, finely chopped

1 tbs sesame seeds, toasted, for garnish

METHOD:

In mixing bowl beat milk, butter, and eggs with hand beater or wire whisk. Next, stir in remaining ingredients all at once and continue to beat until flour is moistened and batter is smooth.

Pre-heat oven to 400°F. Lightly grease bottom and side of round 9"x1½" pan or square 8"x8"x2" pan with butter or margarine. Gently pour batter into pan, place in oven on middle rack, and bake for about 25 to 30 minutes or until bread turns golden brown. Carefully insert toothpick into centre of bread; it should come out clean. Sprinkle toasted sesame seeds on hot bread.

Serve this bread warm with your choice of relish or chutney

Lachedar Paratha

FOR THE ULTIMATE IN INDIAN LEAVENED BREADS, THIS HAS TO BE THE BEST AND IS OFTEN SERVED with bhoona gosht or raahra meat delicacies. My favourite way to enjoy these babies is with any succulent vegetarian curry with paneer. My better half, Sona, makes the best and most wicked Indian breads. Her lachedar parathas are to die for.

INGREDIENTS:

4 cups atta

½ tsp salt

½ cup whole milk

1 tsp Kasoori methi, stems removed and discarded

½ cup clarified butter

METHOD:

To make dough, in shallow dish sift atta with salt. With fist, make a little well in centre of flour and pour in milk and about ½ cup water. Then sprinkle methi over flour and gradually start mixing it, kneading into a soft dough. You may have to add a little more water. When dough is ready cover with moist cloth and keep aside for about 15 minutes.

Divide dough into 12 equal portions and make balls. Lightly dust each ball and roll into 6" discs. Apply butter evenly all over on one side. Make a radial cut and fold disc into a narrow conical shape. Now place flat side of cone on palm

and with other palm, gently compress dough into a thick, flat blob by moving palms in circular fashion. Lightly dust blob with flour and roll again into 8" disc using rolling pin. You may even make dough balls into 6" triangles.

Fry on heated tawa on medium heat until lightly crisp and golden brown, applying butter on both sides.

Squish cooked parathas carefully using both hands and serve hot with your favourite dish.

The dough for these parathas may be seasoned with fresh coriander leaves, mint, cumin, or mashed fennel seeds.

Poori

THE PEOPLE OF CENTRAL INDIA EAT MOSTLY POORIS JUST LIKE NORTH INDIANS EAT TANDOORI ROTIS. In Kenya, the first time I ever had poori was at our Gujarati neighbours' place. They served poori with curried potatoes. Poori is also served in temples or at weddings with masala chickpeas.

My father preferred pooris with a bit of cumin seeds and crushed chilies mixed in the dough. I remember enjoying another version of pooris—pithi poori outside the Red Fort in New Delhi, where it was served with spicy mushy potatoes. These pooris were stuffed with ground lentils and paneer. This delicacy is one of my favourites and often used to be a Sunday morning breakfast at my home.

The following recipe is for basic plain pooris.

INGREDIENTS:

5 cups atta

½ tsp salt

½ cup atta for dusting

Cooking oil for deep-frying

METHOD:

In shallow dish sift atta with salt. With fist, make a little dip in centre of flour and pour in about 1 cup water. Gradually, start mixing flour and knead to make soft dough. You may have to add a little more water. When dough is ready cover with moist cloth and keep aside for about 30 minutes. Then divide dough into 24 equal portions. Make balls, lightly oil them, and cover until oil is ready to fry.

In wok heat oil for frying. Take dough balls and flatten with rolling pin to form discs approximately 4" in diameter.

Gently dip each rolled poori into hot oil and deep-fry until golden brown. Make sure to turn once and gently submerge in oil with spatula. This will make poori puff up.

Serve hot with your favourite potato dish or any other vegetarian dish.

Drunkard's Noodles

DRUNKARD'S NOODLES, OR PAD KEE MAO, IS A CHINESE-INFLUENCED DISH THAT WAS MADE POPULAR by the Chinese people living in Laos and Thailand. In Thai, "kee mao" literally means drunkard.

There are several theories on the naming of this dish. One states its origins stem from the use of rice wine in preparation, but no alcohol is added in any of the original Thai recipes. Another story claims that someone who came home drunk made something to eat with whatever ingredients were available. Another slight variation on this theory describes someone using whatever ingredients remained in stock to cook a side dish to palliate the effects of alcohol consumption. Yet another theory states that this noodle dish is so spicy one needs to drink plenty of beer to cool off the heat. Thus, the name "drunkard's noodles" seems very appropriate. I suggest enjoying with a cold brewski for the ultimate dining experience.

INGREDIENTS:

8 oz broad pad thai noodles

10 oz chicken thigh fillet, sliced into bite-sized pieces

8 medium-sized shrimp, shelled, deveined, with tails on

2 shallot or scallion stems, cut into 2" pieces

½ cup Thai basil leaves, loosely packed

1 tsp garlic, finely chopped

8 firm cherry tomatoes, halved

½ medium white onion, sliced

2 tbs fresh Thai chilies, chopped

1 green bell pepper, cut into strips

½ tsp white pepper

2 eggs

3 tbs canola or peanut oil

4 tbs black soy sauce

1 tbs light soy sauce

1 tbs palm sugar

3 tbs oyster sauce

2 tbs nam pla (fish sauce)

3 tbs rice vinegar

METHOD:

Place pad thai noodles in mixing bowl, pour boiling water over noodles, and set aside for 5 minutes or until softened. Drain when ready.

In separate mixing bowl add black soy sauce, light soy sauce, palm sugar, oyster sauce, nam pla, and rice vinegar and mix well.

Next, heat oil in wok over high heat, add garlic and chilies, and cook for about 15 seconds. Immediately add chicken and fry until cooked, about 2 minutes, remove chicken with slotted spoon, and set aside. Add shrimp, cook for 1 minute, remove with slotted spoon, and add to cooked chicken. Next, break eggs into wok and lightly scramble until set. Add shallots or scallions and sliced onions, peppers along with white pepper, and drained noodles and mix well. Stir-fry for 1 minute, pour sauce all over, and add chicken, shrimp, and cherry tomatoes. Mix well and cook to allow sauce to coat noodles. Remove from heat and add basil leaves. As soon as they wilt, serve noodles.

Missi Roti

THIS BOOK WOULD BE INCOMPLETE WITHOUT THIS PARTICULAR RECIPE, OR MY SON WOULD NEVER forgive me, as this happens to be one of his favourite Indian breads. He has always claimed that his mom makes them the best and I agree. As mentioned earlier, Punjabis are robust people with robust appetites. Their mornings often begin with these rotis served with butter and yogurt. Leftover rotis make an excellent midday snack and can be enjoyed cold with a spiced cup of tea.

INGREDIENTS:

1 lb whole-wheat flour, sifted

5 tbs gram flour, sifted

1 cup fresh methi leaves, chopped

1 medium onion, finely diced

1 tbs fresh ginger root, finely chopped

2 finger hot green chilies, finely chopped

1 tsp red chili powder

½ tsp garam masala

Salt to taste

1 tbs clarified butter

3 tbs plain yogurt, well beaten

Clarified butter for pan-frying

Butter and plain yogurt

METHOD:

In shallow pan add flours and rest of ingredients. Mix thoroughly, gradually add water, and knead mixture to form stiff dough. Cover dough with moist cloth and let sit for 30 minutes.

Make about 8 lemon-sized balls and roll each into a 7" round disc. Cook on hot griddle or tawa, lightly greasing both sides until golden brown.

Serve hot with additional butter and plain yogurt.

Gobi Paratha

STUFFED PARATHAS MAKE EXCELLENT BREAKFAST BREAD OR A WONDERFUL ADDITION TO YOUR NEXT picnic basket. They are usually served with butter, plain yogurt, and pickles. Parathas can be stuffed with potatoes, daikon, paneer, or ground meat and cooked on a heated tawa.

INGREDIENTS:

5 cups atta

½ cup atta for dusting

½ cup clarified butter or vegetable oil

FILLING:

½ lb cauliflower, coarsely grated

2 tbs fresh ginger root, finely chopped

3 finger hot green chilies

2 tbs fresh coriander leaves, chopped

1 tsp red chili powder

½ tsp cumin seeds

1 tsp pomegranate seeds

Salt to taste

METHOD:

In mixing bowl add all ingredients for filling and mix well. Taste and make any necessary seasoning adjustments. Cover and set aside.

For dough, in shallow dish sift atta. With fist, make a little dip in centre of flour and pour in about 1 cup water. Gradually, start mixing flour and knead to make soft dough. You may have to add a little more water. When dough is ready cover with moist cloth and keep aside for about 30 minutes. Then divide dough into 10 equal portions. Make balls, lightly dust them with atta, and cover with moist cheesecloth until ready to stuff.

Place each dough ball on lightly floured surface and flatten with rolling pin into round disc approximately 4" in diameter. Using a tablespoon, place about 1½ tbs filling into middle of disc and gently bring dough up, covering filling. Pinch dough to seal neatly. Flatten stuffed dough again with rolling pin to about 7" to 8" in diameter.

Place stuffed paratha on heated tawa and cook partially on both sides by turning over once. Apply butter or oil on both sides and pan-fry over medium heat until crisp and golden brown.

Serve piping hot with 1 tsp butter on top and plain yogurt and pickles on side. A cup of masala tea would turn this dish into a complete breakfast.

CRISPY NOODLES

Ultimate Pad Thai With Meat And Shrimp

MAKING PAD THAI AT HOME IS "EASY PEASY," SO HERE IS MY RECIPE ADAPTED FROM THE NOODLES I often ate on the streets of Bangkok in Thailand. This preparation has become very popular amongst my friends and family. I am very pleased to share it with my foodie friends.

INGREDIENTS:

1 pkg pad thai noodles

½ lb shrimp, shelled and deveined

¼ lb BBQ'd pork or boneless chicken, sliced

½ carrot, julienned

¼ cup green peppers, julienned

¼ cup red peppers, julienned

¼ cup firm tofu, sliced

1 medium onion, sliced

6 shiitake mushrooms, soaked and sliced

2 eggs, partially beaten, made into omelette, then cut up

2 green chilies, julienned

¼ cup peanuts, toasted and crushed

¼ cup fresh bean sprouts

¼ cup fresh coriander, chopped

3 tbs pad thai sauce, with tamarind

1 tbs nam pla (fish sauce)

2 tbs dark soy sauce

1 tbs garlic paste

1 tbs. Mag's Hot Chili Oil*

4 tbs cooking oil

Salt to taste

*Mag's Hot Chili Oil is my signature oil (see page 74). Please feel free to use any hot oil available at the market.

METHOD:

Soak noodles in boiling hot water for about 10 minutes or until softened but not mushy. Drain and rinse noodles in cool water and set aside. In hot wok add both oils and as soon as it starts to heat, add fresh garlic and stir-fry well. Immediately, add shrimp and stir-fry for 1 minute. Then add following ingredients:

BBQ'd pork or sliced chicken, green and red peppers, onions, mushrooms, carrots, and green chilies. Stir well. You should be cooking on high heat. Next, add pad thai sauce, nam pla, and soy sauce and mix all ingredients well. Then add drained pad thai noodles and keep stirring. Taste and make any necessary adjustments for heat or salt. Next, add tofu and when noodles are heated through garnish with bean sprouts, peanuts, cut-up eggs, and chopped coriander.

Serve piping hot with quartered fresh limes, fresh Thai green chilies, crushed peanuts, and hot chili sauce on side.

FUSILLI IN A CREAMY SAUCE WITH MUSHROOMS AND SHRIMPS

Thai-Style Noodles

THIS DISH IS SOMEWHAT SIMILAR TO THE POPULAR SINGAPORE FRIED RICE NOODLES. THE BIG DIF-ference here is that this version has no curry powder. Personally, I like these noodles better. I often make changes to suit the availability of ingredients. The following is an easy and a delicious preparation.

INGREDIENTS:

250 gm rice stick noodles

200 gm raw baby shrimp, peeled

200 gm boneless and skinless chicken or BBQ pork, diced small

½ medium onion, thinly sliced

1 tsp garlic, minced

1 tsp chili sauce

1 tsp palm sugar

1 tbs light soy sauce

1 tbs nam pla (fish sauce)

150 gm bean sprouts, washed and drained

2 whole eggs, beaten

Salt to taste

Cooking oil

GARNISH:

3 sprigs green onions, chopped

Fresh coriander leaves, chopped

2 tbs blanched peanuts, toasted and chopped

1 lime, cut into 8 wedges

Thai green chilies

METHOD:

In pot boil about 2 litres water and add rice noodles. Cook for about 3 to 4 minutes, making sure not to overcook. Immediately, remove noodles and drain. Spread onto oiled cookie sheet to prevent further cooking. Otherwise, noodles become very mushy.

In frying pan heat 1 tbs oil and make a fine crepe with beaten egg. When egg is fully cooked remove and cool. Roll up cooled crepe, thinly shred, and set aside.

Heat about 3 tbs oil in wok and add shrimp and meat of your choice plus garlic. Cook shrimp and chicken. Now add chili sauce, palm sugar, nam pla, and soy sauce and mix well. Add drained noodles to wok along with bean sprouts and half the egg shreds and stir well, making sure to heat thoroughly.

Pile noodles onto serving platter and garnish with green onions, coriander, toasted chopped peanuts, and remainder of egg shreds. Arrange cut pieces of lime and Thai chilies around serving platter and serve hot.

PASTA WITH CHICKEN
AND MUSHROOMS

Spicy Hakka Noodles With Meat And Shrimp

HAKKA NOODLES ARE ONE OF THE MOST POPULAR INDO-CHINESE DELICACIES IN INDIA AND ARE NOW even found in many other countries. This type of cuisine is the adaptation of Chinese seasonings and cooking techniques to Indian tastes through a larger offering of vegetarian and non-vegetarian dishes.

This kind of fusion cooking was introduced to India by a small group of Chinese residents of Hakka origin, who lived in Kolkata over a century ago. Today, Indo-Chinese food has become an integral part of the Indian culinary scene and is also enjoyed by Indian and Chinese communities in Malaysia, Thailand, Britain, Australia, East Africa, Singapore, and all over North America.

There are numerous restaurants in Hong Kong, Indonesia, Malaysia, Singapore, and Canada serving Hakka cuisine. In India this cuisine is immensely popular and widespread, but interestingly it bears no resemblance to traditional Hakka or Chinese dishes. Noodles here are quickly stir-fried with a spicy "Indian-Chinese" flavoured sauce, crunchy vegetables, and sometimes eggs and meat.

Hakka noodles are made from plain or egg noodles, stir-fried with sauces and crunchy vegetables. Chicken, pork, and shrimp may be used in these easy and fast-cooking recipes. I have been cooking Indo-Chinese dishes for a long time. I love these oodles of noodles with a medley of seafood and meat and loads of crunchy veggies. Here is how you too can make this popular Asian dish. It takes a bit of elbow grease in chopping and preparing, but is well worth it! Please note that my recipe is a non-vegetarian preparation, but you may make it vegetarian by omitting any meat, eggs, or shrimp.

INGREDIENTS:

8 oz pkg Hakka noodles or rice vermicelli

1 tbs corn oil for coating noodles

5 tbs peanut oil or corn oil

2 Thai hot green chilies, chopped

1 large onion, sliced

½ cup scallions, sliced on a bias

1 cup cabbage, finely shredded

½ cup carrots, julienned

1 stalk celery, sliced on a bias

½ cup white mushrooms, sliced

½ cup red or green bell peppers, sliced

2 whole eggs, slightly beaten

½ lb medium shrimp, shelled and deveined

½ lb chicken breast, boneless, thinly sliced

½ cup bean sprouts, washed, for garnish

MARINADE:

2 tbs dark soy sauce

1 tbs Sriracha sauce

1 tbs garlic paste

1 tbs ginger paste

SAUCE:

1 tbs tomato puree

2 tbs dark soy sauce

1 tbs oyster sauce

1 tbs Sriracha sauce

1 tsp garlic paste

1 tbs rice vinegar

1 tbs red chili flakes, dried

¼ tsp black pepper powder

1 tsp sesame oil

METHOD:

In bowl mix all ingredients for marinade. Marinate shrimp and chicken separately in small bowls for 1 hour. Next, in separate bowl mix all ingredients for sauce and keep aside.

Now bring enough water to a boil in pot with a little salt. Add noodles and cook according to instructions on package. Make sure not to overcook noodles, otherwise they will become mushy. Drain and rinse noodles immediately to rid of starch and stop any further cooking. Once noodles are rinsed and fully drained, gently massage them with 1 tbs oil and keep aside.

Next, heat about 2 tbs oil in wok and quickly stir-fry chicken and shrimp separately. Drain and keep aside. Save any leftover marinade. In same wok quickly fry and scramble eggs and promptly remove to impart rustic look. Keep aside.

In same wok heat remaining oil and quickly stir-fry on medium to high heat Thai chilies, sliced onions, cabbage, carrots, celery, mushrooms, scallions, and bell peppers for a few minutes and toss well.

Next, add drained noodles, toss mixture well, and add prepared sauce and any leftover marinade. Mix well and as soon as all noodles are coated with sauce, add chicken, shrimp, and eggs. Toss mixture and lastly garnish with bean sprouts. Serve these oodles of noodles piping hot. You may want to serve chopped green chilies in mixture of vinegar and soy sauce for extra heat and bite.

Suggestion: This may seem like a tedious process, but the trick is to be fully prepared and organized with all the chopping and slicing—even the meat, eggs, and shrimp may be fried ahead of time, and on the day of serving just assemble everything and get cooking!

COASTAL FISH KOFTAS

Usually made with ground fish mixed with herbs and spices , are formed into balls balls, ovals or cylindrical shapes.

Fish and Seafood

Ambarsari-Style Fish Pakoras

THIS IS ANOTHER CLASSIC RECIPE FROM MY FAMILY'S KITCHEN THAT HAS TRAVELLED ACROSS THE seas. For this creation usually surmai or halibut fillets are best. Tilapia, cod, or haddock fillets work well too. For those who do not care for strong-smelling fish, tilapia is the answer. If you like basa, it would work equally well in this preparation. But please try to avoid using any oily fish.

The amount of fish used will depend upon the number of people you are serving. Usually about six to eight ounces per person should be plenty. This delicacy goes a lot faster when served with drinks; therefore you may have to adjust the quantity accordingly.

INGREDIENTS:

1 kg fish fillets of choice, cut into 2"x1" pieces

1 fresh lemon

Salt and freshly ground pepper to taste

6 finger hot green chili peppers, chopped

2 tbs ginger root, grated

2 tbs garlic, finely chopped

½ cup coriander leaves, washed

1 tsp ajwain

1 tsp tandoori masala

1 tbs cornstarch

1 tbs hot chili powder

¼ cup fresh coriander stems, cleaned and finely chopped

1 cup besan

Vegetable oil for deep-frying, or good-quality mustard oil

METHOD:

Squeeze fresh lemon juice onto cut-up fish pieces and rub with salt and freshly ground black pepper. Let fish rest at room temperature for about 1 hour.

In food processor add hot green chilies, ginger root, garlic cloves, and fresh coriander leaves and pulse to fine paste. Then add ajwain, tandoori masala, and cornstarch and mix well. Add chili powder, taste, and adjust seasonings as necessary.

Drain and save liquid from marinated fish and smother fine paste on fish pieces, ensuring paste covers fish well and evenly. Next, add about half of besan to fish pieces and mix well so all pieces are neatly covered with besan batter. If besan is not enough you may add a little more and mix. If mixture feels too dry, then add saved marinade liquid to fish and mix well. Let fish sit for at least 2 hours in fridge before deep-frying. Just before frying add chopped coriander stems to fish and mix well.

Heat oil to medium-high heat in wok or fryer and deep-fry fish pieces to a golden, crisp finish. Serve piping hot with your favourite chutney and lemon or lime wedges. This style of fish is so popular that I have to caution you that you can never cook enough to go around, so always have generous portions for serving.

Garlic Shrimp And Scallops In Spicy Sauce

THIS IS TRULY A FUSION DISH ADAPTING THE CHINESE TECHNIQUE OF QUICK STIR-FRYING AND USING spices from India and Thailand. A fairly simple and quick recipe, it should be prepared just before serving.

INGREDIENTS:

1 kg jumbo shrimp, peeled and cleaned, with tails on

1 lb large scallops

3 tbs cooking oil

1 medium onion, diced

1 tsp garam masala

½ tsp turmeric

1 tbs garlic paste

1 tsp fresh garlic, chopped

1 tbs fresh ginger root, chopped

2 Thai red chili peppers, finely sliced

50 gm bamboo shoots, sliced

1 tbs tomato paste

2 tbs sweet chili sauce

1 tsp nam pla (fish sauce)

1 tbs hoisin sauce

1 tbs cornstarch, dissolved in ¼ cup cold water

2 tbs fresh coriander leaves, chopped

METHOD:

Wash shrimp and ensure dark vein is removed and discarded. Using sharp knife cut down centre of shrimp to remove vein.

In wok heat oil and add chopped onions, garam masala, and turmeric and stir-fry for 1 minute. Then add garlic, ginger, and chili pepper. Cook for another minute on high heat, add shrimp and scallops, and stir well. As soon as shrimp start to curl and change colour, add bamboo shoots, tomato paste, sweet chili sauce, nam pla, and hoisin sauce. Mix well and heat through, stirring constantly.

Finally, add dissolved cornstarch, mix well, and as soon as sauce starts to thicken transfer shrimp onto serving platter. Garnish with coriander and serve hot with steamed rice.

Ambarsari Masala Fish

THE CITY OF AMRITSAR IS WELL KNOWN FOR ITS GOLDEN TEMPLE AND AUTHENTIC PUNJABI CUISINE. Zaikka of the Punjab comes from this holy city. For decades we have enjoyed papads and warrians from Amritsar, but my all-time favourite has been the fried Ambarsari fish.

Recently, when I was in Chennai in the south of India, one day around lunchtime we ended up in a neighbourhood that offered three classy restaurants—the Duchess, Shogun, and Kaaraikudi—along with the Dhaba. It was a tough choice, but we ended up going to the Dhaba. This eatery featured Afghan and Persian cuisines and surprisingly amongst many amazing delicacies had the Ambarsari masala fish on its menu. To my surprise this fish was one of the best preparations that I had had in a long time. It was marinated and spiced similarly to the way many Punjabis prepare it in their homes, and the flavours and seasonings lingered in my mouth all day long.

This experience inspired me to adapt and create a recipe like the one we enjoyed at the Dhaba. The fish that restaurant used were surmai and halibut, but you may use any firm fish for this recipe, such as tilapia, cod, snapper, or any other non-oily white fish of your choice.

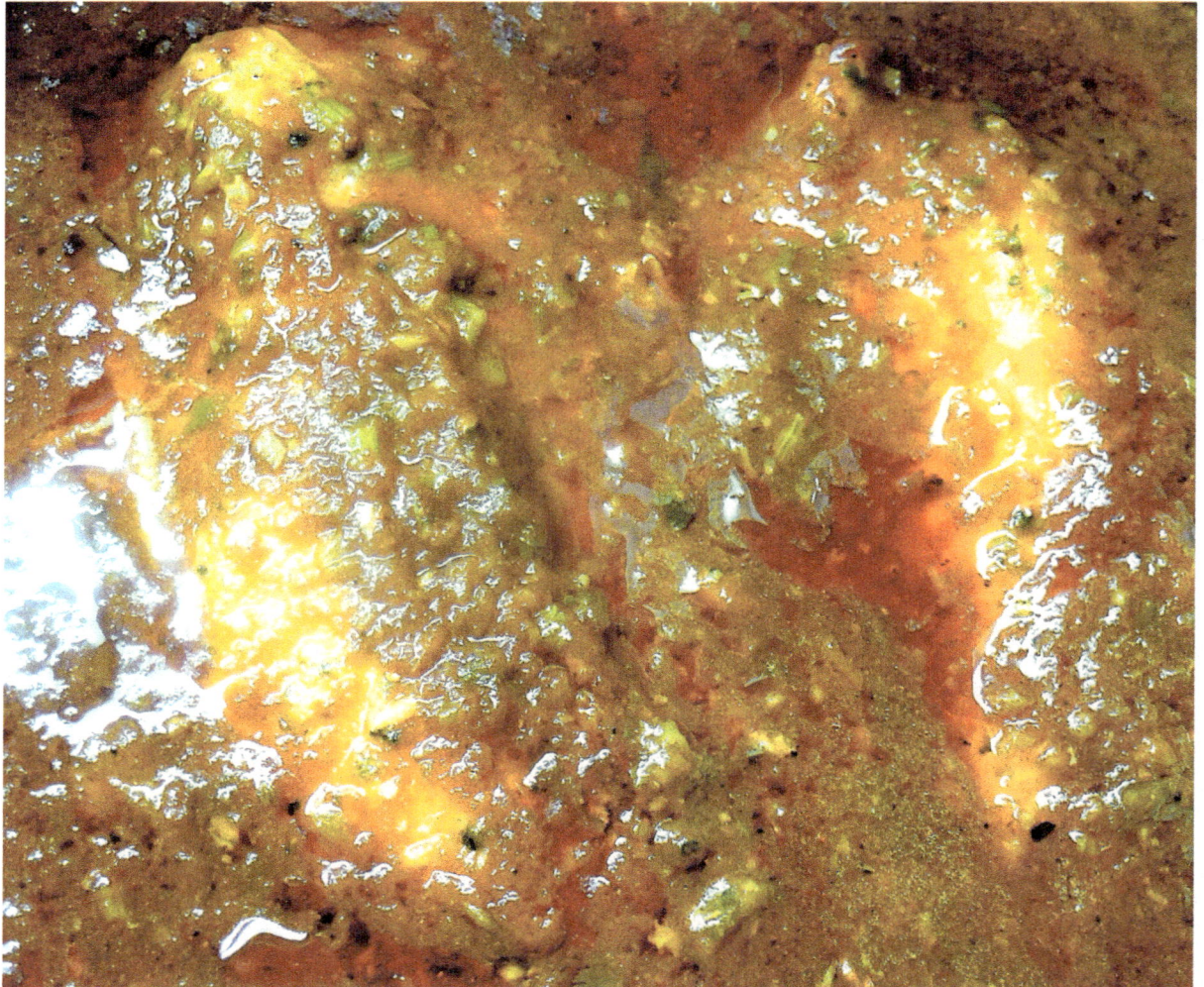

INGREDIENTS:

1 lb fish fillet of choice, cut into 2-oz pieces

1 fresh lemon

1 tsp ajwain, lightly rubbed

½ tsp garlic paste

½ tsp ginger paste

Salt and hot red chili powder to taste

1 medium onion, finely chopped

1 tsp coriander seeds, coarsely crushed

½ tsp cumin seeds, rubbed

½ tsp turmeric powder

1 tsp garam masala

3 green cardamom pods, lightly crushed

1 tbs Kasoori methi

1 pinch nutmeg powder

1½ cups ripe tomatoes, diced

2 tbs clarified butter

3 tbs mustard oil

Fresh coriander for garnish

Green chilies for garnish

Ginger root, julienned, for garnish

METHOD:

In mixing bowl add pieces of fish pat-dried with paper towel. Squeeze juice of fresh lemon on fish and add ajwain, garlic and ginger pastes, salt, and chili powder. Mix fish well and let marinate for at least 1 hour or more. Next, in heated non-stick frying pan add clarified butter and quickly pan-fry fish lightly. Save any marinade left in bowl. Remove fried fish and any fat from pan and keep aside.

Next, in different saucepan heat mustard oil and let it smoke. Then add diced onions, coriander seeds, cumin seeds, and cardamom pods. Sauté mixture for a few minutes, then add turmeric, garam masala, Kasoori methi, and nutmeg and combine well, ensuring that mixture does not scorch and onions do not burn. Add tomatoes, scrape leftover marinade, and add to pan. Keep stirring sauce until it is nicely cooked and oil separates. Turn heat off and taste sauce to make any final adjustments with salt and chili powder.

Place fried fish on top of masala and very gently smother sauce all over fish pieces. Cover pan and let sit for a few hours before serving.

Just before serving carefully heat fish thoroughly and plate on platter. Garnish fish with coriander, ginger, and green chilies. Serve this amazing preparation with steamed rice or lachedar parathas. If eating this delicacy with rice, enjoy it with your fingers for the ultimate authentic taste experience!

Pineapple Shrimp Curry

IN BANGKOK MANY RESTAURANTS SERVE THIS DELICACY. IT IS USUALLY FAIRLY HOT AND THE PINE-apple chunks help cut the heat down. This dish is also served with fresh chunks of mangoes and jackfruit.

INGREDIENTS:

1 lb jumbo shrimp, shelled, deveined, with tails on

2 tbs red curry paste (see page 24)

1 tsp fresh ginger root, julienned

1 tbs nam pla (fish sauce)

2 cups coconut milk

1 cup fresh pineapple chunks

3 kaffir lime leaves, coarsely cut

1 tsp palm sugar

2 tbs lime juice

1 tbs fresh coriander leaves, chopped

METHOD:

In saucepan add about 4 tbs coconut milk, cook it with red curry paste and ginger, and keep stirring. When fat from milk separates add shrimp, nam pla, kaffir lime leaves, and sugar. Stir well and as shrimp start to change colour add remaining coconut milk and pineapple chunks. Bring to a boil, add lime juice, and transfer curry to serving dish. Garnish with fresh coriander and serve hot with steamed rice.

Jumbo Shrimp In A Light Spicy Coconut Curry Sauce With Squash And Yellow Zucchini

THIS DELICACY BRINGS BACK FOND MEMORIES FROM PATTAYA BEACH IN THAILAND. PATTAYA IS A FEW hours away from Bangkok and is well known for its beaches and resorts.

Until the 1960s, Pattaya was a small fishing village. During the Vietnam War, American servicemen started to visit Pattaya for rest and relaxation. As a result, it developed into a popular beach resort; now greatly expanded, it attracts over four million visitors a year. Fishermens' huts along the beach were replaced by resort hotels, like the Hilton Hotel situated right on Beach Road in central Pattaya, and retail stores, including Asia's largest beachfront shopping mall, the Central Festival Pattaya Beach Mall.

Equally exquisite is the food from this region, particularly the seafood delicacies. The few days that I spent at this beautiful heaven on earth, I enjoyed a variety of seafood delicacies like tom yum soup, Pattaya mussels in lemongrass sauce, fresh octopus satay, fresh catch of the day cooked whole in exotic spices, and the best pad thai in all of Thailand.

The following recipe has been adapted from the wonderful foods I ate in Thailand. You may substitute boneless chicken, firm fried tofu, firm fish, or different vegetables and mushrooms into this recipe. However you prepare it, the end result is going to be phenomenal.

INGREDIENTS:

1 lb large shrimp, shelled, deveined, with tails on

1 tbs garlic chili paste

1 tbs Worcestershire sauce

1 medium-sized opo squash, peeled and cubed into 1" pieces

1 large-sized yellow zucchini, washed and cubed into 1" pieces

2 tbs clarified butter

1 tbs oil

3 shallots, finely chopped

1 tsp fresh garlic paste

1 stalk fresh lemongrass, dried outer shell discarded

3 kaffir lime leaves, centre vein removed, finely chopped

1 tbs lime rind, finely grated

1 tbs fresh ginger root, chopped

1 tsp galangal, finely chopped

1 finger hot green chili pepper, finely chopped

1 tsp turmeric powder

1 tbs fresh coriander stems, chopped

1 cup vegetable stock or chicken stock

1 cup coconut milk

Salt to taste

2 tbs fresh lemon juice

1 tbs fresh coriander, chopped

METHOD:

With rolling pin mash lemongrass stalk and finely chop it. It is always best to do this just before you start to prepare this delicacy.

In mixing bowl add cleaned shrimp, chili paste, and Worcestershire sauce. Mix well and let marinate for 1 hour or so.

In large saucepan, heat butter. Add shallots, garlic, turmeric powder, lemongrass, and kaffir lime leaves. Stir-fry all ingredients for about 2 minutes.

Add lime rind, ginger root, chili pepper, coriander stems, and stock. Season with salt, mix well, and bring to a boil.

Add cubed zucchini and squash and cover pot. Cook until vegetables are slightly done. Do not overcook. Remove pot from heat and set aside.

Next, heat frying pan and add oil. As soon as oil gets hot add marinated shrimp and sauté on high heat for a few minutes. Immediately add shrimp to saucepan with vegetables and stir gently. Add coconut milk to pan and mix well.

Just before serving heat sauce to ensure shrimp and vegetables are thoroughly warmed. Garnish with coriander leaves and serve with steamed rice or noodles of your choice.

Mussels In Kaffir Lime And Lemongrass Sauce

THIS DELICACY BRINGS BACK FOND MEMORIES OF BANGKOK'S STREET VENDORS. THE SEAFOOD FROM this region is particularly divine, and the few days that I spent here, every day I enjoyed a bowl of these mussels before each meal.

INGREDIENTS:

1 lb live mussels

2 tbs clarified butter

3 shallots, finely chopped

1 tsp fresh garlic paste

1 stalk fresh lemongrass, with dried outer shell discarded

3 kaffir lime leaves, with centre vein removed, finely chopped

1 tbs lime rind, finely grated

1 tbs fresh ginger root, chopped

1 finger hot green chili pepper, finely chopped

1 tbs fresh coriander leaves, chopped

1 cup white wine or vegetable stock

Salt to taste

2 tbs fresh lemon juice

1 tbs fresh coriander stems, chopped

1 lemon, cut into 8 wedges

Crusty garlic bread

METHOD:

Using small knife, carefully scrape off beard from mussels and wash them under cold running water. Discard any open or damaged mussels. Keep washing until all sand is removed. Drain mussels and keep in fridge or a cool place.

With rolling pin mash lemongrass stalk and finely chop it.

In large saucepan heat butter, shallots, garlic, lemongrass, and kaffir lime leaves. Stir-fry all ingredients for about 2 minutes.

Alaskan King Crab Legs In A Spicy Garlic-Gingercurried Glaze

WHENEVER OUR CHILDREN ARE VISITING US FROM VANCOUVER, ANY SEAFOOD DELICACY IS A MUST, as they love seafood of all kinds. Recently, I laid my hands on the finest crop of Alaskan king crab legs at my neighbourhood fishmonger.

When I brought this prize catch home, we had a tough time deciding whether we should steam the legs and have them with peri peri butter, cook them in a spicy sauce, or make them in a curry sauce. You guessed it: a new dish was created!

When enjoying this delicacy, please be forewarned that you may want to discard your cutlery, as this is something that has to be experienced with your hands. The legs turn out so tasty that you'll be tempted to give "finger-licking and lip-smacking good" a new meaning. The best part is when you are about to clean the wok, as you'll surely want to wipe it clean with a piece of bread. This dish embodies the true joy of cooking and enjoying good food at home with your loved ones and friends.

If you buy frozen legs, it is recommended that crab legs thaw overnight in your refrigerator. If you're in a big hurry, king crab can be placed under cold running water to speed the thawing process. A useful tip is to drain the frozen legs as they are defrosting by placing them on a rack in a watertight container.

INGREDIENTS:

1 kg Alaskan king crab legs, fully thawed

5 tbs clarified butter

1 tbs coconut oil

1 medium onion, finely chopped

½ cup green onions, finely chopped

4 hot green chilies, chopped

1 tbs garlic paste

1 tbs ginger root, chopped

2 tbs red Thai curry paste

2 tbs soy sauce

1 large tomato, finely diced

1 tbs tomato paste

¼ cup fresh coriander, stems and roots, chopped

1 tsp palm sugar

1 fresh lime

1 tbs fresh coriander leaves

METHOD:

Cut crab legs into 6"-long pieces and slit lengthwise.

In wok heat butter and stir-fry crab legs for about 4 minutes, stirring constantly. Remove and drain fried legs and set aside in plate.

In same wok with drained butter add coconut oil, onions, green chilies, garlic paste, ginger root, red curry paste, and soy sauce. Mix all ingredients well and sauté for about 3 to 5 minutes on high heat. Add diced tomatoes and paste along with coriander stems and roots. Stir well and add sugar.

Continue to cook mixture, occasionally stirring until fat starts to separate from sauce. Please note that there is no need to add salt, as legs already have sea salt. Next, add legs into wok and mix well, ensuring all legs are well coated with glaze. As soon as legs get nicely warmed, immediately plate on serving platter, squeeze juice of 1 lime all over, and garnish with coriander leaves. Serve this succulent and scrumptious delight hot with steamed rice. Indulging by dipping a piece of hot naan or a layered paratha in the rich glaze would be a heavenly experience.

Baked Pacific Salmon With Dill-Garlic Sauce

I ENJOYED THIS DELICACY AT A RESTAURANT IN THE SOOK REGION NEAR VICTORIA, BRITISH COLUMBIA. The freshness of the fish just blew my mind and the simplicity of its preparation has since left an everlasting memory of the butter sauce infused with fresh dill.

INGREDIENTS:

2 lb fresh Pacific salmon fillets

1 lemon

½ cup white wine

8 tbs cold butter, cut into 16 pieces

1 tsp dill weed

½ tsp garlic, minced

Salt and freshly ground black pepper to taste

METHOD:

Squeeze juice of ½ lemon on fish and season with salt and pepper. Pre-heat oven to 375°F. Place fish in ovenproof baking dish and bake for approximately 10 minutes. Fish should be firm but not dry.

Add wine, dill, and garlic in small saucepan. Reduce mixture on heat and keep stirring until almost dry. Remove saucepan

from heat and quickly add butter while whisking briskly. When butter has been incorporated, allow sauce to rest for a few minutes, then spoon it over hot salmon fillets and serve immediately.

Garnish salmon with slices of remaining lemon and serve with saffron rice and grilled vegetables.

Coastal Fish Kofta Curry

KOFTAS HAIL FROM SOUTHEAST ASIA AND THE MIDDLE EAST. THEY ARE USUALLY MADE FROM GROUND meat mixed with herbs and spices, are formed into balls, ovals, or cylindrical shapes, and are cooked in spicy sauces or gravies or simply grilled. There are hundreds of variations of this dish, ranging from spicy lamb koftas grilled on the streets of Morocco and Istanbul, to curried vegetable and nutty paneer koftas served with rice or naan in India, Pakistan, and Afghanistan. If you happen to be travelling through Kashmir, you will likely encounter gushtaba, a velvety-soft lamb kofta flavoured with cardamom and cooked gently in delicately spiced hung yogurt and cream on low heat. Though the most commonly used meat choices include beef, lamb, pork, and chicken, in the Far East, seafood koftas are very popular, and in some parts of India, seafood koftas cooked in coconut milk curry or rich, spicy tomato curry sauce are consumed with rice.

Over the years, I have enjoyed several varieties of koftas in many different countries. My all-time three favourites are chicken koftas cooked in a spiced methi curry, Amritsari mutton koftas, and above all, my aunt Mrs. Trilochan Suri's fabulous fish koftas.

Decades ago when I visited the Suris in the coastal city of Mombasa, Kenya, Mrs. Suri treated us to her amazing fish koftas with plain rice. To this day, I have not forgotten that unique and tantalizing experience. Without trying to explain to you the taste and flavours, I am risking disappointing Mrs. Suri by sharing the version I was inspired to create by my beloved aunt. I hope you will agree with me that it is outstanding and enjoy it as much as I do.

INGREDIENTS FOR KOFTAS:

1 kg fresh cod, haddock, or tilapia fillets

1 fresh lemon

1 small onion, finely chopped

2 tsp fresh ginger, finely chopped

1 tsp garlic paste

2 green chilies, finely chopped

2 tbs fresh coriander, finely chopped

½ tsp Kasoori methi, rubbed

1 tsp ajwain seeds, rubbed between palms

1 small potato, boiled, chilled, and finely mashed

2 egg whites, beaten

Salt and pepper to taste

Flour for dusting

Mustard oil for frying

INGREDIENTS FOR CURRY:

5 tbs vegetable cooking oil

1 cup onions, finely chopped

1 tbs ginger paste

1 tbs garlic paste

2 green chilies, finely chopped

1 tsp turmeric

1 tsp ajwain seeds, rubbed

1 tsp garam masala

1 tbs deggi mirch

2 cups ripe tomatoes, finely diced

8 cups boiling water

2 tbs coriander stems, finely chopped

2 tbs fresh coriander leaves for garnish

Salt to taste

METHOD:

In mixing bowl add fish fillets and ensure they are boneless and clean. Squeeze juice of 1 lemon, mix well, and let sit for a few minutes. Next, place fillets on clean chopping board and, using cleaver or sharp knife, carefully finely chop fillets. Put chopped fish back into mixing bowl and all kofta ingredients except dusting flour and mustard oil. With hands knead mixture well until all ingredients are very well blended. Cover bowl and place in fridge for 1 hour.

After 1 hour shape fish mixture into small balls about 1" in diameter by rolling mixture gently between moist palms. Keep balls on flat dish and cover.

In small wok heat mustard oil on high heat and allow it to smoke. As soon as oil has started to smoke turn heat down. Dust rolled balls lightly with flour and gently drop them into hot oil without overcrowding. Fry to a light golden brown finish. With slotted spoon remove fried balls and place on paper towel.

Once all balls are fried and kept aside, start to make sauce by heating oil in saucepan and sauté chopped onions until lightly browned. Then add ginger and garlic pastes, turmeric, garam masala, deggi mirch, ajwain seeds, and salt. Keep stir-frying for a few minutes. Then add diced tomatoes and keep cooking until oil starts to separate. Next, add coriander stems and 8 cups boiling water and bring sauce to a boil. Turn heat to medium and let sauce reduce a little. Simmer for about ½ hour. Check seasoning and make any necessary adjustments. Gently slide in fish balls one at a time into simmering sauce. Let fish balls simmer for another 10 minutes. Plate koftas in serving platter, garnish with fresh coriander, and serve hot. You may want to let this preparation rest in fridge overnight for best results.

Serve this coastal delicacy with hot steamed basmati rice or lachedar parathas. Radish and onion salad makes a good accompaniment.

Manchurian Chili Pepper Fish

FOR A LONG TIME IN MANY PARTS OF INDIA, THE CHINESE HAVE MADE HAKKA AND MANCHURIAN styles of cooking very popular. This type of Chinese cooking is fairly hot and very compatible with many fiery hot Indian delicacies. More recently Chinese cooks from India have opened restaurants in Toronto and other parts of Canada and have introduced this new cuisine, and it is no surprise that it has taken over like a wild fire—there aren't enough restaurants to meet the enormous demand.

This new trend in Chinese cooking has indeed inspired me to share such recipes from my kitchen. For starters, I'll feature a fish dish that can be easily adapted for chicken, shrimp, or vegetables.

INGREDIENTS:

2 lb tilapia or cod fillets, boneless, cut into 1"x2" pieces

1 lemon

½ tsp garlic powder

Salt and pepper to taste

2 whole bunches spring onions, finely chopped

2 red chilies, dried

1 tbs ginger paste

1 tbs garlic paste

1 cup fresh tomatoes, chopped

3 finger hot green chilies, sliced on a bias

1 tbs Sichuan peppers, stems discarded

½ cup fresh coriander stems, chopped

1 tbs Sriracha sauce

1 tbs soy sauce

2 tbs hoisin sauce

2 tbs fresh coriander leaves, chopped

1 tbs fresh ginger root, julienned

1 tbs butter

3 tbs cooking oil

1 onion, halved and sliced

½ cup green or red sweet peppers, julienned

Fresh coriander for garnish

METHOD:

In mixing bowl place fish pieces and add garlic powder, salt, and pepper and mix well. Now squeeze juice from lemon onto fish and mix well. Cover bowl and let fish marinate for at least 1 hour.

In heated saucepan add 2 tbs cooking oil and butter. Add chopped green onions and dried chilies to pan. Make sure to chop spring onions, including green parts. Sauté onions for about 5 minutes and then add garlic, ginger, and green chilies and keep stirring. Next, add Sriracha sauce and keep stirring for another minute. Then add tomatoes and coriander stems and mix well.

Cook sauce for another 5 minutes and then add soy sauce, hoisin sauce, and Sichuan peppers and continue to stir and cook. Sauce should be almost ready when fat starts to separate. Immediately pour marinade juice from bowl into saucepan and cook for another minute or so. Check for seasonings and make any necessary adjustments. Gently add fish pieces into saucepan and carefully stir fish into sauce so all pieces are well coated. Cover saucepan and let fish simmer in sauce on low heat for about 6 minutes or until fully cooked.

In small frying pan heat remaining oil, add sliced onion and julienned peppers, and stir-fry on high heat for 1 minute. Then add crunchy onions and peppers to saucepan and gently mix well with fish. Plate fish on serving platter and garnish with fresh coriander. Serve piping hot with steamed basmati rice.

Spicy Yellow Curry Coconut Mussels

I ENJOYED THIS APPETIZER IN PATTAYA, A COASTAL RESORT IN THAILAND ABOUT TWO HUNDRED kilometres from Bangkok. It was by accident that I discovered this amazing dish; a restaurant that had run out of its famous Thai fish cakes offered these mussels as a substitute. I had no choice and opted for this dish. I liked it so much that it has now become a specialty in our household.

INGREDIENTS:

4 lb fresh cultivated mussels, washed in cold water and cleaned

2 tbs clarified butter

1 medium onion, finely diced

1 tbs yellow Thai curry paste

2 green chilies, finely chopped

3 kaffir lime leaves

1 tbs fresh ginger root, chopped

1 tsp garlic paste

½ cup ripe tomatoes, pureed

Salt to taste

1 cup coconut milk

Fresh coriander for garnish

Green onions, chopped, for garnish

Fresh ginger root, julienned, for garnish

METHOD:

In deep saucepan heat butter and sauté diced onions and chilies for a few minutes. Next, add kaffir lime leaves, ginger, and garlic paste and mix well, cooking mixture for a few minutes. Then add tomatoes, curry paste, and salt, stir sauce, and then gently add coconut milk. Bring to a boil and immediately add mussels, cover pot, and cook until all mussels have fully opened.

Immediately plate mussels and garnish with fresh coriander, green onions, and ginger root. Serve with garlic or plain baguette or buttered naan. Add lime rind, ginger root, chili pepper, coriander stems, and stock. Season with salt, mix well, and bring to a boil. Add cleaned mussels and cover pot. Cook until all mussels have opened and immediately transfer to serving bowl.

Garnish with coriander leaves and fresh lemon wedges. Serve with plain crusty bread or garlic bread. Serve in smaller portions as appetizer.

Pan-Seared Ginger-Glazed Mahi-Mahi Steaks

SOME PEOPLE WHO ENJOY MAHI-MAHI ROUTINELY BELIEVE THAT THE FISH THEY ARE COOKING IS A form of dolphin. Some justify their choice by declaring that mahi-mahi is a primitive form of dolphin without the behaviours and intelligence of more commonly known species. In fact mahi-mahi is not a species of dolphin or even a relative at all. It is a water-breathing, ray-finned fish distantly related to the perch.

The reason for this common misconception is that restaurants often call the mahi-mahi fish "dolphin" on their menus. In scientific terms, the word dolphin refers exclusively to mammals of the Delphinidae family, and not to any fish.

While dolphin lovers can breathe easy and continue to eat their mahi-mahi without the fear of biting into a mammal, the fish does carry one major negative drawback for environmentalists. Catching mahi-mahi by the long-line fishing system is considered to be very unfriendly to the environment: the nets have massive amounts of by-catch and often destroy sea turtles, sharks, and, yes, indeed actual dolphins. Seafood lovers should best avoid mahi-mahi caught by this common method and instead opt for fish caught with a line-and-pole method.

The first time I enjoyed this delicacy was in Hawaii, where mahi-mahi is common and cooked in many different ways. We are very fortunate here in Ontario to get a good supply of mahi-mahi, and in our household it is one of the favourite seafood items enjoyed by all.

This dish bursts with flavour and combines the taste sensations of sweet, sour, and hot. It can be prepared in a snap and is absolutely delicious.

INGREDIENTS:

4 fresh mahi-mahi steaks

2 tbs clarified butter

All-purpose flour, sifted, for dusting

MARINADE:

1 tbs garlic paste

2 tbs ginger root paste

1 tbs light soy sauce

1 tsp deggi mirch or smoked paprika

1 tsp hot chili oil paste

Juice of 1 fresh lemon

2 tbs honey or agave syrup

½ tsp black pepper, freshly ground

Salt to taste (please taste marinade for salt, as soy sauce may have enough)

GARNISH:

Fresh coriander leaves, chopped

1 fresh lime, sliced into rounds

METHOD:

In large mixing bowl add all ingredients for marinade and mix well. Add fish fillets to marinade and mix thoroughly. Allow fish to marinate for at least 3 to 4 hours at room temperature.

Gently remove each fish fillet from marinade, shake off liquid, and dust with finely sifted flour. In hot frying pan add clarified butter and gently slide fish fillets into pan.

Sear fish to a golden brown finish on each side, about 4 to 5 minutes. Repeat process until all fillets are fried.

Serve fish piping hot with steamed rice and mango salsa. Garnish with sliced lime and fresh coriander. You may also serve dollar fries, asparagus, beans, snow peas, and sautéed sliced mushrooms and onions with this preparation.

Pan-Seared Tilapia

THESE FISH FILLETS ARE A MUST AT EVERY MAGON GATHERING WITH FAMILY AND FRIENDS. IN THIS preparation East takes over West in both taste and flavour—a finger-licking good experience in it's true sense.

INGREDIENTS:

4 fresh tilapia fillets

MARINADE:

2 tbs garlic paste

2 tbs ginger root paste

1 tbs light soy sauce

1 tbs cornstarch

1 tbs deggi mirch

1 tbs hot chili oil paste

Juice of 1 fresh lemon

Salt to taste (please taste marinade for salt, as soy sauce may have enough)

All-purpose flour, sifted, for dusting

Cooking oil for searing

GARNISH:

Fresh coriander leaves, chopped

1 fresh lime, sliced into rounds

METHOD:

In large mixing bowl add all ingredients for marinade and mix well. Add fish fillets to marinade and mix thoroughly. Allow fish to marinate for at least 3 to 4 hours at room temperature.

Gently remove each fish fillet from marinade, shake off liquid, dust with finely sifted flour, and sear in hot frying

pan with oil. Cook fish to a golden brown finish on each side. Repeat process until all fillets are fried.

Serve fish piping hot with mango salsa and garnish with sliced lime and fresh coriander. You may also serve dollar fries, asparagus, beans, snow peas, and sautéed sliced mushrooms and onions.

Pan-Seared Red Snapper
In Spicy Orange Sauce

A TANGY GINGER-ORANGE SAUCE, SEASONED WITH GARLIC AND CORIANDER STEMS, REALLY BRINGS out the best in these red snapper fillets. If you cannot find red snapper any white fish will work fine.

INGREDIENTS:

1 lb red snapper fillet, boneless

Salt and pepper to taste

1 tbs chili paste

Juice of ½ lemon

½ cup all-purpose flour

2 tbs cornstarch

1 tsp garlic paste

Vegetable oil for frying

2 tbs bamboo shoots, julienned

½ medium onion, sliced

1 finger hot green chili, sliced

1 stalk green onion, including green parts, sliced on a bias

2 celery stalks, sliced on a bias

½ bell pepper, julienned

SAUCE:

2 tbs butter

½ tsp garlic paste

1 tsp fresh ginger paste

1 tbs honey

½ cup fresh orange juice

1 tsp orange peel, grated

2 tbs fresh coriander stems, chopped

Fresh coriander for garnish

Ginger root, julienned, for garnish

METHOD:

Pat-dry fish with paper towel and cut fillets into 2"x1" chunks. Place them in bowl, add salt and pepper, chili and garlic pastes, and lemon juice. Mix well and let marinate for a few hours.

Start making sauce by melting butter in saucepan. Add garlic and ginger pastes, honey, and orange juice. Stir well and bring mixture to a boil. As soon as it starts to boil turn heat to simmer and add orange peel and coriander stems. Mix well and let sauce simmer for about 5 minutes. Keep sauce warm.

In separate bowl add flour and cornstarch and mix well. Gently add fish pieces, shaking off any excess marinade. Make sure all fish pieces are evenly coated. In wok heat oil and carefully fry fish to a golden brown crispness. Transfer fried fish onto paper towel to absorb excess oil.

Blanch all vegetables in boiling water for a few minutes and drain. Transfer drained vegetables onto serving platter and place fried fish on top. Finally, drizzle ginger-orange sauce all over fish and garnish with fresh coriander and ginger root. Serve hot with steamed rice.

Penne Rigate In Mustard Mushroom Sauce With Shrimp

THIS IS A VERY SIMPLE PASTA DISH THAT CAN BE PREPARED WITH SEAFOOD, CHICKEN, OR JUST vegetables. It can be made with a spicy tomato sauce or a rich, velvety cream-and-cheese sauce.

INGREDIENTS:

3 cups penne rigate, cooked according to package instructions

1 lb large shrimp, shelled, deveined, with tails on or off

3 tbs butter or olive oil

2 shallots, finely chopped

1 cup fresh white mushrooms, finely chopped

½ tsp ginger paste

½ tsp garlic paste

½ cup green peas, fresh or frozen

1 stalk celery, sliced on a bias

½ cup carrots, julienned or cut into shoestrings

1 tbs Dijon mustard

1 cup half-and-half

1 tbs Parmesan cheese

Salt and freshly ground black pepper to taste

½ tsp hot sauce of choice

1 tbs parsley or coriander, finely chopped

METHOD:

In saucepan heat butter or olive oil and add chopped shallots and mushrooms. Sauté mixture for a few minutes. Next, add ginger and garlic pastes, stir well, cook for 1 minute, and then add peas, celery, and carrots. Mix well and cook for a few minutes. Then gently add half-and-half, Parmesan cheese, and Dijon mustard, mix well, and

turn heat to medium. Add shrimp, salt and pepper, and hot sauce, and let mixture simmer for a few minutes. Do not overcook shrimp. Finally, add cooked penne, mix well into sauce, and heat pasta in sauce. Plate pasta in serving dish and garnish with parsley or coriander. Serve hot with salad of choice and garlic bread.

Seafood Medley In Mustard Mushroom Cream Sauce With Shrimp

THIS SEAFOOD LASAGNA IS A RICH, SATISFYING DISH, ADAPTED FROM SEVERAL DIFFERENT KINDS OF lasagna I have enjoyed over the years. This loaded "crown jewel" seafood medley, married with two kinds of pasta in a rich, creamy cheese sauce, is always a hit at our family gatherings and one of my prized recipes.

The sauce used in lasagna is a necessary component and may differ according to region. Usually, sheet-shaped pasta and a cheesy sauce, most often Béchamel, are used in the preparation of most lasagna recipes. Tomato-based sauces are also very common. Traditionally, lasagna is prepared with vegetables, like eggplant, and meat, but nowadays seafood seems to be a favourite addition as well.

The foodie in me loves to give a twist to the traditional preparations without taking away from the original dish's integrity.

INGREDIENTS:

24 jumbo pasta shells, cooked according to package instructions

6 lasagna strips, cooked according to package instructions

36 large pasta shells, cooked according to package instructions

1 lb large shrimp, shelled, deveined, with tails off

1 cup salad shrimp, coarsely chopped (smaller cleaned shrimp)

1 lb seafood medley, including bay scallops, calamari, white fish tidbits, and chopped octopus

5 tbs butter or olive oil

2 shallots, finely chopped

1 cup fresh white mushrooms, finely chopped

½ tsp ginger paste

½ tsp garlic paste

1 stalk celery, finely chopped

½ cup green peas

½ cup carrot, finely diced

1 tbs Dijon mustard

1 cup half-and-half

1 tbs Parmesan cheese

Salt and freshly ground black pepper to taste

½ tsp hot sauce of choice

1 tbs parsley, finely chopped

1 cup mozzarella cheese, shredded

Note: No herbs are used so as to emphasize the marriage of flavours between the seafood and creamy cheese. However, you may wish to use dill, oregano, or tarragon.

METHOD:

In saucepan heat 3 tbs butter or olive oil and add chopped shallots and ½ cup chopped mushrooms. Sauté mixture for a few minutes. Next, add ginger and garlic pastes, stir well, cook for 1 minute, and then add celery, green peas, and carrots. Combine well and cook mixture for a few minutes, then gently add half-and-half, Parmesan cheese, and Dijon mustard and mix well, turning heat down to medium. Next, add seafood medley, salt and pepper, and hot sauce and let mixture simmer for a few minutes until it thickens. Do not overcook mixture.

Slightly season large shrimp with salt and pepper and sauté lightly in 1 tbs butter. Set aside.

In separate pan, heat remaining butter and add remaining mushrooms and chopped salad shrimp, chopped parsley, salt, and pepper. Sauté mixture until mushrooms and shrimp are slightly cooked. Remove pan from stove and let mixture cool. Once cooled, fill cooked shells with mixture and keep aside.

Slightly butter ovenproof dish and lay 3 sheets cooked lasagna on bottom. Pour ½ seafood sauce all over and cover with remaining lasagna sheets. Pour remaining sauce over pasta and save a little for final garnish. Next, place filled shells on top of sauce and sprinkle with any sauce left over. Gently place sautéed shrimp all over dish, and sprinkle with Parmesan and mozzarella cheeses.

Place dish into pre-heated oven at 325°F. Cook for a few minutes and let cheese melt to a golden brown finish. Serve hot with salad of choice or garlic bread.

Farfalle In Mustard Mushroom Sauce With Shrimp

SPECIALLY CREATED FOR MY DEAR FRIENDS FROM PAKISTAN, TAHA AND SOPHIA, this is a very simple pasta dish that can be prepared with seafood, chicken, or vegetables. It can be made with a spicy tomato sauce or a rich, velvety cream-and-cheese sauce.

INGREDIENTS:

3 cups farfalle, cooked according to package instructions

1 lb large shrimp, shelled, deveined, with tails on or off

3 tbs butter or olive oil

2 shallots, finely chopped

1 cup fresh white mushrooms, finely chopped

½ tsp ginger paste

½ tsp garlic paste

½ cup green peas, fresh or frozen

1 stalk celery, sliced on a bias

½ cup carrots, julienned or cut into shoestrings

1 tbs Dijon mustard

1 cup half-and-half

1 tbs Parmesan cheese

Salt and freshly ground black pepper to taste

½ tsp hot sauce of choice

1 tbs parsley or coriander, finely chopped

METHOD:

In saucepan heat butter or olive oil and add chopped shallots and chopped mushrooms. Sauté mixture for a few minutes. Next, add ginger and garlic pastes, stir well, and cook for 1 minute, then add peas, celery, and carrots. Mix well and cook for a few minutes. Then gently add half-and-half, Parmesan cheese, and Dijon mustard and mix well, turning heat to medium. Next, add shrimp, salt and pepper, and hot sauce and let mixture simmer for a few minutes. Do not overcook shrimp. Finally, add cooked farfalle, mix well into sauce, and gently heat pasta in sauce. Plate in serving dish and garnish with parsley or coriander. Serve hot with salad of choice and garlic bread.

Peri Peri Buttered Grilled Shrimp

A UNIQUE AFRICAN-PORTUGUESE PEPPERY BUTTER-GRILLED SHRIMP DISH, THIS IS AN EXCELLENT yet simple preparation I enjoyed in Durban, South Africa. The key ingredients are the authentic peri peri peppers.

INGREDIENTS:

2 lb large shrimp, shelled, deveined, with tails on

MARINADE:

¼ cup unsalted butter

Juice of 1 lemon

¼ tsp lemon rind

2 tbs peri peri pepper powder

½ tsp garlic paste

Salt and freshly ground pepper to taste

METHOD:

In small saucepan on medium heat melt butter and add remaining ingredients. Cook for a few minutes, stirring sauce. Remove from heat and marinade is ready to be used.

Add shrimp to marinade, mix well, and let shrimp marinate for at least 2 hours before grilling or pan-frying.

Next, skewer shrimp onto wet bamboo skewers or metal skewers and cook to perfection on fairly hot grill for about 3 minutes on each side.

Serve hot on top of rice pilaf of choice or with hot buttered naan and salad.

Lobster In A Light Spicy Coconut Curry Sauce

QUITE A FEW YEARS AGO WHEN I TRAVELLED TO ZANZIBAR, EAST AFRICA, I HAD THE OPPORTUNITY to try many exotic curried seafood delicacies at several beachfront shack restaurants, and this particular lobster preparation was amongst my favourites. I also recall enjoying something very similar and equally succulent in Goa. I am confident that I have replicated this delicacy to perfection and am pleased to share it here.

INGREDIENTS:

1 large lobster

1 medium onion

1 bunch green onions

4 fresh curry leaves

¼ cup fresh ginger root

4 hot green chilies

2 tbs fresh garlic paste

1 tbs crushed red chili in oil

3 ripe tomatoes, finely chopped

1 tsp deggi mirch

1 tbs tamarind sauce

1 tsp turmeric powder

Salt and pepper to taste

1 small can coconut milk

Fresh coriander, chopped, for garnish

Vegetable cooking oil

METHOD:

In large pot bring water to a boil and gently drop lobster in. Cook for about 8 minutes. Carefully remove lobster from water. Let cool, then gently separate claws and tail from head. Using dull edge of cleaver or big knife, crack claws and save. Now gently remove tail meat from shell and ensure shell remains intact. Clean head and shells and save them for garnish.

Cut tail meat into small chunks and keep aside. Finely chop green chilies, onion, and green onions, including half the green part, and julienne ginger root.

In hot wok add cooking oil and quickly fry shell and claws for 1 minute. Remove and keep aside. Next, add lobster meat, chili oil, and garlic paste and sauté for a few minutes. Remove lobster meat and keep aside.

Next, sauté chopped onions, green onions, ginger, and hot chilies. As onions start to brown, add garlic paste and cook for 1 minute or so. Then add turmeric powder along with chopped tomatoes, salt, and pepper and continue to cook and stir sauce until oil starts to separate. Next, add tamarind paste, deggi mirch, and coconut milk and mix well. Then add sautéed lobster meat to sauce and mix well. Cook mixture for a few minutes, ensuring not to overcook.

Plate lobster curry on large serving platter. Place fried body shell and claws on top of curry and arrange to form lobster shape. Garnish with fresh coriander and dish is ready to be served. You may want to serve some lemon or lime wedges with this curry.

Serve lobster hot with steamed rice. You may also enjoy with hot buttered naan or rotis.

Alaskan King Crab Legs In Black Bean Sauce

LATELY WE HAVE BEEN GETTING LOADS OF THE FINEST CROP OF ALASKAN KING CRAB LEGS AT OUR neighbourhood fishmonger's, and whenever I see these babies I can't help but drool and grab some for dinner.

INGREDIENTS:

1 kg fresh Alaskan king crab legs

5 tbs clarified butter

1 medium onion, sliced

4 hot green chilies, chopped

1 tbs garlic paste

1 tbs ginger root, chopped

1 tbs black bean sauce in chili oil

1 tbs red curry paste

1 tbs nam pla (fish sauce)

1 tbs dark soy sauce

1 medium tomato, diced

1 tbs tomato paste

¼ cup fresh coriander stems, chopped

½ cup white wine

½ tsp granulated sugar

1 fresh lime

1 tbs fresh coriander leaves

METHOD:

Cut crab legs into 6"-long pieces and slice them in half lengthwise. In wok heat butter and stir-fry crab legs for about 4 minutes, stirring constantly. Remove and drain fried legs and place aside on plate.

In wok add onion, green chilies, garlic paste, ginger root, black bean sauce, curry paste, nam pla, and soy sauce. Mix all ingredients well and sauté for another 3 minutes. Add diced tomatoes and paste along with coriander stems. Stir well, gently pour wine, and add sugar.

Cook sauce, occasionally stirring until half of liquid has evaporated. Now add crab legs to sauce and cook until fat separates from sauce and legs are nicely coated.

Remove legs onto serving platter, squeeze juice of 1 lime all over, and garnish with coriander leaves. Serve piping hot with steamed rice.

When indulging in this delicacy, please be forewarned that you might discard your knife and fork, as this is something that has to be enjoyed with your hands! This is the true joy of cooking and enjoying good food.

Spicy Black Pepper Crab In Garlic-Ginger Sauce

RECENTLY WHEN TRAVELLING IN SINGAPORE WE HAD THE OPPORTUNITY TO TRY SEVERAL EXOTIC seafood delicacies at many eateries, and this crab dish was simply amazing. I think I have replicated this specialty to perfection here and am very pleased to share it with you.

INGREDIENTS:

2 large fresh crabs

1 medium onion

¼ cup fresh ginger root

4 hot green chilies

2 tbs fresh garlic paste

1 tbs black pepper, coarsely ground

1 tbs tomato paste

2 tbs Worcestershire sauce

2 tbs hoisin sauce

1 tbs white vinegar

Salt to taste

Fresh coriander, chopped, for garnish

Vegetable cooking oil

METHOD:

Carefully remove shell and separate legs of crab. Using dull edge of cleaver or big knife, crack legs for sauce to seep in through shell. Clean body shells and save them for garnish.

Finely chop onion and green chilies and julienne ginger root.

In hot wok add cooking oil and quickly fry both body shells. Keep aside. Next, add crab legs with 1 tbs garlic paste and sauté legs for a few minutes. Add salt and mix well. Keep crab warm.

Then sauté chopped onions, ginger, hot chilies, and remaining garlic paste. As onions start to brown add tomato paste and cook for 1 minute or so. Next, add black pepper along with hoisin sauce, white vinegar, and Worcestershire sauce and mix well, cooking sauce for a few minutes. Add sautéed crab legs to sauce and stir well. Taste sauce and make any necessary adjustments. Cover wok and allow crab to heat through thoroughly. You may wish to add some water to wok to make dish more saucy. Do not overcook crab.

Plate crab legs on serving platter. Place fried body shells for garnish along with some fresh coriander and crab is ready to be served. Serve hot with steamed rice. You may enjoy sauce with naan, rice, or rotis.

Mama Sarge's Bajan Fish And Chips

IN BARBADOS, COUCOU AND FLYING FISH ARE PREPARED WITH CORNMEAL AND OKRA, AND TOPPED with an aromatic sauce of tomato, onion, chives, thyme, fresh pepper, garlic, and other herbs. The recipe for coucou was passed down from African slaves who came to the island in 1644. The fish can be steamed, battered and fried, or grilled.

Barbados has many popular local fish such as kingfish, tuna, barracuda, and red snapper, but it is hailed as "The Land of the Flying Fish." Flying fish are very prevalent in warm water—and they do fly! They can fly distances of up to one hundred yards above the water's surface at around thirty miles per hour. This allows them to escape predators such as swordfish, tuna, and other larger fish. This fish can be easily identified by its silvery-blue skin, large fins, and lopsided tails. It is breathtaking to see the flying fish soar above the ocean. In fact, the image of the flying fish can be seen on the national logo for Barbados.

Some years back we were on a family vacation in Barbados and had the opportunity to enjoy the fresh fruits of the sea. At Rockley Beach we found a gem of a place, a family-run restaurant called Mama Sarge's Fish and Chips. We had its Bajan pan-fried red snapper with coleslaw and jerked pan-fried chips. This meal by far was the best meal we had on the island. We were so impressed that we ate there almost every day. The day we were to return home, my son insisted that we should have our last lunch there, and in enjoying our meal, we almost missed our flight!

Upon our return to Canada, my son challenged me to replicate the fish preparation that we enjoyed so much on the island. It took me almost a year to perfect the recipe and the marinade. This marinade has become very popular in our kitchen and is used for chicken, pork, fish, and shrimp.

INGREDIENTS:

2 lb fresh red snapper fillets or any other fish of choice
Oil for frying

2 lb red potatoes, peeled, cut into wedges, and parboiled
All-purpose flour for dredging

MARINADE:

1 bunch green onions, finely chopped
½ cup fresh basil, finely chopped
2 tbs ginger paste
1 tbs garlic paste
6 finger hot green chili peppers, chopped
1 Scotch bonnet pepper, finely chopped
1 tbs Bajan hot sauce (Barbadian hot sauce)
½ cup fresh lemon juice

1 tsp mustard powder
¼ tsp nutmeg powder
½ tsp all-spice powder
1 tbs brown sugar
1 tbs Worcestershire sauce
2 tbs olive oil
½ tsp pepper, freshly ground
Salt to taste

METHOD:

In food processor add all marinade ingredients and pulsate to form fine paste. In mixing bowl add fish fillets, rub with marinade paste, and mix well. Allow fish to marinate for at least 6 hours.

In separate bowl add parboiled potato wedges and gently rub marinade all over wedges.

In large frying pan, heat oil. Dredge fish fillets in flour and add to pan. In second pan, heat oil, add potato wedges, and fry them to a golden brown crispness. Keep eye on fish and gently flip them over, making sure that all fish are fried to perfection.

Serve fish hot with potato wedges, peppered beans, and fresh lemon slices. Rice with pigeon peas makes a good accompaniment to this dish; homemade garlic bread goes well too.

Lobster Thermidor

FRESH LOBSTERS ARE SUPERB WHEN COOKED THE TRADITIONAL WAY BY SIMPLY STEAMING OR BOILING.

Boiling: Fill large lobster pot three-quarters full of salted water; use 1 tbs sea salt for each quart water. Bring water to a rolling boil. Gently immerse live lobsters in pot, making sure to fully submerge. Cover pot and begin timing, making sure to keep water boiling, and use the following standard:

1- to 2-lb lobsters should be boiled for about 18 minutes.

2-lb or larger lobsters should be boiled for about 22 to 25 minutes.

Steaming: Add about 3" of salted water into large pot; use 1 tbs sea salt for each quart water. As soon as water starts to steam, place live lobsters in pot and cover tightly. Start timing, and steam lobsters using same standard mentioned above.

Should you wish to eat your lobsters at a later time, you may partially boil or steam them for about 6 minutes less than the times outlined above. Make sure you dunk your partially boiled or steamed lobster in cold water for a few minutes and then drain and refrigerate. These lobsters can be safely refrigerated for a maximum of 48 hours. Reheat the lobsters in boiling water and enjoy them to your liking. Gently crack the claws and remove the meat, and with a scissor cut underneath the tail and remove the tail carefully without breaking the shell. The tail portion has a vein containing waste, so make sure to remove it before eating. Enjoy the succulent meat with clarified butter or use it in your favourite delicacy.

Lobster thermidor is a French dish consisting of a creamy mixture of cooked lobster meat, egg yolks, and cognac or white wine, stuffed into a lobster shell. It can also be served with an oven-broiled cheese crust, typically Gruyère. Please note that the traditional sauce must contain mustard powder.

This delicacy originated in 1894 at Marie's, a Parisian restaurant. Due to the expensive and extensive preparation involved, lobster thermidor is usually considered a dish primarily for the rich and for special occasions. My first experience enjoying this delicacy was in Mombasa. Ever since tasting the first morsel of this lobster goodness forty years ago, I have been in love with this delicacy and often cook it for my friends and family. Over the years I have kept adjusting my ingredients and the following recipe is as authentic as it can get.

INGREDIENTS:

2 medium lobsters, cooked, about 2 lb each6 tbs butter

2 shallots finely chopped

¼ tsp tarragon, dried

¼ tsp thyme

½ lb fresh white mushrooms, sliced

1½ cups fresh fish stock

¼ cup white wine or cognac

½ cup double cream or whipping cream

½ tsp hot English mustard powder

2 egg yolks

1 tbs fresh lemon juice

2 tbs fresh parsley, chopped

Salt and freshly ground black pepper to taste

½ cup Parmesan or Gruyère cheese, freshly grated

METHOD:

Gently separate claws, tails, and heads of lobsters. Carefully remove all meat. Cut meat into bite-sized chunks and keep aside. Please ensure tails remain intact. Thoroughly clean them and remove any ligaments or legs. Pat-dry tails and keep aside.

Melt half of butter in large skillet over medium heat. Add chopped shallots and sliced mushrooms, cooking and stirring until tender. Add tarragon, thyme, and mustard powder and mix well. Gently add fish stock, white wine or cognac, and double cream. Bring to a boil, and cook until reduced by half. Mix in parsley, salt, and pepper.

Next, melt butter in pan and sauté lobster meat until fully warmed. Add warmed lobster to reduced sauce and gently stir in egg yolks and lemon juice. Taste mixture and make any necessary adjustments.

Pre-heat broiler. Place lobster tail shells on ovenproof dish and gently spoon lobster mixture into tails, so mixture is heaped but not overflowing. Next, sprinkle Parmesan and Gruyère cheeses over top of lobster mixture.

Broil for 3 to 4 minutes, just until golden brown. Serve immediately on individual dishes. You may serve with saffron rice or oven-roasted potatoes and buttered asparagus. You may also garnish with fresh mango slices and cherry tomatoes.

Shrimp Zanzibari

THIS RECIPE BRINGS BACK SOME FOND MEMORIES FROM THE COASTAL REGION OF EAST AFRICA, PARticularly Zanzibar. I had this succulent creation on one of the ships of the Sultan of Zanzibar. My dear uncle, the late Sardar Amrik Singh Suri, was a good friend of the sultan and I recall during one of our visits to Mombasa, the ship was docked there and the family was invited to dine with royalty. It was a once-in-a-lifetime experience for me and I will cherish those moments forever. Of course, as a young lad I was more interested in the food than the ship's decor or the company. I particularly remember the shrimp delicacy cooked in a rich, tasty, spicy coconut sauce. I have cooked this dish many times with fish, shrimp, and chicken, and the results have always been remarkable. Now I am pleased to share my recipe with you to enjoy without having to leave home to go to Zanzibar.

INGREDIENTS:

1 lb jumbo shrimp, shelled, deveined, with tails on

3 tbs coconut oil

4 cloves

3 green cardamom pods, lightly mashed

½ tsp cumin

1 stick cinnamon, 1" long

½ tsp turmeric

2 finger hot green chillies, finely chopped

1 medium onion, finely chopped

1 tsp garlic paste

1 tbs ginger root paste

¾ cup ripe tomatoes, crushed

1 small potato, peeled and cut into 8 pieces

1 small red or yellow bell pepper, cut into 8 pieces

1 cup coconut milk, whisked

Salt and pepper to taste

Fresh coriander leaves, chopped

METHOD:

In saucepan heat about 3 tbs oil and add cloves, cardamom, cinnamon stick, cumin, and chopped onions. Continue to sauté mixture for about 5 minutes. Stir constantly to avoid any scorching and allow spices to infuse aroma.

When onions turn light golden brown, add ginger and garlic pastes and chilies and stir well. Immediately add turmeric powder and mix well. Cook for 1 minute and add crushed tomatoes. Let tomatoes blend well, then add salt and pepper to sauce. Add potatoes and cook mixture for about 8 to 10 minutes until oil starts to separate from sauce and potatoes are fully cooked.

Next, gradually add shrimp to sauce and cook for a few minutes. Do not overcook. Finally, add bell peppers and coconut milk. Cover pot and let rest until ready to serve.

Just before serving turn heat on high and bring sauce to a quick boil. Garnish dish with coriander leaves and serve with good-quality steamed basmati rice or buttered naan or bread of choice.

Poached Pacific Salmon With Dill And Pink Peppercorn Sauce

I ENJOYED THIS DELICACY AT A FANCY RESTAURANT IN VICTORIA, BRITISH COLUMBIA. I MUST ADMIT it was the freshest catch of the day from the Pacific region and the taste was divine. I take a lot of pride in preparing this fish for my friends. In my opinion Pacific salmon is the best, but you may wish to use fresh Atlantic salmon.

INGREDIENTS:

2 lb fresh Pacific salmon fillets, cut up into equally sized large pieces

½ lemon

½ cup red wine

1½ cups table cream

3 tbs butter

1 tsp dill

½ tsp garlic paste

1 tbs black pepper, coarsely ground

Salt to taste

1 tbs green onion, finely chopped

METHOD:

Squeeze juice of ½ lemon onto fish and season with salt. In shallow frying pan, heat butter and lightly fry fish. Gently transfer onto serving platter. Fish should be firm but not fully cooked.

Add wine, dill, and garlic to same frying pan with butter. Add black pepper and cream to pan and mix well. Bring mixture to a boil, then gently pour sauce over partially fried fish. All fish pieces should be covered with sauce. Cover serving platter with tin foil and place dish in oven pre-heated to 375°F for about 10 minutes.

Take piping-hot poached fish out from oven, remove foil, and garnish with slices of lemon and chopped green onion. Serve with rice pilaf and grilled vegetables.

PESHAWARI LAMB KEBABS

Meat

Achari Murgh

MY MOTHER'S FAMILY HAILS FROM SHIMLA, AND WHENEVER WE USED TO DRIVE FROM DELHI TO VISIT my granny, we always made a pit stop in the Shivalik Hills near Kalka in Himachal Pradesh at a tiny place called Dhalli. There was a small shop, a hole in the wall where the owners sold various meat pickles made from pork, mutton, deer, and other game. Dad always bought a small container of mountain goat and pork meat pickle for Granny, and we made it a habit to take a care package back to Delhi with us on our return trip.

My grandfather and dad were great cooks and used to create some amazing delicacies. One of my dear dad's best creations was pickled mutton meatballs and pork, and he never shared these recipes with anyone but my mom. By using my devastating charm, however, I eventually managed to convince my mother to reveal Dad's best-kept secret, and now I think I have mastered the art of meat pickling. Here I am sharing an achari murgh delicacy adapted from Dad's collection of treasured recipes that will certainly blow your mind and make you crave more.

"Achari" means pickle, and this chicken dish is made with all the spices one would normally use in making an Indian pickle. The flavours and seasonings improve over time in this extremely aromatic and delicious preparation. This recipe is spicy and very flavourful, and has no store-bought ready-made mixes, which may have preservatives and additives. Like any other curried delicacy, plan to prepare this dish well ahead of serving time, as it will taste even better a day or two later.

INGREDIENTS:

1 kg chicken, skinless and cut up

2 sticks cinnamon

6 black peppercorns

5 whole cloves

½ tsp turmeric

Salt and pepper to taste

4 tsp mustard oil

½ cup vegetable oil

1 tsp mustard seeds

1 tsp coriander seeds, crushed

4 whole red chilies, dried

1 tbs garlic paste

1 tbs ginger paste

1 cup onions, finely sliced

1 tsp red chili powder

1 pinch asafoetida

1 tsp cumin seeds

1 tsp kalonji

1 tbs mustard seeds, ground

1 oz jaggery or brown sugar

3 tbs boiled white vinegar

1 tbs malt vinegar

¼ cup tomato paste

1 tbs finger hot green chili, chopped

1 tbs fresh coriander leaves, chopped

1 tbs ginger root, julienned (optional)

METHOD:

Clean and cut up a whole chicken. In pot add mustard oil and heat to a smoking point. This will help in removing pungent mustard aroma and bitter taste from oil. Next, add cinnamon sticks, turmeric, black peppercorns, cloves, and chicken and stir well. Turn heat down to medium, add salt and pepper, and continue to stir-fry until meat is almost tender. Remove pot from heat, gently transfer chicken pieces and its juices to separate dish, and set aside.

Next, add vegetable oil to pot and heat along with dried red chilies and mustard seeds. As soon as mustard seeds start to crackle add sliced onions and garlic and ginger pastes and sauté until mixture has browned. Then add asafoetida, cumin seeds, kalonji, and ground mustard seeds and mix well. Next, add tomato paste and cook until it forms into rich, thick sauce. Keep stirring to ensure that sauce does not scorch. If sauce gets too dry, then add a little saved juice from chicken. As soon as oil starts to separate from sauce, add cooked chicken, vinegars, and jaggery. Stir mixture well and cook meat on medium to high heat, stirring constantly until surface of chicken acquires brownish hue and fat separates from sauce. At this stage, taste masala and make any necessary adjustments to seasoning. Transfer chicken to serving dish and when ready to serve gently reheat and garnish with chopped green chilies and fresh coriander leaves. You may also garnish with julienned ginger root.

Serve hot with tandoori roti or naan. Pickled small red onions in malt vinegar are an excellent accompaniment to this gastronomic delight.

Achari Lamb Chops

OVER THE YEARS, I HAVE TRIED TO REPLICATE MY GRANDFATHER'S RECIPE FOR THIS DISH, AND MY mother tells me that I have almost perfected it to his standards. This is a very creative dish that takes lamb to a different level in taste and flavour. Its pickle aroma is enough to tickle any palate.

INGREDIENTS:

1 kg spring lamb chops

4 cups water

2 sticks cinnamon

1 bay leaf

6 black peppercorns

½ tsp turmeric

Salt and pepper to taste

4 tsp mustard oil

½ cup vegetable oil

1 tsp mustard seeds

5 whole cloves

1 tsp coriander seeds, crushed

4 whole red chilies, dried

1 tbs garlic paste

1 tbs ginger paste

1 cup onions, finely sliced

1 tsp red chili powder

1 pinch asafoetida

1 tsp cumin seeds

1 tsp kalonji

1 tbs mustard seeds, ground

1 oz jaggery or brown sugar

3 tbs boiled white vinegar

1 cup fresh tomatoes, diced

1 oz ratan jot in cheesecloth bag (optional)

1 tbs finger hot green chili, chopped

1 tbs fresh coriander leaves, chopped

METHOD:

Have butcher cut chops from spring lamb and have bone chopped about 4" long. Clean meat and put into pot with about 4 cups water, turmeric, cinnamon, bay leaf, peppercorns, salt, and pepper. Bring water to a boil and then reduce heat and let simmer covered until meat is almost tender. Remove pot from heat, gently take out chops, and drain stock and save. Discard all spices from stock.

Add mustard oil to pot and heat to a smoking point. This will help remove pungent mustard aroma and bitter taste from oil. Next, add dried red chilies, cloves, and mustard seeds. As soon as mustard seeds start to crackle, add sliced onions and garlic and ginger pastes and sauté until mixture has browned. Remove and discard red chilies from pot. Then add asafoetida, cumin seeds, kalonji, and ground mustard seeds and mix well. Now add tomatoes and cook until thick paste forms. Keep stirring to ensure that paste does not scorch. If masala gets too dry then add a little saved stock. Next, add cooked lamb chops, vinegar, jaggery, about 1 cup of stock, and ratan jot bag and stir well. Cook meat on medium to high heat, stirring constantly until tops of chops acquire a brownish hue and fat separates from masala. At this stage, taste masala and make any necessary adjustments to seasoning. This delicacy is now ready to be served. Transfer chops to serving dish. Discard ratan jot bag. Finally, garnish with chopped green chilies and fresh coriander leaves. You may also garnish with julienned ginger root.

Serve hot with tandoori roti or naan. Pickled small red onions are an excellent accompaniment to this delicacy as well.

Stir-Fried Beef With Bok Choy

BOK CHOY IS AN EXTREMELY IMPORTANT INGREDIENT IN THIS PREPARATION. ALTHOUGH THERE ARE other vegetables in this recipe, try not to exclude bok choy.

INGREDIENTS:

3 tbs peanut oil

1 tbs fresh garlic, crushed

1 lb sirloin steak, trimmed and cut into thin strips

1 head bok choy, including green leaves, cut into 1" pieces

1 cup snow peas

6 spring onions, chopped

1 red bell pepper, cored, deseeded, and sliced into ¼" strips

1 green bell pepper, cored, deseeded, and sliced into ¼" strips

½ cup baby corn

2 tbs oyster sauce

2 tbs soy sauce

1 tbs cornstarch

METHOD:

In wok heat oil and add garlic and beef. Gently sear beef for a few minutes until just browned.

In the meantime quickly blanch all vegetables and add them to wok, stir-frying for another few minutes.

In cup mix oyster sauce, soy sauce, 3 tbs cold water, and cornstarch and mix well. Gently add to centre of beef and vegetables, stir, and as sauce thickens, immediately plate in serving dish and serve with steamed rice or rice noodles.

Chicken Zanzibari

THIS RECIPE BRINGS BACK SOME FOND MEMORIES FROM THE COASTAL REGION OF EAST AFRICA, PARticularly Zanzibar. I had this succulent creation on one of the ships of the Sultan of Zanzibar. In this delicacy, chicken is cooked in a rich, spicy coconut sauce.

INGREDIENTS:

2 lb chicken drumettes, skinned and cleaned

Cooking oil

3 cloves

3 green cardamom pods, lightly mashed

1 stick cinnamon, 1" long

½ tsp turmeric

2 finger hot green chilies, finely chopped

1 tsp garam masala

1 large onion, finely chopped

1 tbs garlic paste

1 tbs ginger root paste

½ cup tomatoes, crushed

2 tbs tomato paste

1 cup coconut milk

Salt and pepper to taste

Fresh coriander leaves, chopped

Note: Drumettes are the small drumsticks attached to the wings of the chicken. Use only the drumsticks. Or, you may want to use larger drumsticks or thighs, but make sure you cut them in twos.

METHOD:

In saucepan heat about 3 tbs oil and add cloves, cardamom, cinnamon stick, and chopped onions. Sauté mixture for about 5 minutes, stirring constantly to avoid any scorching and allowing spices to infuse aroma.

When onions turn light golden brown in colour, add ginger, garlic, and chillies and stir well. Immediately add garam masala and turmeric and mix well. Keep stirring for a few minutes and then add crushed tomatoes and paste. Let tomatoes blend well, add salt and pepper, and cook mixture for about 5 minutes until oil starts to separate from sauce.

Now add chicken (please note that you may use any cut of chicken for this dish; however, the chicken must be skinless). Keep cooking and stirring meat on medium heat until almost done. Do not overcook. Cover pot and let rest until ready to serve. For best results, let chicken rest for a few hours before serving.

Just before serving turn on heat to medium and warm chicken. Then add coconut milk, stir well, bring to a quick boil, and serve immediately. Garnish dish with coriander leaves and serve with good-quality steamed basmati rice.

Tandoori-Style Chicken

THE TRUE INDIAN VERSION OF THIS DISH IS ALWAYS COOKED IN A SPECIAL CLAY OVEN, OFTEN AT temperatures over eight hundred degrees. The first time I had this authentic dish was in Delhi at the famous Moti Mahal restaurant. It has taken me almost three decades to perfect this delicacy by cooking it in a convection oven.

INGREDIENTS:

1 chicken, skinned and quartered

½ cup plain hung yogurt

1 tbs lemon juice

1 tsp vinegar

1 tsp garlic, minced

1 tsp fresh ginger, peeled and minced

1 tbs raw papaya paste

1 tsp coriander powder

½ tsp cumin powder

1/8 tsp cloves, ground

½ tsp red pepper powder

2 tbs clarified butter

½ tsp reddish-orange food colour (optional)

Salt and pepper to taste

METHOD:

Make gashes in drumsticks and thighs as well as breasts of chicken with sharp knife. In large bowl add chicken pieces, lemon juice, and vinegar. Season with salt and pepper and rub seasoning into gashes. Let sit for at least 1 hour.

In separate bowl add all remaining ingredients and mix well to form reddish-orange paste. Remove chicken pieces from bowl and discard fluid. Add chicken to paste, rubbing paste into chicken, and cover all pieces well. Place bowl in fridge for at least 12 hours. Occasionally stir chicken during marinating process.

Pre-heat oven to 500°F. Place chicken pieces on baking dish and cook for about 25 minutes or until done. Serve hot in serving platter and garnish with lemon wedges and onion rings. For an exotic presentation you may use sizzling platter lined with onion rings and peppers, and before bringing it to table squeeze lemon juice for extra sizzle.

Tandoori chicken is best served with naan and a simple onion-tomato salad or pearl onions pickled in malt vinegar.

Ground Meat Koftas

THIS IS MY MOTHER'S SPECIALTY PASSED ON TO HER BY MY DAD. IT JUST SO ALSO HAPPENS TO BE MY son's favourite dish using minced goat meat or minced chicken. This is one of those preparations that tastes better after it has cured in the fridge for at least a day or two.

INGREDIENTS FOR KOFTAS:

1 kg minced goat or chicken (pork or beef may also be used)

1 tsp green cardamom seeds, coarsely ground

½ tsp cinnamon powder

2 tbs brown onion paste

2 tsp fresh ginger, finely chopped

1 tsp garlic paste

4 green chilies, finely chopped

1 tbs fresh coriander, finely chopped

1 tsp Kasoori methi, rubbed

1 tbs cumin seeds, rubbed between palms

1 tbs aloo bukhara, seeded and chopped

1 tbs fine bread crumbs

2 egg whites, beaten

Salt and pepper to taste

INGREDIENTS FOR CURRY:

5 tbs cooking oil

1 cup onions, finely chopped

2 tbs ginger paste

2 tbs garlic paste

1 tsp turmeric

1 tsp garam masala

1 tbs deggi mirch

½ tsp Kasoori methi

2 cups tomatoes, finely diced

1 tbs tomato paste

8 cups boiling water

3 tbs coriander leaf stems, finely chopped

2 tbs fresh coriander leaves for garnish

Salt to taste

METHOD:

In mixing bowl add all kofta ingredients and mix well. Shape small balls about 1" in diameter by rolling meat gently between moist palms. Keep balls on flat dish and refrigerate.

For sauce heat oil in large saucepan and sauté chopped onions until lightly browned. Then add ginger, garlic paste, turmeric, garam masala, deggi mirch, Kasoori methi, and salt. Stir mixture well and keep stir-frying until onions start to brown. Then add diced tomatoes and paste and, stirring constantly, cook until fat separates. Add coriander stems and 8 cups of boiling water and bring sauce to a boil. Gently slide in meatballs one at a time into boiling sauce. As soon as sauce comes to a boil again after all meatballs are in, cover pot and let simmer until meatballs are fully cooked and soft.

Garnish with fresh coriander and let kofta curry rest in fridge overnight for best results. Serve hot with steamed basmati rice or lachedar parathas.

Please note that if you are using goat meat it may take a bit longer to soften up. You may need to use a pressure cooker to achieve softer balls.

Minced pork and beef also make excellent-tasting koftas; chicken koftas taste best when cooked in a coconut curry sauce.

Masaledar Champan

THIS RECIPE USES NO FAT TO COOK. THE CHOPS HAVE A DELIGHTFUL CUMIN FLAVOUR AND CAN BE served both as appetizers or a main course dish.

As a variation, I have cooked this recipe using chicken drumsticks and pork ribs instead of lamb chops. Steamed basmati rice makes an excellent accompaniment to the pork ribs.

INGREDIENTS:

3 lb spring lamb chops

1 cup onions, chopped

½ cup tomatoes, crushed

1 tbs tomato paste

3 tbs ginger paste

3 tbs garlic paste

1 cup plain yogurt

1 tsp red chili powder

1 tsp garam masala

Salt to taste

2 tsp cumin seeds, coarsely ground

2 tbs ginger root, julienned, in fresh lemon juice

METHOD:

Heat wok and add yogurt and crushed tomatoes. Mix well and gently add chops, onions, garlic, ginger, chili powder, garam masala, and salt. Stir all ingredients and bring to a boil. Turn heat to medium, cover pot, and let simmer until chops are almost tender. Remove chops and keep aside.

Now continue to stir-fry sauce until reduced to half. Add cumin and cook sauce for another few minutes, then add chops, mix well, and cook for another few minutes, stirring constantly.

Plate chops in serving platter and garnish with julienned marinated ginger. Serve chops with tandoori rotis or naan.

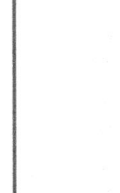

Kashmiri Rogan Josh

THE ORIGIN OF THIS DELICACY IS OFTEN THE SUBJECT OF DISPUTE. SOME CLAIM THIS AROMATIC LAMB dish is of Persian origin whilst others claim it is one of the signature "Wazwan" dishes that originated in Kashmir. "Rogan" in Persian means "oil" and "josh" means "heat" or "passion." Thus, rogan josh means meat cooked in oil at high heat. Please note that "rogan" also means "red," which is the colour of the prepared dish.

Regardless of its origin, this dish is very popular in South Asian restaurants across the globe. I have enjoyed it in many different places and every time had a unique flavour experience.

While the traditional preparation uses whole dried chilies that are deseeded, soaked in water, and ground to a paste, non-traditional shortcuts use either Kashmiri chili powder available in Indian stores marketed as deggi mirch, or hot paprika. It is interesting to note that there has been commercial modification worldwide, creating in particular a tomato-based meat dish that imitates rogan josh. While tomatoes add a different flavour to the dish, which is fully acceptable, this version is very distinct from that of the traditional Kashmiri rogan josh.

My dad often used to cook this dish on Sundays. It is believed that Moghlai cuisine has a strong Persian influence, and Dad would say that the Moghuls introduced rogan josh to Kashmir. There is a common saying in Indian culture: "Enjoy the mangoes and don't bother counting the trees." The same applies here; I suggest enjoying the recipe and not worrying about its origin.

INGREDIENTS:

500 gm mutton leg meat, cut up

5 tbs clarified butter or mustard oil, smoked

1 small pinch asafoetida, diluted in water

1 tbs deggi mirch powder

1 black cardamom pod, crushed

5 green cardamom pods, bruised

1 stick cinnamon

5 cloves

1 tbs ginger powder

1 tbs fennel seeds, powdered

1 tsp garlic paste

1 tbs ginger paste

2 tbs onion paste, browned

1 cup hung yogurt, whisked

1 cup warm water

1 pinch saffron, diluted in warm water

Salt and freshly ground pepper to taste

1 tsp fresh ginger root, finely julienned, for garnish

1 tsp fresh coriander leaves for garnish

METHOD:

Wipe meat clean with kitchen towel but do not wash meat.

In heavy-bottomed pot, heat clarified butter or oil and add black and green cardamom pods, cinnamon stick, cloves, and fennel and ginger powders. As soon as spices become aromatic add meat and asafoetida and stir meat well. Cover pot and stir occasionally until all juices from meat dry up.

Next, add ginger and garlic pastes, browned onion paste, whisked yogurt, and deggi mirch. Mix well, add salt and pepper, and continue to cook until meat is well browned. Finally, add about 1 cup warm water along with diluted saffron, stir meat well, and cook until tender and sauce has thickened and reduced and fat starts to separate. For best results let cooked meat rest for a few hours before serving. Quickly heat up meat and transfer rogan josh to serving platter. Garnish with julienned ginger root and fresh coriander leaves. Serve hot with khamiri roti, lightly buttered naan, or jeera rice.

Kenyan-Style Pork Chops With Gravy

THE CHEF AT THE BAOBAB LODGE IN KILIFI, A COASTAL RESORT IN KENYA, PREPARED THIS DISH FOR us. The chops were very tender and when I asked the chef how this was achieved, he shared the secret that placing good-quality pork in a moderate oven after browning makes them very tender.

INGREDIENTS:

4 pork loin chops, trimmed (8 oz each)

1¼ cups all-purpose flour

Salt and peri peri pepper to taste

2 tbs butter

½ cup chicken broth

½ cup light cream

METHOD:

Pre-heat oven to 275°F.

In mixing bowl add 1 cup flour along with salt and pepper. Mix well. Melt and heat butter in heavy skillet. Dredge pork chops in seasoned flour and place pork in skillet. Cook chops on both sides until evenly browned. Remove chops from skillet, transfer onto baking sheet, and place in warm oven. Save fat in skillet for gravy.

Add remaining flour into skillet, whisk well, and cook for about 3 minutes, stirring vigorously. Gently whisk in broth and cream. Add salt and freshly ground black pepper to gravy. Reduce heat to low and simmer for 10 minutes, stirring frequently. Taste gravy and make any necessary adjustments.

Remove pork from oven and top with hot gravy. Chops can be served with mashed potatoes and buttered carrots.

Stir-Fried Beef With Broccoli In Black Bean Sauce

I HAVE TRIED TO COOK THIS DISH WITH OTHER MEAT LIKE CHICKEN AND PORK, BUT FOR REASONS unknown, beef truly brings out the flavours and does justice to this recipe. Try it for yourself and be the judge.

INGREDIENTS:

1 lb tender beef, rump or sirloin

1 tbs dark soy sauce

1 tsp oyster sauce

½ tsp sugar

1 medium onion, sliced

1 tbs fresh ginger root, finely sliced

1 tsp garlic paste

1 medium bunch fresh broccoli, cut into florets

¼ cup beef stock

2 tbs black bean sauce

1 tbs cornstarch

2 tbs spring onions, chopped

2 tbs cooking oil

METHOD:

Thinly slice beef and cut into narrow strips. Place beef in mixing bowl and add dark soy sauce, oyster sauce, and sugar. Mix well and allow beef to marinate for at least 1 hour, turning occasionally.

In wok heat oil and stir-fry onions, ginger, and garlic for 1 minute. Transfer mixture into dish and put aside. Now add beef to wok and stir-fry on high heat until beef changes colour. Add onion mixture to wok and stir. In meantime quickly blanch and drain broccoli and add it to wok along with black bean sauce. Mix well.

In small cup dissolve cornstarch in beef stock and pour over meat. Gently stir over high heat and as soon as sauce starts to thicken, transfer to serving dish and garnish with chopped spring onions.

Serve hot with steamed rice.

Raahra Meat

MOST PUNJABI MEN TAKE GREAT PRIDE IN THEIR INDIVIDUAL VERSIONS OF THIS MEAT DELICACY. IT also offers them the opportunity to showcase the art of bhoona, a technique of braising and stir-frying to create a tasty dry masala.

I recall my grandfather and father preparing this dish, followed by my older brother and cousins creating this recipe to impress their friends. Now, my son and my nephews are on the verge of mastering this art.

INGREDIENTS:

2 kg spring lamb or goat meat, cut up

½ lb lean lamb, coarsely ground

½ cup yogurt

Salt to taste

½ cup clarified butter

2 black cardamom pods, slightly mashed

10 green cardamom pods, slightly mashed

2 bay leaves

2 cinnamon sticks

2 cups onions, chopped

3 tbs ginger paste

4 tbs garlic paste

4 tsp coriander powder

½ tsp turmeric powder

1 tsp red chili powder

2 cups tomatoes, chopped

2 tbs tomato paste

1 tbs cumin seeds

2 tbs ginger root, julienned

2 tbs fresh coriander leaves, chopped

METHOD:

Remove any excess fat and clean meat. Then add to mixing bowl, whisking in yogurt, salt and pepper, and 1 tbs fresh garlic paste. Mix well and let meat marinate for at least 3 hours.

In heavy-bottomed pot heat butter and add cardamom pods, bay leaves, and cinnamon sticks and sauté over medium heat for 30 seconds. Add chopped onions and sauté until lightly browned. Now add remaining ginger and garlic pastes along with coriander powder, turmeric, and red chili powder. Stir well and cook until moisture has evaporated, making sure paste does not scorch.

Gradually add meat to marinade. Bring mixture to a boil, reduce heat, and let simmer until meat is tender. You may need to add a little warm water at regular intervals to keep meat from sticking. Turn heat up and add tomatoes, tomato paste, and ginger, stir well, and add ground lamb. Now the process of bhoona starts. Rub cumin seeds between palms and sprinkle all over meat. Bhoona until meat pieces are fully wrapped around this rich golden brown masala and fat starts to separate. Check meat for doneness to your liking. If you like it well done, then cook for longer.

Plate on platter and garnish with fresh coriander leaves and more julienned ginger root. Serve hot with tandoori rotis or lachedar parathas. Naan is another option. Some like this dish with jeera rice as well.

Peshawari Kebabs

THIS RECIPE COMES FROM PESHAWAR, THE MOST NORTHWESTERN OF DISTRICTS IN OLDEN BRITISH India. This area is predominantly occupied by Afghans, whose cuisine is influenced by people from Afghanistan and Uzbekistan.

INGREDIENTS:

1 kg lamb cubes, boneless
1 tsp black cumin seeds
1 tsp garam masala
1 tsp garlic paste
1 tsp ginger paste
1 lemon

2 tbs raw papaya paste
2 tsp red chili powder
½ cup yogurt
Salt to taste
¼ cup clarified butter

METHOD:

In mixing bowl add black cumin, garam masala, garlic, ginger, papaya paste, red chili powder, yogurt, and salt. Mix all ingredients into a nice paste. Add lamb cubes to paste and mix well. Allow meat to marinate for a few hours.

Thread meat pieces onto metal skewers and cook on charcoal grill for about 4 minutes or until half done.

Remove skewers from grill and let cool for about 10 minutes. Baste meat with clarified butter and cook again for about 8 minutes, occasionally turning skewers to brown meat evenly. Gently remove meat from skewers onto platter lined with lettuce leaves. Garnish meat with sliced red onions and lemon wedges. Peshawari kebabs go great with tandoori naan or Afghan rice.

Makhni Chicken (Butter Chicken)

ALTHOUGH THE ORIGIN OF THIS RECIPE HAILS FROM NORTHERN INDIA, THIS DELICACY HAS BECOME so popular that it is now served at practically any festive occasion all over the world where Indians reside. In Britain as well as North America non-Indians are equally fond of this dish and enjoy it with naan and jeera rice. I have tried butter chicken in many countries and the recipe varies from place to place. The recipe that I am sharing here with you is my favourite. Please note that I am using a whole cut-up chicken and not just the boneless white chicken meat that is used by the majority of restaurants and households.

INGREDIENTS:

1 kg whole chicken, skinned, cleaned, and cut into small pieces

½ cup hung yogurt

1 tsp garlic paste

2 tbs tandoori masala

½ tsp green cardamom seed powder

½ tsp cinnamon powder

Salt and pepper to taste

BUTTER SAUCE:

¼ cup clarified butter

½ small onion, finely chopped

1 tbs ginger paste

1 tbs garlic paste

1½ cups ripe tomatoes, crushed

¼ cup water

3 green chilies, finely chopped

1 tsp deggi mirch

Salt to taste

1 cup full cream

1 tbs honey

1 tbs coriander leaves, finely chopped

1 tbs ginger root, finely julienned

2 tbs almond flakes, toasted

Pinch of saffron, dissolved in 1 tsp warm milk

METHOD:

In large bowl add chicken and in separate mixing bowl add yogurt, garlic paste, tandoori masala, cardamom and cinnamon powders, salt, and pepper and mix well. Add mixture to chicken and make sure all pieces are well coated. Let chicken marinate for at least 4 hours.

In saucepan melt half of butter and add chopped onions and ginger and garlic pastes, and sauté mixture until it turns light brown in colour. Add tomatoes and water, bring to a boil, and simmer sauce for about 10 minutes. Sauce should turn a bright red colour. Using hand blender puree sauce until silky smooth.

Next, spread marinated chicken onto cookie sheet and brush with remaining melted butter. Cook chicken in pre-heated oven at 400°C until done and golden brown.

Add cooked chicken pieces and any liquid on cookie sheet to pureed sauce along with cream, honey, and saffron and mix well. Simmer gently for another 5 minutes and delicacy is ready for plating and garnishing.

Plate chicken on serving platter and garnish with coriander and almonds. Serve hot with rice pilaf, tandoori naan, or rotis. Roomali rotis or lachedar parathas would be excellent with this creation too.

Kasoori Methi Murgh

AS WITH ANY DELICACY, THE FRESHEST INGREDIENTS MAKE THE DISH TASTE BETTER. SIMILARLY, THIS recipe tastes better with fresh fenugreek if available. The world's finest fenugreek comes from Qasur in Pakistan. Dried fenugreek from this region is now available all over the globe and marketed as "Kasoori methi." This dried methi is an excellent substitute for the fresh vegetable and is also extensively used to enhance the flavours of both vegetarian and meat delicacies. I recall that whenever my father prepared this recipe using fresh fenugreek locally grown in Kenya, he always added the dried Kasoori methi to enhance the flavour of regular methi. A liberal pinch of this ingredient works like magic in improving taste; it is a must in all kitchens. Try a pinch even in your daals and you will agree with me.

Punjabis are known to cook their meat with spinach, fenugreek, or the combination of both, and my favourite happens to be the methi murgh served with lachedar parathas.

You may prepare the following recipe with fresh or dried methi—the choice is entirely yours.

INGREDIENTS:

1 whole chicken (about 1 kg)
½ cup hung plain yogurt
1 tsp red chili powder
1 tbs salt

½ cup clarified butter
2 cloves
4 green cardamom pods, lightly mashed
1 black cardamom pod, lightly mashed

1 stick cinnamon, about 1" long

1 cup onions, finely chopped

2 tbs fresh garlic paste

2 tbs fresh ginger paste

4 finger hot green chilies, finely chopped

1 tsp turmeric powder

3 cups fresh fenugreek leaves, washed and chopped
(about 1 cup Kasoori methi, if using dry product)

Salt to taste

1 cup fresh ripe tomatoes, crushed

1 tbs fresh ginger root, julienned, for garnish

METHOD:

Skin and clean chicken, cut into small pieces, and place into mixing bowl. Add salt and red chili powder to chicken and mix well. Whisk in yogurt, mix well with chicken, and allow chicken to marinate for at least 1 hour or more.

In heavy-bottomed pot, heat clarified butter and add all dry spices. Sauté over medium heat until spices begin to crackle and release aromas. Immediately add onions and sauté until golden brown. Then add chopped chilies, garlic and ginger pastes, and turmeric powder and stir well. Add salt. Next add chopped fenugreek leaves and crushed tomatoes, mix well, and cook for about 15 minutes or more, until juices from

tomatoes and fenugreek almost dry up and butter starts to separate from mixture.

If preparing dish with dry Kasoori methi, then add it to pot along with pastes and crushed tomatoes.

Next, add marinated chicken to pot and stir well. Continue to stir and cook chicken in methi masala until done and fat starts to separate again. Taste chicken and adjust seasoning to your liking. Transfer chicken to serving dish and garnish with julienned ginger root. Serve hot with freshly baked naan or tandoori rotis. Personally, I love this dish with lachedar parathas and an onion salad.

Jeera Chicken

THIS DISH CAN BE SERVED AS AN APPETIZER OR AS A MAIN COURSE ENTRÉE. IT USED TO BE SERVED at many dinner parties I attended in Kenya, and most of the hosts always cooked this succulent delicacy on a tawa. However, if you do not have a tawa, it can be easily cooked in a shallow pan or wok.

INGREDIENTS:

1 kg chicken pieces, skinless, with bones cut up small

4 tbs clarified butter

1 medium onion, finely sliced

1 tbs ginger root, julienned

½ tsp garlic paste

2 medium tomatoes, diced

4 finger hot green chilies, chopped

2 tbs cumin seeds, coarsely ground

1 tsp cumin seeds, roasted

½ tsp black peppercorns, coarsely ground

Salt to taste

2 tbs fresh coriander leaves, chopped

1 fresh lemon

METHOD:

In shallow pan or wok, heat butter and sauté onions until golden brown. Add ginger, garlic paste, and tomatoes. Stir mixture and cook on medium-high heat for 5 minutes until a nice paste forms. Add chilies, cumin, salt, and chicken. Continue stirring and cover pan, occasionally stirring meat, and cook on medium heat until chicken is almost cooked and fat starts to separate.

Sprinkle cumin and black peppercorn on meat and mix well. Let meat rest for 1 hour before serving.

Just before serving heat chicken through and plate it on serving platter. Garnish with fresh coriander and squeeze fresh lemon juice over meat. Serve hot with tandoori rotis or naan.

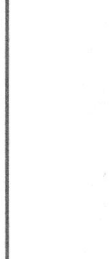

Goan Pork Vindaloo

THE PORTUGUESE BROUGHT THIS DELICACY TO GOA, AND IT SOON BECAME A POPULAR DISH OFTEN served during special occasions.

For the English this delicacy is tongue-searing, but it wasn't always that way. When the Portuguese introduced this dish, it was adjusted to fit local conditions: There was no wine vinegar in India, so priests fermented their own from palm wine. Local ingredients like tamarind, black pepper, cinnamon, and cardamom were also incorporated, and most importantly the addition of chili peppers imported to India from the Americas was a legacy of Portugal's global empire. When the British occupied India from 1797 to 1813, they were delighted to discover this East-meets-West food, as well as Christian Goan cooks, who, free of caste and religious restrictions, were happy to make beef and pork dishes beloved by ex-pats.

Vindaloo, like many earlier delicacies, met the same fate when it was exported to England—it became another hot curry. The tang of vinegar disappeared along with the practice of marinating the meat, and the balance of different spices was lost under a blistering use of excessive chilies. Goa still has many versions that go back to the good old days when cinnamon and cardamom provided an earthy elegance, and the heat was kept in check.

A good vindaloo is spicy and tangy at the same time, and leaves your taste buds tingling for more. I have savoured vindaloos from all over, and personally, I like the one that my neighbours from Goa in Nairobi used to cook, often using lamb, beef, and chicken.

The hotter the dish, the better it is, and for some reason, all vindaloo dishes taste better when they are eaten a day later. If you plan to serve this dish to your guests, please forewarn them about its spicy heat.

INGREDIENTS:

2 lb pork loin, boneless, cut into 1" cubes

10 chili peppers, dried, stemmed, and seeded

1" piece cinnamon stick

1 tsp cumin seeds

6 green cardamom pods

4 whole cloves

½ tsp whole black peppercorns

½ tsp turmeric powder

1 tbs white vinegar

1 tbs vegetable oil

Salt to taste

¼ cup vegetable oil

4 onions, chopped

2 tbs garlic paste

2 tbs ginger root, chopped

2 green chilies, seeded and cut into strips

1½ cups boiling water

¼ cup red wine vinegar

METHOD:

Grind chili peppers, cinnamon stick, cumin, clove, cardamom, peppercorns, and turmeric with mortar and pestle or electric coffee grinder until spices are coarsely ground. Transfer spice mixture to small mixing bowl, add 1 tbs white vinegar and oil, and mix well to create a smooth paste. Season with salt.

In large mixing bowl add cubed pork and spice paste, and mix well until evenly coated. Cover bowl with plastic wrap and marinate overnight in fridge.

Next, heat vegetable oil in large pot over medium-high heat. Add onions, garlic, and ginger and cook until golden brown.

Add marinated pork and cook for about 5 minutes, stirring regularly to avoid any scorching. Then add boiling water and reduce heat to simmer, covering pot and allowing to cook for about 30 minutes or until pork is tender. Next, add sliced chilies and wine vinegar. Cook vindaloo uncovered to allow sauce to thicken.

Check salt seasoning and make any necessary adjustments. Garnish with fresh coriander and sliced red onions and serve hot with bread rolls or steamed rice.

Chicken Jalfrezi

CHICKEN COOKED WITH VEGETABLES IS LIKE A SPICY STEW AND IS A GREAT DELICACY FOR YOUR NEXT family gathering. In northern and central Africa a similar dish is served with couscous on special occasions.

INGREDIENTS:

2 lb chicken, boneless and sliced about ¼" thick

1 medium onion, finely chopped

1 tbs fresh garlic paste

1 tbs fresh ginger paste

1 tsp turmeric

1 tsp garam masala

1 cup fresh tomatoes, ground

1 tbs tomato paste

Salt and pepper to taste

Cooking oil

VEGETABLES:

1 zucchini, sliced

1 medium onion, sliced ¼" thick

1 green pepper, sliced

1 red pepper, sliced

¼ cup fresh mushrooms, sliced

¼ lb snow peas, cleaned and washed

1 carrot, thinly sliced on a bias

1 stalk celery, sliced 1/8" thick on a bias

2 hot green chilies, finely sliced

GARNISH:

4 sprigs green onion, finely chopped

1 tbs fresh ginger root, julienned

Fresh coriander leaves, chopped

METHOD:

In shallow frying pan or wok fry chicken with a little salt and brown it, ensuring not to overcook. Remove chicken pieces and set aside. Now add onions, garlic, and ginger root and sauté for a few minutes. Add turmeric, garam masala, tomatoes, and paste. Next, add salt and pepper and stir well. Cook mixture until it turns into a rich paste and oil starts to separate. Turn off heat and add cooked chicken to pan.

In saucepan boil enough water to submerge all vegetables. Add some salt to water and gently drop in all vegetables. Wait for a few minutes and as soon as water starts to boil again, quickly drain all vegetables thoroughly and add them to pan with sauce and chicken. Mix chicken and vegetables well in sauce and turn heat on. As soon as meat and vegetables heat through, remove pan from heat and serve piping hot on serving platter.

Garnish with fresh coriander, ginger root, and green onions. You may add a few slices of fresh firm tomatoes to your garnish as well. This dish may be served with steamed basmati rice or your favourite Indian bread.

Chicken Tikka

THIS APPETIZER HAS TO BE ONE OF THE MOST POPULAR SNACKS SERVED WITH COCKTAILS. THERE ARE many different recipes for this delicacy. However, the following is my favourite; I have often prepared it for large gatherings and served it as a side dish rather than as an appetizer. It has always been a hit.

INGREDIENTS:

2 lb chicken breast, boneless and cubed into 1" pieces

¼ cup hung yogurt

2 tbs garlic paste

2 tbs ginger paste

½ tsp cumin powder

½ tsp mace or nutmeg powder

½ tsp green cardamom powder

½ tsp turmeric powder

1 tsp red chili powder

4 tbs white vinegar

2 tbs besan

Salt to taste

4 tbs vegetable oil

Butter for basting

1 lemon, sliced into 8 wedges

2 tbs fresh coriander leaves, chopped

METHOD:

Prepare marinade in large bowl by whisking yogurt and rest of ingredients. Now add chicken pieces and mix well in marinade. Set aside for at least 3 hours before cooking.

Pre-heat oven to 400°F. Skewer chicken, making sure to add space between each piece. If using bamboo skewers make sure to soak them in cold water for a few hours, to keep bamboo from burning. This dish is best when cooked in a tandoor, but an oven does a fairly good job too. You may wish to use a charcoal BBQ as well or cook on a large tawa. If cooking in oven or on charcoal grill, roast meat for about 8 to 10 minutes, basting at least twice on all sides. It will take about 5 minutes to cook in traditional tandoor.

When tikkas are fully cooked, serve them piping hot garnished with lemon wedges and fresh coriander leaves. You may even squeeze fresh lemon juice on top before serving.

PERI PERI CHICKEN

Pudina Chutney Lamb Chops

ALL ALONG OLD DELHI'S BUSTLING ROADS ARE STREET VENDORS WHO SELL THE MOST MOUTHWATER-ing Punjabi and Moghlai delicacies: stuffed kulchas, grilled and fried meat, fish, tandoori rotis, fruit chaats, and spiced vegetables. All these delicacies make old Delhi a wandering gourmet's delight and a unique epicurean experience.

Lamb and mint go hand in hand, and minty lamb chops are a unique recipe in old Delhi. Over the years I have often prepared these babies for my social gatherings.

INGREDIENTS:

12 meaty lamb chops, trimmed

2 green chilies, chopped

2 cinnamon stick pieces, 1" long

4 cloves

1 bay leaf

3 cloves fresh garlic, chopped

1 tbs ginger root, chopped

1 lb white potatoes, boiled, mashed, and seasoned with salt and pepper

3 whole eggs, beaten

4 tbs bread crumbs

Salt to taste

Oil for frying

MINT CHUTNEY:

3 tbs fresh mint leaves

2 tbs fresh coriander leaves

1 small unripe mango, peeled, chopped, with stone removed

1 tbs granulated sugar

2 green chilies, chopped

1 small onion, chopped

Salt to taste

GARNISH:

Onion rings, sliced

1 lemon, cut into 8 wedges

Coriander leaves, finely chopped

METHOD:

In saucepan add 4 cups hot water along with chops, green chilies, cinnamon, cloves, bay leaf, chopped garlic, ginger root, and salt. Boil chops until tender but not overcooked. Remove chops and allow to cool. Discard juices and whole spices.

Add all ingredients for mint chutney to blender and pulsate until smooth. Coat cooled chops with fine layer of chutney and then wrap fine layer of mashed potatoes evenly all over meaty part of each chop, exposing bone.

Beat eggs and dip coated chops into egg wash, and then roll them in bread crumbs. Place chops on wax paper–lined cookie sheet without overlapping and chill for about 10 minutes.

In the meantime, heat vegetable oil in wok and deep-fry chops until golden brown. Remove chops with slotted spoon, drain excess oil, and place chops on paper towel. Arrange chops on serving platter and garnish with thinly sliced onion rings, lemon wedges, and sprinkled coriander leaves.

Serve hot with cocktails or as an accompaniment at your buffet table. You can enjoy these chops with lachedar parathas or tandoori naan.

Murgh-E-Nawabi

THIS IS ONE OF MY FAVOURITE GRILLED CHICKEN RECIPES. IT'S NOT TOO SPICY YET VERY FLAVOURFUL and tasty. This simple creation owes much to Mughlai cuisine. I recall that my grandfather always asked for this chicken appetizer whenever he invited guests for cocktails before the main dinner. The only difference in my recipe is the omission of saffron. You may wish to use it in your preparation.

INGREDIENTS:

1 whole chicken, skinless and cut (approximately 2 lb)

4 finger hot green chilies, finely chopped or ground

60 ml white vinegar

2 tsp white pepper

½ tsp mace powder

4 tsp ginger paste

4 tsp garlic paste

1 cup hung yogurt

½ cup full cream

Butter and salt as required

METHOD:

In mixing bowl combine chilies, pepper, mace, salt, garlic paste, ginger paste, and vinegar. If using saffron, mix a pinch in 1 tsp warm water and add to mixture. Rub mixture into chicken pieces and let sit for about ½ hour. Add hung yogurt and cream to chicken and mix well. Allow chicken to marinate for at least 4 hours or more.

Skewer chicken pieces 1" apart and keep dish underneath to catch drippings. Metal skewers are best to use and if using wooden skewers make sure to soak them in water before using.

Pre-heat oven to 375°F. Cook chicken in hot oven or on charcoal grill for about 10 to 12 minutes until done. Remove skewers and let them rest to allow excess moisture to drip off. Baste chicken with butter and grill again for about 3 minutes.

Serve piping hot with sliced onion rings and lemon wedges. You may want to serve this appetizer on a heated sizzler for that extra flair and show.

Lahori Murgh Do Piaza

MY FATHER USED TO TALK ABOUT THIS RECIPE AND ITS ORIGINS IN LAHORE, NOW IN PAKISTAN. I recall him saying, "Jinney Lahore nahin dekhieya, oh janamaya hi nahin." ("He who has not seen Lahore has not lived at all.")

Since the days of Maharaja Ranjit Singh, Lahore was not only a seat of imperial power, but a great centre for cosmopolitan culture. This is where life was lived to its fullest extent and high standards for Punjabi cuisine were established. Lahore has often been called the "Paris of the East." It attracted scholars, scientists, painters, poets, musicians, and dancers. Above all, the greatest chefs from all over loved to make Lahore their home. I am pleased to share one of Lahore's prized delicacies here to keep its culinary flame alive.

INGREDIENTS:

1 kg chicken, skinless and cut into small pieces

½ cup clarified butter

2½ cups onions, chopped

5 tbs ginger paste

5 tbs garlic paste

1 tbs deggi mirch

1 tsp turmeric powder

1 tsp red chili powder

Salt to taste

¼ cup fresh coriander leaves, chopped

1 tbs fresh mint leaves, chopped

½ cup blanched cashews

Peanut oil for deep-frying nuts

2 tbs onions, sliced and deep-fried

1 tbs garam masala

METHOD:

In wok heat peanut oil and fry cashews until lightly browned. Drain nuts and spread on paper towel to cool.

In heavy-bottomed pot heat clarified butter and sauté onions until lightly browned. Add ginger, garlic, deggi mirch, turmeric, red chili powder, and salt. Stir mixture well and cook for 1 minute. Then add chicken pieces and stir well, cooking for a few minutes.

Add about 2½ cups boiling water to chicken and simmer until tender and firm. Make sure not to overcook. Taste curry and make any necessary adjustments.

Remove chicken curry to serving dish and garnish by sprinkling garam masala, nuts, and deep-fried sliced onions. Serve hot with your favourite bread or basmati rice.

Stir-Fried Chicken With Chilies And Fresh Basil

THIS WAS ONE OF THE FIRST THAI DISHES THAT I LEARNED BY WATCHING MY MOTHER COOK. IT IS fairly simple, quick, and easy to prepare. Just one caution—when cooking, the chilies and oil fumes may be overpowering. Make sure your kitchen is well ventilated.

INGREDIENTS:

1 lb chicken breast, skinless and cubed

3 tbs peanut oil

4 red chilies, dried

2 finger hot green chilies, sliced on a bias

4 spring onions, chopped

1 tsp chili oil sauce

1 tsp garlic paste

1 tsp fresh ginger root, julienned

2 tbs dark soy sauce

1 tsp nam pla (fish sauce)

1 tbs palm sugar

½ cup fresh Thai basil leaves, without stems

METHOD:

In wok heat oil and add red chilies, green chilies, and chili sauce. Stir-fry mixture for 1 minute and then add chicken cubes. Stirring constantly, cook chicken on high heat until it turns white. Then add spring onions, garlic, and ginger. Stir well and cook for another 2 minutes, then add soy sauce, nam pla, and palm sugar. Mix well, toss in basil leaves, and stir-fry for another minute.

Remove chicken to serving platter and serve piping hot with rice.

Note: You need not add any salt to this recipe, as the soy sauce and nam pla are usually very salty.

Leg Of Lamb

THIS DELICACY USED TO BE MY DAD'S FAVOURITE; HE OFTEN COOKED IT ON HIS DAYS OFF, USUALLY on Sunday afternoons. The process was tedious and took almost two days from the time the meat was purchased to the time it hit the dining table. Of course, to be an ultimate success, any good recipe has to be prepared with tender, loving care and passion, without any shortcuts. I used to watch my dad prepare this recipe with keen interest and have since carried on his legacy.

Please note that it is better to use fresh lamb for this recipe, as frozen imported meat does not fare well. For best results this dish is best cooked in a clay oven, though the results are equally good when cooked in a BBQ with a cover or in a regular oven.

INGREDIENTS:

1 leg fresh spring lamb, with most of fat removed (approximately 4 lb)

4 oz fresh garlic, crushed

4 oz fresh ginger root, ground

2 hot green chilies

1 large onion, ground, with juice drained

½ cup fresh coriander

½ tsp cinnamon powder

½ tsp cumin powder

¼ tsp cloves, ground

¼ tsp cardamom, ground

1 cup fresh yogurt or sour cream

Pinch of good-quality saffron

4 tbs clarified butter

Juice of 1 lemon

Salt and pepper to taste

METHOD:

Make sure that leg of lamb is clean and make some slits with sharp knife in thigh meat about 1" apart. The slits do not have to be very deep; about 1" will do.

Now add all remaining ingredients to grinder and pulse into a paste. If using whole spices, toast them a little and grind them first before adding any wet ingredients. Taste paste for seasoning and make any necessary adjustments. Apply paste generously to leg and let marinate overnight in fridge. Take leg out from fridge at least 2 hours before cooking.

Pre-heat oven to 350°F. Place leg on ovenproof dish and slide into oven. Periodically check meat and keep basting with any of its released juices. If meat starts to brown too quickly, cover with tin foil and bake. Cook meat to your liking, but it should not take any longer than roasting a large 4-lb bird, about 30 to 40 minutes.

When meat is done, remove from oven. Let it rest for ½ hour before carving and serving. Garnish with red onion rings, lemon wedges, green chilies, and coriander leaves. Serve with your favourite Indian bread or rice.

Gushtaba

THE ULTIMATE FORMAL BANQUET IN KASHMIRI CUISINE IS THE ROYAL WAZWAN. THIS BANQUET offers thirty-six or more courses, many of which are preparations of meat cooked by master chefs.

This extravagant feast of delectable delights concludes with the gushtaba, a very exclusive dish served before dessert and a cup of Kashmiri kahwa, green tea flavoured with saffron, cardamom, and almonds. Such a meal truly showcases Kashmiri hospitality at its best and offers a memorable dining experience.

I feel very privileged to have had the opportunity to take part in a "Kashmir Ka Zaika" Taste of Kashmir Fair in Mumbai several years ago and thoroughly enjoyed several delicacies such as mutton yakhni, rogan josh, rista, tabak maaz, gushtaba, dum aloo, tamatar chaman, and phirni. This zaika gave me a good sense of what a royal Wazwan banquet would be like. Maybe one day I'll enjoy Wazwan too.

Later when I visited Srinagar in Kashmir, I ate gushtaba for the second time on a houseboat and loved it so much that ever since, whenever I travel or dine out, if this dish is on the menu, I always order it.

Gushtaba are velvety-soft lamb balls flavoured with cardamom and cooked gently in delicately spiced hung yogurt and cream on low heat. For some time now, I have been on a mission to recreate this delicacy that I enjoyed in Kashmir. Chef Rocky Mohan is a world-renowned Wazwan chef and an author of several books on this wonderful cuisine. I had the opportunity to meet with him in Toronto, and during that brief visit, I learned a lot about Kashmiri cooking. Here I bring you my version of this culinary delight.

INGREDIENTS:

1 kg lamb, finely ground

12 green cardamom pods, seeded and crushed

1 whole egg, well beaten

1 tbs clarified butter

2 tsp deggi mirch

1 tbs salt

1½ lt warm water

3 bay leaves

2 tbs fennel powder

1 tbs cumin powder

1 tsp cinnamon powder

1 tsp coriander powder

1 tbs ginger powder

1 tbs fresh mint leaves, finely chopped

1 tbs cumin seeds

3 tbs clarified butter

1 onion, finely chopped

1 tsp garlic paste

6"x6" piece of cheesecloth

2 black cardamom pods, crushed

2 cinnamon sticks, 1" long

6 whole cloves

1 tsp cumin seeds

1½ cups hung yogurt

½ cup full cream

Fresh coriander for garnish

METHOD:

In mixing bowl add lamb, green cardamom seeds, 1 tsp deggi mirch, egg, 1 tbs clarified butter, and half of salt and mix well. For this preparation it is extremely important to pound meat in mortar and pestle extensively so meat achieves velvety-smooth consistency. Once done pounding, with wet hands form nice, smooth, round meatballs about the size of golf ball or larger and set aside.

Next, in large saucepan add water, remaining salt, deggi mirch, fennel, cumin, coriander, ginger, and cinnamon powders, bay leaves, and fresh mint leaves, and bring water to a boil. Gently slide meatballs into boiling water and continue to cook on medium heat until all liquid evaporates. Remove bay leaves from pan and discard. Remove meatballs from pan, cover, and keep aside.

In clean saucepan heat butter and add cheesecloth pouch containing cardamom, cinnamon sticks, bay leaves, cloves, and cumin. Next, add chopped onions and garlic paste and sauté mixture until golden brown. Remove spice pouch and discard, and grind browned onions into a paste. Next, gently whisk in yogurt and cream and simmer mixture for about 5 minutes. Then add cooked meatballs with any liquid to yogurt-cream sauce. Gently stir and simmer mixture for another 6 to 8 minutes on low heat.

Plate delicacy on serving platter and garnish with fresh coriander. Serve hot with rice or naan.

Gosht Beli Ram

MY GRANDFATHER OFTEN SPOKE ABOUT THE LEGENDARY CHEF BELI RAM, THE UNDISPUTED "KING OF Punjabi Cooking" prior to the partition between India and Pakistan. My granddad's bhoona lamb delicacy used to be an integral part of every major banquet he created that was inspired by Lahore's master chef. My father often cooked this delicacy on Sundays, and as a child I always enjoyed watching him prepare this awesome dish, later perfecting the art of making it myself. Unfortunately, I never got to taste Chef Beli Ram's creation, so it is difficult to say how close my version comes to the Real McCoy. Nor did I ever have the chance to serve my cooking to my dad; he left us all at a very early age.

In paying tribute to this legendary chef and my dear dad, I have attempted to replicate this delightful creation and take pleasure in sharing my recipe here with you. In this recipe I use spring lamb hind meat, but you may use goat or mutton. Please note that goat meat takes a little longer to cook than spring lamb.

INGREDIENTS:

4 lb spring lamb, hind legs cut up

3 cups plain hung yogurt

2 cups onions, diced

6 tbs ginger root paste

5 tbs garlic paste

4 finger hot green chilies

3 cinnamon sticks, about 1" long

6 cloves

8 green cardamom pods, crushed

1 black cardamom pod, crushed

2 tbs heaped Kashmiri deggi mirch

½ cup clarified butter

6 tsp coriander seeds

Salt to taste

Fresh coriander for garnish

Ginger root, julienned, for garnish

METHOD:

Have butcher clean and remove any visible fat from lamb and discard. It is best to use assorted cuts of spring lamb cut into 1½" chunks for this dish.

Place meat into mixing bowl. In smaller bowl add yogurt, ginger root, garlic paste, green chilies, deggi mirch, and salt. Mix all ingredients well and add to meat, combining thoroughly. Let meat marinate at least overnight at room temperature or in refrigerator, and stir meat at least twice while marinating.

In heavy-bottomed pot, heat butter, add coriander seeds, and sauté over medium heat until seeds start to crackle. Then add cinnamon, cloves, and cardamom pods. Sauté spices for a few minutes, then gently add chopped onions and brown them. Once onions are golden brown add marinated lamb along with marinade. Stir well for a few minutes, add deggi mirch, mix well, cover pot, and simmer until meat is tender and firm but not overdone. While meat is simmering make sure to stir to avoid scorching.

Uncover pot and increase heat to high. Keep stirring meat until fat starts to separate, moisture has absorbed, and meat gets a nice reddish-brown finish. Taste and adjust seasoning as needed.

Serve hot in serving dish and garnish with fresh coriander leaves and julienned ginger root. This delicacy goes great with tandoori rotis or lightly buttered naan. Roomali rotis would also make an excellent accompaniment along with pickled red onions.

Pan-Seared Beef Tenderloin With Wild Mushrooms And Shallot Sauce

I ENJOYED A SIMILAR KIND OF MEAL ON A FLIGHT FROM TORONTO TO FRANKFURT AND WAS INSPIRED to replicate the recipe for my family upon my return.

INGREDIENTS:

4 beef fillet medallions (6 oz each)

2 tbs good-quality olive oil

3 oz mushrooms, portobello or shiitake, diced

2 shallots, diced

1 tbs butter

2 tbs flour

½ cup beef broth

½ cup red wine

Salt and pepper to taste

METHOD:

Season beef medallions with salt and pepper. Heat oil in heavy skillet over medium-high heat and sear beef on both sides, about 1 minute each side. Remove beef to plate and let sit.

Now add butter to skillet, add mushrooms and shallots, and cook until limp. Whisk in flour and cook for 2 minutes while stirring. Slowly whisk in broth and wine, bring to a boil, keep stirring, then reduce heat and simmer for 15 minutes. Season reduced sauce with salt and pepper. In serving platter place drained pieces of beef and add liquid from beef to sauce. Mix well. Pour hot sauce over beef and serve with pasta, rice pilaf, and buttered veggies of choice.

Shinwari Karahi Chicken

WITH THE RECENT MIGRATION OF AFGHANS TO ENGLAND, CANADA, AND THE USA, WE ARE SEEING more and more Afghan and Shinwari restaurants cropping up in neighbourhoods everywhere where there is a sizeable Asian population nearby.

During my last visit to London, I had the opportunity to visit a few of these newer restaurants and observed that these establishments served extremely delicious authentic halal Afghan cuisine in relaxed contemporary surroundings and paid the utmost attention to the quality of service and detail.

In Pakistan and India there are endless recipes for several karahi dishes. In London the karahi chicken delicacy that I tried was typical of Khyber Pakhtoonkhwa, claimed to be the "original" karahi chicken. You will find this sort of preparation in Peshawar's Namak Mandi, and it is named along with meat tikka and kebabs as one of the famous dishes of the Pashtun tribes of the entire frontier region.

This recipe in particular is based on the style of the Shinwari tribe of Pashtuns. It is known in Pakistan for being very delicious while containing no ground spices besides black pepper. Green chilies and juicy ripe tomatoes give this dish its unique and clean flavour. It makes its appearance on London restaurant menus and at wedding catering in India and Pakistan as Shinwari karahi. Following my dining experience in London, I was inspired to replicate what I enjoyed there and am very pleased to share my recipe here.

INGREDIENTS:

1 whole chicken, skinless, cut into pieces

¼ cup cooking oil

4 green chilies, slit

1 tsp ginger paste

1 tsp garlic paste

2 tomatoes, coarsely pureed

2 tomatoes, cut into ¼" cubes

1 tsp black pepper, coarsely ground

Salt to taste

1 fresh lime

Fresh cilantro, chopped, for garnish

Ginger root, julienned, for garnish

Green onions for garnish

METHOD:

In a karahi (wok) heat oil, add slit green chilies, and sauté until they change colour. Remove chilies with slotted spoon and set aside for garnish. Next, add ginger and garlic pastes to karahi and cook until golden brown. Immediately add chicken pieces. Stir well and allow chicken to brown a bit. Then add pureed tomatoes and salt. Continue to gently stir chicken and cook until chicken is almost done and oils start to separate. Next, add tomato cubes and black pepper and gently stir chicken. Lower heat, cover karahi, and allow chicken to cook for another 3 minutes. Turn off heat and you should have a rich, thick sauce laden with chunky rustic tomatoes that are still a bit raw and have not fully broken down into the sauce.

Plate chicken on platter and squeeze lime juice all over it. Garnish with julienned ginger root, fresh coriander, green onions, and fried chilies.

Mag's Jerk Pork

SOME YEARS AGO I HAD JERK PORK IN BARBADOS FOR THE FIRST TIME. I ENJOYED IT SO MUCH THAT I set out to replicate the delicacy with some variations to suit my liking. The marinade in this recipe can be used for chicken and fish as well.

INGREDIENTS:

2 lb lean pork, cut into strips 1"x2" long

MARINADE:

1 bunch green onions, finely chopped

½ cup fresh basil, finely chopped

2 tbs ginger paste

1 tbs garlic paste

6 finger hot green chili peppers, chopped

1 Scotch bonnet pepper, finely chopped

1 tbs Bajan hot sauce or Tabasco

½ cup fresh lemon juice

1 tsp mustard powder

¼ tsp nutmeg powder

½ tsp allspice powder

1 tbs brown sugar

1 tbs Worcestershire sauce

2 tbs olive oil

½ tsp pepper, freshly ground

Salt to taste

METHOD:

In food processor add all marinade ingredients and pulsate to form a fine paste. In mixing bowl add cut-up pork and marinade paste and mix well. Allow pork to marinate for at least 6 hours.

Grill pork on BBQ until done or cook in saucepan on high heat and keep stirring until all liquid has dried. Then lay pork pieces onto cookie sheet and place under broiler of oven.

Keep an eye on the meat, and as soon as it starts to get golden brown pull it out of oven.

Serve hot and garnish with coriander leaves and freshly squeezed lemon juice. Rice with pigeon peas makes a good accompaniment to this dish; homemade garlic bread goes well too.

Bhoona Spicy Spring Lamb With Turnips

WHEN I WAS GROWING UP IN KENYA, MOST PUNJABI MEN TOOK GREAT PRIDE IN THEIR INDIVIDUAL versions of this meat delicacy. Preparing this dish also offered them the opportunity to showcase their patience and the art of bhoona, a technique of braising and stir-frying meat in rich, semi-dry masalas.

I recall my grandfather and father preparing this dish, an example my older brother and cousins eventually followed to impress their friends. My son and nephews are now on the verge of mastering this culinary art as well. Here, I am extremely pleased to share my family's recipe with you.

INGREDIENTS:

2 kg spring lamb, cut up, bone in or without (goat leg meat works too)

½ cup yogurt

Salt and pepper to taste

½ cup clarified butter

4 medium-sized fresh turnips, peeled and cut into 4 pieces

2 black cardamom pods, slightly mashed

8 green cardamom pods, slightly mashed

2 bay leaves

2 cinnamon sticks

1 tbs coriander seeds, slightly crushed

2 cups onions, finely chopped

4 tbs ginger paste

4 tbs garlic paste

2 tsp coriander powder

½ tsp turmeric powder

1 tsp red chili powder

1 tsp Kasoori methi

3 cups ripe tomatoes, finely crushed

1 tbs cumin seeds

2 tbs ginger root, julienned

2 tbs fresh coriander leaves, chopped

METHOD:

Remove and discard any excess fat and clean meat. Then add meat to mixing bowl, whisking in yogurt, salt and pepper, 2 tbs fresh garlic paste, and 2 tbs ginger paste. Mix well and let meat marinate for at least 3 hours.

In heavy-bottomed large pot heat butter and add cut-up turnips. Fry until light brown, then remove with slotted spoon and keep aside. Next, add to pot both kinds of cardamom pods, bay leaves, cinnamon sticks, coriander seeds, and Kasoori methi. Mix well and sauté spices over medium heat for 30 seconds. Then add chopped onions and sauté until lightly browned. Now add remaining ginger and garlic pastes along with coriander powder, turmeric, and red chili powder. Stir well and cook briefly, ensuring onion paste does not scorch.

Gradually add meat to marinade. Bring mixture to a boil, then reduce heat and let simmer until meat starts to tenderize, ensuring meat is constantly being stirred to avoid any scorching. You may need to add a little warm water at regular intervals to keep meat from sticking to bottom of pan. Next, turn heat up, add tomatoes, and stir well. Now the bhoona process starts. Rub cumin seeds between palms and sprinkle all over meat. Add fried turnips and continue to bhoona meat until meat pieces and turnips are fully wrapped around rich reddish-brown masala and fat starts to separate. Check meat for doneness to your liking. If you like it well done, then cook for longer.

Plate meat on serving platter and garnish with fresh coriander leaves, julienned ginger root, and some sliced fresh finger hot chili peppers. Serve hot with tandoori rotis or lachedar parathas. Buttered naan or jeera rice are also options. A nice onion and tomato salad with daikon makes a good accompaniment to this meal as well.

Please note that if you are not fond of turnips, then use potatoes or Punjabi tindas instead.

Chettinad Pepper Kohzi

DURING OUR LAST VISIT TO CHENNAI, INDIA, I WAS FORTUNATE TO HAVE MY FILL OF ALL KINDS OF dosas, idlis, and sambar. But I was yearning to venture into some other delights from the south and thus had an interesting chat with one of the chefs at the hotel where we were staying. He suggested Chettinad cuisine from the Chettinad region of Tamil Nadu in South India. He claimed that this cuisine is one of the spiciest and most aromatic in India and is famous for using a variety of different spices in preparing mainly non-vegetarian delicacies. People from this region consume lots of seafood, chicken, and lamb, but refrain from eating beef and pork.

Chettinad cooks use star anise and kalpasi, a lichen known as the "black stone flower," or patthar ke phool. In addition, tamarind or malt vinegar, whole red chilies, and fennel seeds are also used along with cinnamon, cloves, bay leaves, curry leaves, mustard seeds, black peppercorns, cumin seeds, and fenugreek. The use of these different spices gives Chettinad cuisine pungent and aromatic flavours with lots of heat.

The chef was so generous that he offered to prepare "Chettinad Pepper Kohzi" for us. It was an amazing and unforgettable experience indulging in this peppery aromatic chicken delicacy, which we thoroughly enjoyed with parathas. Interestingly, when I tasted this chicken it reminded me of Kenyan joggos, country chickens, and the chef confirmed that Chettinad cooks indeed prefer to use naatu kohzi—country chickens—which makes this dish extremely delicious. Using country chickens may mean longer cooking times, but trust me, it's worth it.

The chef verbally shared his recipe and I took copious mental notes. Upon returning to Canada, I tried replicating it and have finally succeeded in making the following authentic Chettinad delicacy.

INGREDIENTS:

1 kg country chicken, skinless, cut into pieces, and washed

1 large onion, finely chopped

2 tbs ginger paste

1 tbs garlic paste

¼ cup curry leaves

2 small cinnamon stick pieces

1 tsp turmeric powder

1 tsp hot chili powder

Salt to taste

5 tbs coconut oil

1 tbs tomato paste

1 cup tomatoes, chopped

1 tbs tamarind paste, or 2 tbs malt vinegar

Fresh coriander for garnish

MASALA:

1 tbs cumin seeds

1 tsp fennel seeds

1 tsp mustard seeds

1 tsp coriander seeds

2 tbs black peppercorns

4 red chilies, dried

2 cloves

1 star anise

2 small pieces kalpasi

1 tbs unsweetened coconut, desiccated

METHOD:

In heated pan add all ingredients for freshly ground masala and lightly toast until fragrant. Immediately remove from heat, grind spices in mortar and pestle, and keep aside.

Next, in saucepan heat coconut oil, add curry leaves, cinnamon pieces, and onions, and sauté mixture for a few minutes. Then add ginger and garlic pastes along with turmeric and chili powders. Stir well to avoid any scorching. Add chopped tomatoes, mix well, and cook until tomatoes are well blended and form a nice sauce.

Add chicken and salt. Stir well and cook chicken for about 30 minutes, making sure to stir while cooking. Halfway through cooking process, add ground masala to mixture. Once chicken is almost done, turn heat down and add tamarind paste or malt vinegar and tomato paste and mix well. Continue to simmer until chicken is fully cooked, but not overdone, and fat starts to separate. Transfer to serving platter and garnish lightly with fresh coarsely ground black pepper and fresh coriander. Serve with steamed rice, parathas, or hot naan.

Chicken Korma

"KORMA" IS DERIVED FROM THE TURKISH WORD FOR ROASTING OR GRILLING, AND HAS ITS ROOTS IN Mughlai cuisine. Traditionally, a korma is defined as a dish where meat or vegetables are braised in their own juices, stock, and yogurt or cream. The korma cooking style is similar to all other braising techniques, in that the meat or vegetable is first cooked briskly or seared using high heat and then subjected to long, slow cooking using moist heat and a minimum of added liquid. The pot may be sealed with dough during the last stages of cooking as well. This technique covers many different styles of korma.

The flavour of a korma is based on a mixture of spices, including ground coriander and cumin, combined with yogurt at a lower temperature and incorporated slowly and carefully with the meat juices to avoid curdling. A korma can be mildly spiced or fiery and may use lamb, chicken, beef, or game. Some kormas combine meat and vegetables such as squash and turnips. Sometimes the term shahi (royal) is used for some kormas, indicating its status as a prestigious dish, rather than an everyday meal, as well as its association with royalty.

In the United Kingdom, a korma usually refers not to a particular cooking technique but to a curry with a thick, cream-based sauce or gravy. The kormas in UK restaurants are invariably mildly spiced and may often feature nuts, usually almonds or cashews.

Navratan korma is a vegetarian korma made with vegetables and either paneer or nuts—or sometimes both. "Navratan" means nine gems, and it is common for the recipe to include nine different vegetables.

There are variations between individual kormas and other "curry" recipes. Chili, garlic, and ginger are often used, but the precise method of preparation results in widely different flavours. Bay leaves or dried coconut may be added, the latter being a predominantly South Indian flavouring.

INGREDIENTS:

1 kg chicken, skinless, boneless, and cut into 1"cubes

½ cup blanched cashews, coarsely ground

3 tbs clarified butter

1 tsp garlic paste

1 tsp fresh ginger root paste

3 green cardamom pods, mashed

1 cinnamon stick, about 1" long

1 small bay leaf

1 large onion, finely chopped

½ tsp garam masala

½ tsp turmeric, ground

1 green chili, finely chopped

1 large fresh ripened tomato, finely chopped

Salt and pepper to taste

½ cup chicken stock

½ cup heavy cream

½ cup plain hung yogurt

Fresh coriander, chopped, for garnish

5 whole cashews for garnish

METHOD:

Heat clarified butter in saucepan over medium heat. Open cardamom pods and add to pan along with bay leaf and cinnamon stick. Stir and cook for 1 minute. Now add onion and garlic and ginger pastes, and stir well. Let onions and mixture sauté for a few minutes and then add garam masala, turmeric, chopped chili, and salt and pepper. Cook for another few minutes and add chicken cubes and chopped tomatoes.

Let chicken cook on high heat for about 8 minutes, making sure to occasionally stir it. As soon as fat starts to separate, blend chicken stock, heavy cream, hung yogurt, and ground cashews, gently pour mixture over chicken, and stir well. Cover pot with airtight lid and let korma simmer for another 5 minutes on low to medium heat.

Just before serving, heat korma, plate in serving dish, and garnish with fresh chopped coriander, a few whole cashews, and julienned ginger root. Serve hot with rice, naan, or rotis. My personal preference is to enjoy with hot lachedar parathas.

Please note that this dish tastes even better if served at least 6 to 10 hours after it is cooked.

Kenyan-Style Butter Chicken

WHEN I WAS GROWING UP, DESI MEN IN EAST AFRICA, PARTICULARLY IN KENYA, WOULD TAKE GREAT pride in being Sunday afternoon chefs. Usually, friends would get together in someone's garage or backyard with chilled beverages and cook up a storm. Whatever they cooked was prepared with tender, loving care and every last bit was consumed. These men had absolutely no hang-ups about setting the table or having the right and appropriate accompaniments for a meal that was painstakingly being prepared. At such gatherings, no one even bothered to make rotis or parathas; loaves of simple white bread worked wonders with whatever was cooked.

I remember gate-crashing several of these cookouts that my elder brother or cousins would organize, and I always managed to steal a bite or two to taste the delicacies prepared by these jovial and exuberant young master chefs.

I am pleased to share a very simple and much healthier butter chicken recipe here. You will be blown away to know that this dish has no cream, onions, tomatoes, or other usual spices in the so-called authentic butter chicken preparation.

INGREDIENTS:

½ lb clarified butter or ghee

2 whole chickens, skinned, cleaned, and cut up small

4 hot green chilies, finely chopped

2 tbs fresh ginger paste

2 tbs fresh garlic paste

1 tbs deggi mirch

Fresh black pepper, coarsely ground

Salt to taste

1 bunch green onions

1 lemon

1 lime

½ cup fresh coriander, chopped

METHOD:

In large mixing bowl place cut-up chicken and add green chilies, ginger paste, garlic paste, deggi mirch, salt, and pepper. Mix well and let meat marinate for at least a few hours.

Make sure to stir meat at short intervals. Gently remove any liquid released during marinating process and save in separate bowl. Now in heated pot add clarified butter and gently add marinated chicken, stirring it. Constantly stir to avoid any scorching of meat. Continue process until chicken is fully cooked and has golden brown finish. If chicken is taking longer to cook and getting dry, you may add drained marinade liquid to pot. Taste to check seasonings and make any adjustments desired. One tip to keep in mind is that butter usually has salt, so exercise caution when adding salt. Another note is to use only butter for recipe, as oil or any other fat would not make this dish credible—"Butter makes it better." As soon as chicken is done plate it on serving platter and garnish with slices of lime and lemon, fresh coriander, and chopped green onions. Get creative and make some fancy flowers out of two sprigs of green onion to jazz up dish. Finally, squeeze some lemon or lime juice over chicken.

BHOONA LEG OF
LAMB AND CHOPS

Chat Patte Tangri Kebabs
(Lollipop Chicken)

SOME YEARS AGO I HAD JERK CHICKEN IN BARBADOS FOR THE FIRST TIME. I ENJOYED IT SO MUCH that I was inspired to replicate the recipe with some variations to suit my liking. In creating a fusion delicacy I was reminded of the Thai chicken that I had in Bangkok and nyama choma in Kenya, and I decided to blend the three flavours to develop a stellar marinade. This marinade can be used for chicken, fish, or any other meat.

INGREDIENTS:

20 fresh chicken drumsticks, skinned and cleaned

MARINADE:

1 whole bunch green onions, finely chopped

½ cup fresh basil, finely chopped

1 tbs lime rind, finely chopped

3 tbs ginger paste

2 tbs garlic paste

6 finger hot green chili peppers, chopped

1 Scotch bonnet pepper, finely chopped

3 tbs Thai sweet chili sauce

¼ cup fresh lemon juice

1 tsp mustard powder

¼ tsp nutmeg powder

½ tsp allspice powder

1 tbs brown sugar

3 tbs Worcestershire sauce

1 tbs dark soy sauce

1 tbs tamarind paste

3 tbs olive oil

1 tsp pepper, freshly ground

1 tsp peri peri pepper powder

Salt to taste

METHOD:

In food processor add all marinade ingredients and pulsate to form a fine sauce. In large mixing bowl add drumsticks, make sure all pieces have a slight gash in meaty part of leg, and pour marinade all over meat. Mix well, making sure all pieces are well glazed with marinade. Allow meat to marinate overnight or 12 hours, stirring at least 3 times. Keep meat in fridge and remove for 1 hour or so before cooking.

Pre-heat oven to 425°F. Place marinated chicken onto baking sheet and spread pieces without overcrowding.

Place chicken in pre-heated oven on middle rack and cook until almost done. Baste and turn chicken pieces to ensure even cooking. Just before removing chicken from oven, turn broiler on to give chicken a slight charred finish. Keep an eye on kebabs and as soon as they start to get golden brown and charred, pull them out of oven. Serve hot and garnish with coriander leaves, green chilies, and freshly squeezed lemon juice.

You may wish to grill kebabs on BBQ on medium-high heat, basting often until fully done.

GRILLED PORK CHOP
KENYAN STYLE

Dhaba-Style Mattar Keema

THIS DELICACY HAS A MUGHLAI CUISINE INFLUENCE BOTH IN FLAVOUR AND USE OF SPICES, MINUS the nuts. I also call it sookha bhoona kharda keema. I am pretty confident that you will love this simple yet elegant preparation.

INGREDIENTS:

2 lb lamb or mutton, minced

½ lb fresh green peas

2 tomatoes, chopped

1 medium onion, sliced

6 tbs oil

1 cinnamon stick, 2" long

6 green cardamom pods, crushed

½ tsp cumin seeds

6 whole black peppercorns

6 cloves

½ tsp coriander seeds, crushed

Salt to taste

¼ tsp turmeric

1 tsp deggi mirch

1 tsp ginger paste

1 tsp garlic paste

2 green chilies, chopped

½ tsp garam masala

Fresh coriander for garnish

Ginger root, julienned, for garnish

Chilies for garnish

Lemon for garnish

METHOD:

Heat large pot or wok and add following spices: cinnamon, cardamom, cumin, peppercorns, cloves, and coriander seeds, and lightly toast them until aromas of spices are released. Then add oil and stir well. Immediately add sliced onions and lightly sauté them. Add ginger and garlic pastes and mix well. Add salt, turmeric, deggi mirch, and chopped chilies and mix well. Then add minced meat and stir-fry for a few minutes. Add peas and chopped tomatoes, and continue to stir. Add about 1 cup hot water, cover pot, and cook on medium heat until meat has tenderized and water evaporates. You may need to add a little more water if meat does not tenderize.

Continue cooking and stirring until oil starts to separate. Once meat is fully cooked, plate it on serving platter and sprinkle garam masala powder. Like most curried dishes, the food tastes best after about 8 to 10 hours of cooking. Garnish with fresh coriander leaves, green chilies, and julienned ginger root and squeeze with fresh lemon juice. Serve hot with rice, naan, or tandoori rotis. I love this keema preparation with lachedar parathas for breakfast. Leftover keema makes excellent roti rolls or grilled sandwiches.

JERK CHICKEN

Nihari (Hot And Spicy Lamb Shanks)

THIS HOT AND SPICY DELICACY IS BEST EATEN IN THE EARLY HOURS OF THE MORNING. FROM THE kitchens of the Nawabs to the side and back lanes of Old Delhi near the Jama Masjid, nihari has had an exciting culinary journey over the years. My nephew Rup of the famous "Josh" band often raves about this delicacy that he so often indulges in while on tours in Pakistan. Sometimes, I feel as if he is full of nihari.

When I was in Delhi recently, I tried this delicacy for the first time by chance. One early morning we went to the Red Fort area for aloo curry and peethi pooris for breakfast and ended up having a bowl of nihari. First, I was intrigued by a handwritten sign outside one of the roadside eateries that read, "Nihari available from 5 AM to 8 AM." Soon I learned that nihari is served as soon as the morning prayers end at the Jama Masjid, so one must get up early to enjoy this delicacy, or you will be out of luck.

With the sun still under the covers, happy, eager faces line up outside these eateries and are seen polishing off plates of nihari—meat cooked in hot, spicy gravy. Since I had to quell my hunger early in the morning, I ordered this delicacy, not realizing that this particular nihari was made with beef shanks. I had little difficulty digesting even the first morsel. Later, I discovered that nihari can be made with lamb, goat, or chicken, and my yearning to enjoy this much-talked-about delicacy got me thinking about these different preparations. I could now relate to what Rup talked about every time he returned from his music concerts in Pakistan.

Nihari involves the slow cooking of meat with the stock in large vessels, sealed with dough. Since the meat is cooked overnight over a slow fire, these vessels are called shab deg, or overnight vessels. Since the nihari involves a cooking time of 6 to 8 hours for beef, one has to watch the lamb or chicken, as they would overcook easily.

Nihari tastes best with khameeri rotis, naan, or phulkas. Since it is so heavy on the stomach, be prepared to have a nap after indulging. Cooked brains and bone marrow are often served with nihari, and the Hyderabad version contains lamb bones and tongue.

The secret to cooking the best nihari lies in proportion management. We all buy our best ingredients from the market but when it comes to producing the best taste, I strongly believe that it lies in the hands of the cook and in what proportions and sequence he or she is going to mix the masala.

Today I am sharing with you a very delicious and traditional slow-cooked lamb shank stew. Traditionally, this stew is cooked slowly overnight and eaten as breakfast on early chilly mornings, but you can enjoy it for lunch or dinner. This is a spicy stew with wonderful flavours and aromas of different spices, which give much-needed warmth during the winter months. I am dedicating this recipe to the "Josh" boys.

INGREDIENTS:

4 lamb shanks and 2 lb leg of lamb, cut up

1 bay leaf

2 cinnamon sticks, 1" long

4 tsp ginger paste

4 tsp garlic paste

1 large onion, thinly sliced

1 tsp red chili powder

2½ tsp nihari masala

1 tsp salt

2 tbs whole-wheat flour

1 piece fresh ginger, julienned, 1" long

¼ cup cilantro, chopped

1 lemon, cut into wedges

NIHARI MASALA:

2 tbs fennel seeds

2 tbs cumin seeds

4 green cardamom pods

1 black cardamom pod

8 cloves

15 whole black peppercorns

1 tsp ginger, ground

¼ tsp nutmeg powder

¼ tsp cinnamon powder

1 bay leaf

METHOD:

To prepare nihari masala, add all ingredients into spice grinder and grind to fine powder form. Sift powder through a fine sieve to remove any rough pieces and store in airtight container in cool place. You can keep this for about 1 month.

To boil shanks, in large pot add lamb shanks and cut-up meat along with 2 tsp ginger paste, 2 tsp garlic paste, bay leaf, 1 cinnamon stick, 1 tsp salt, and 5 cups water. Boil shanks on low-medium heat until meat is tender, for about 2 to 3 hours (make sure to add a little more water if water starts to dry out too fast; there should be enough water in pot to cover meat.)

Once meat is done, use slotted spoon to carefully remove meat from liquid and keep aside. Measure stock (liquid), add water if needed to make 4 cups, and keep in separate container. Discard bay leaf and cinnamon. You can do this step up to 2 days in advance. Keep meat and stock together while you store them in refrigerator, and remove meat from stock just before you start to put stew together.

To make nihari stew, in non-stick saucepan or pot, heat oil over medium heat. When oil gets hot, add sliced onions and stir-fry constantly until they turn golden brown. Don't overfry or onions will burn.

Add remaining 2 tsp ginger paste and 2 tsp garlic paste and do a quick stir. Add 1 cup reserved stock to pan, cover pan, and let everything cook on low heat for 5 to 6 minutes, until liquid starts to dry out and onions turn very soft.

Add shanks to pan along with chili powder and nihari masala. Sauté gently for a few minutes and make sure meat doesn't break down. Add 3 cups remaining stock (if stock is less than 3 cups add water). Give stew a gentle stir and cover pan. Simmer on low heat for 10 minutes.

In the meantime, in small bowl, combine flour with ½ cup water. Stir well.

After stew has simmered for 10 minutes, add flour mixture to pan, stirring gently. Cover pan and let simmer for another 10 to 15 minutes on low heat. Check once or twice to ensure gravy is not drying out.

Remove pan from heat and let stand for 10 minutes with lid on before serving. When ready to serve, add salt and garnish stew with ginger, cilantro, and lemon wedges. Serve hot with phulkas, naan, or any bread of choice. Sliced red onions, green chilies, and slices of fresh lemon would be an excellent accompaniment.

Seekh Kebabs From Nairobi

THIS PARTICULAR KEBAB IS VERY FAMOUS IN THE CITY OF NAIROBI AND ALL OVER EAST AFRICA. "Seekh" means "skewer" in the Punjabi language and seekh kebabs are cooked on metal skewers. These kebabs are made using many different varieties and combinations of minced meat, spices, and seasonings. Often these kebabs are eaten as appetizers with cocktails or simple meals of daal and phulkas or naan and good onion salad.

These days, as rolls and wraps are becoming popular, so are seekh kebab rolls and wraps. Try serving this recipe in rolls or wraps using your favourite trimmings. No matter how you prepare these babies, everyone will be sure to love them.

My first experience eating these kebabs was at Sardar Budh Singh's butchery in Nairobi. He used to sell the best freshly cut meat in the mornings and seekh kebabs on the street in front of his butchery in the evenings. In my opinion, to this day his kebabs are the best, but the recipe I am sharing with you here fairly closely replicates the flavour, taste, and texture of Sardar Budh Singh's kebabs. Please note that his kebabs were always made of hind leg goat meat.

INGREDIENTS:

2 lb beef, chicken, lamb, or goat meat, ground

1 medium onion, finely chopped

2 tbs fresh ginger root, finely chopped

1 tsp garlic paste

4 finger hot green chilies, finely chopped

4 tbs fresh coriander leaves, finely chopped

1 tbs cumin seeds, rubbed between palms

2 tbs fine bread crumbs

1 tsp Kasoori methi

½ tsp green cardamom powder

¼ tsp cinnamon powder

1 pinch clove powder

1 pinch nutmeg powder

Salt and freshly ground black pepper to taste

Clarified butter for basting

METHOD:

In mixing bowl add meat of choice along with all other ingredients except butter. Mix everything well and divide into 24 equal portions, make balls, and refrigerate for about 1 hour.

Wash metal skewers well and, using moist hands, spread each ball onto middle of skewer, pressing along skewer to wrap meat evenly. Make each kebab about 6" long. If using longer skewers, you may wrap 2 kebabs, ensuring they are about 1" apart.

These kebabs are usually cooked in a moderately hot tandoor for about 4 minutes; otherwise, cook on charcoal grill for about 6 minutes. In Kenya these kebabs are always cooked on charcoal grills. If cooking on grill make sure to turn skewers at regular intervals to cook evenly and avoid burning and too much charring. When kebabs are almost fully cooked and golden brown, baste with clarified butter and slide them off gently onto serving platter. Garnish with sliced onion rings and lemon wedges. Kebabs are best served hot. You may serve on sizzling platter for added flair and a classy touch.

Seekh kebabs may also be cooked in oven or shallow-fried on tawa without skewers. The shape of kebabs can be modified to look like sausages or croquets. Mint or tamarind chutney and lemon wedges are good accompaniments for these kebabs.

BHOONA MURGH

Manchurian-Style Baby Back Pork Ribs

THIS RECIPE IS ALWAYS A HIT AMONGST THE YOUNG AND OLD. IT MAKES THE PERFECT APPETIZER and is one of the most popular finger foods for any occasion. For those who do not eat pork, chicken wings work equally well. One caution: Whenever cooking this delicacy make sure that you prepare a large batch, as this dish will vanish like hot cakes and I can guarantee that you will have no leftovers.

INGREDIENTS:

1 tbs clarified butter

2 lb pork side ribs, cleaned and cut about 2" long

1 bunch green onions, finely chopped

2 oz fresh ginger root, finely chopped

4 cloves fresh garlic, finely ground

2 tbs fresh coriander stems, finely chopped

2 tbs dark soy sauce

2 tbs white vinegar

4 tbs Worcestershire sauce

3 green chilies, finely chopped

1 tbs Sriracha chili sauce

1 tbs tomato paste

Salt and pepper to taste

Fresh cilantro for garnish

Fresh lemon juice for garnish

2 sprigs spring onions, finely chopped

Fresh slices of lemon for garnish

METHOD:

In large bowl mix all ingredients and let sit and marinate at room temperature for about 2 hours.

Place ribs into large pot and cook for about 15 minutes. Keep stirring and ensure that ribs get cooked evenly. Do not overcook meat. You may cover pot for faster cooking. When ribs are almost cooked and all liquid is almost dry, remove from heat and transfer ribs onto cookie sheet or ovenproof dish. Spread ribs evenly on sheet and store in fridge until serving time.

Just before serving, turn broiler on and place ribs into hot oven on

middle rack and broil until golden brown. Be careful to avoid burning.

Remove ribs onto serving platter lined with fresh lettuce, and garnish with fresh lemon juice, chopped cilantro, and chopped spring onions. Serve ribs hot with steamed rice or as an appetizer.

BHOONA SPICY SPRING LAMB

Simple Chicken Curry Inspired By Musical Maestros

PANDIT RAVI SHANKAR'S MUSIC WILL LIVE WITH US FOREVER. A TREMENDOUS MAN AND ARTIST, HE lived an amazing life and was a phenomenal creative force not only in India, but across the globe. I was very fortunate to have met him more than thirty years ago, twice in Saskatoon, Saskatchewan. This was one of my most humbling experiences. Pandit Ji was with the late Ustad Alla Rakha, the tabla maestro, and both of them had requested chicken curry with drumsticks and insisted that it be garnished with julienned ginger root and fresh coriander. They both enjoyed and loved my preparation and blessed me. This recipe is a tribute to these creative geniuses.

INGREDIENTS:

1 whole chicken, skinned, cleaned, and cut, leaving legs intact

¼ cup clarified butter

3 cloves

3 green cardamom pods, lightly mashed

1 cinnamon stick, 1" long

1 bay leaf

½ tsp turmeric

2 finger hot green chilies, finely chopped

1 tsp garam masala

1 large onion, finely chopped

1 tbs garlic paste

1 tbs ginger root paste

1 cup fresh ripe tomatoes, crushed

1 tbs tomato paste

1 tbs deggi mirch

Salt and pepper to taste

1 cup warm water

1 tbs ginger root, julienned

Fresh coriander leaves, chopped

METHOD:

In saucepan, heat clarified butter and add cloves, cardamom, cinnamon stick, and chopped onions. You may want to lightly toast these spices in frying pan before adding them to butter along with onions.

Sauté mixture for about 5 to 8 minutes and continue to stir constantly to avoid any scorching.

When onions turn light golden brown, add ginger, garlic, and chilies and stir well. Immediately add garam masala and turmeric and mix well. Keep stirring for a few minutes and then add crushed tomatoes and tomato paste. Let tomatoes blend well and add salt, pepper, and deggi mirch to sauce. Cook mixture for about 5 minutes and continue to stir until butter starts to separate from sauce.

Now add chicken (please note that you may use any cut of chicken for this dish; however, it must be skinless). Cook chicken in sauce for about 5 minutes and add warm water. Mix well and continue to cook, stirring chicken on medium to high heat until almost done. Make sure not to overcook. Cover pot and let rest until ready to serve. For optimal results it is recommended to let chicken rest for at least 6 hours before serving. Chicken curry tastes best the next day.

Just before serving turn on heat to medium and heat chicken, stirring gently. Bring to a quick boil and plate in deep serving dish. Garnish with coriander leaves and julienned ginger root. Serve curry with jeera rice, tandoori rotis, naan, or lachedar parathas.

METHI MURGH

Stir-Fried Sirloin Steak

STIR-FRYING IS A CHINESE COOKING TECHNIQUE IN WHICH INGREDIENTS ARE FRIED IN A SMALL amount of very hot oil while being stirred in a wok. It is believed that this quick, hot cooking seals in the flavours of the foods, as well as preserves their colour and texture.

Wok- or pan-frying may have been used since the Han dynasty for drying grain, not preparing meats or vegetables, but it was not until the Ming dynasty that the wok acquired its modern shape and introduced the method of quick cooking in hot oil. Around the twentieth century, while restaurants and affluent families could afford the oil and fuel needed for stir-frying, boiling and steaming were the most widely used cooking techniques. Stir-fry cooking became predominant over the course of the century as more and more people could afford oil and fuel, and eventually this technique spread beyond Chinese communities into the West.

This cooking technique is considered healthy and a skillful use of vegetables, meat, and fish. Stir-frying uses moderate quantities of fat, and the sauces are not overly rich, yet still very succulent and tasty.

Generally speaking, there are two primary techniques—"chao" and "bao." Both these techniques use very high heat. But whereas chao uses the addition of liquid and ingredients remain softer as a result, bao stir-fries tend to be crispy because of browning or caramelization.

Over the years I have created numerous Asian stir-fried delicacies that I used to teach in my cooking classes; the following recipe is amongst my favourites. I have tried to cook this recipe with other meat, like chicken and pork, but for reasons unknown, beef truly brings out the best flavours and does justice to this recipe. Please do not take my word for it, though; try it for yourself and pass your own judgment.

INGREDIENTS:

2 tbs cooking oil

1 lb fresh strip loin steak

3 red chilies, dried

2 tbs dark soy sauce

1 tbs Sriracha chili sauce

1 tbs garlic paste

1 medium onion, cut into 1" cubes

1 tbs fresh ginger root, julienned

1 medium bunch fresh broccoli, cut into florets

½ cup baby sweet peppers, sliced into rings

1 tbs hoisin sauce

1 tbs chili oil paste

1 tbs cornstarch, dissolved in ¼ cup cold water

2 sprigs spring onions, sliced

Fresh coriander, chopped, for garnish

METHOD:

Thinly slice strip loin steak and cut into narrow strips. Place meat into mixing bowl and add dark soy sauce, garlic paste, and Sriracha sauce and mix well, allowing meat to marinate for at least 1 hour and turning it occasionally.

Next, in wok heat oil and add dried chilies. Immediately add marinated meat with marinade and stir-fry on high heat for about 5 to 6 minutes. As soon as meat starts to brown, add onions, peppers, broccoli florets, and julienned ginger root. Next, add chili oil paste and hoisin sauce and mix well.

Cover wok and cook on high heat for a few minutes. Then pour cornstarch mixture all over meat and veggies in wok. Stir well and as soon as sauce gets thick and all ingredients are glazed, remove wok from heat.

Plate cooked meat and veggies on serving platter and garnish with sliced spring onions and coriander. Serve piping hot with steamed rice.

Grilled Lamb, Chicken, Or Pork Souvlaki With Warm Corn Salsa

SOUVLAKI IS A POPULAR GREEK FAST FOOD CONSISTING OF SMALL PIECES OF MEAT AND SOMETIMES vegetables grilled on a skewer. It is usually served in a pita sandwich with garnishes and sauces, or on a dinner plate, often with fried potatoes and rice. The meat usually used in Greece and Cyprus is pork, although chicken and lamb may also be used. In other countries and for tourists, Souvlaki may be made with meat such as lamb, beef, chicken, and sometimes fish, especially swordfish.

Souvlaki is very popular in our household, and having tried this delicacy at many Greek fairs in different parts of the world, I had my favourite souvlaki at a small kiosk in Geneva, Switzerland.

INGREDIENTS:

1 kg meat of choice, boneless	½ cup bell peppers, chopped
1 tbs garlic paste	1 cup corn on the cob
Juice of 1 fresh lemon	2 tbs olive oil
2 tbs virgin olive oil	Sea salt
1 tbs oregano flakes	Black pepper
2 fresh bell peppers	2 green chilies, chopped
1 large onion	½ cup coriander, chopped
½ cup onions, chopped	Juice of 2 fresh limes

METHOD:

Marinate cubed lamb, chicken, or pork with garlic paste, salt and pepper, oregano flakes, lemon juice, and olive oil. Mix well and let meat marinate for a few hours.

Cut bell peppers and 1 large onion into 1" squares and place in bowl.

Once meat has marinated, skewer cubed lamb, chicken, or pork with 1 onion slice and 1 piece of meat and then 1 piece of pepper. Repeat process until skewer has been filled. Cover skewers with saran wrap and let marinate until ready to cook. It is best to use metal skewers and if using wooden skewers, make sure to soak them in water before threading meat and vegetables.

For salsa, sauté chopped onions, bell peppers, and chilies in olive oil. Add drained corn on the cob and mix well. Next, add some freshly chopped coriander and a sprinkle of sea salt and freshly ground black pepper. Keep salsa warm.

Grill skewers on hot grill and keep turning to cook them evenly and fully.

When souvlaki is ready to be plated, neatly spread warm salsa on one side of plate and place 2 skewers on top. Garnish plate with tomato and lemon slices. Serve hot with garlic bread or warm pita bread. You may wish to serve rice pilaf on the side.

Grilled souvlaki with warm salsa is a great delicacy at any BBQ party. Please make sure to have plenty of these delicious nibbles on hand, as these babies will disappear quickly, and if there are any leftovers, your guests will be fighting over them!

Tabak Maaz

IN 1965 A FEW FRIENDS AND I WERE VISITING JAMMU AND KASHMIR AND PLANNED A TRIP TO Gulmarg and Khilanmarg—"Heaven on Earth"—about fifty kilometres from Srinagar. The enchanting Khilanmarg lies covered with nature's beauty and splendour. Situated two thousand feet above Gulmarg and surrounded by dense forests and deep valleys, Khilanmarg gives splendid panoramic views of the majestic Himalayan peaks, which look greater, closer, and mightier from there. Khilanmarg is carpeted with fragrant and blossoming flowers in spring and becomes a ski-run destination for its visitors in winter. We never wanted to come back from this heaven, as it was so serene and peaceful.

It was a bright, sunny day in Khilanmarg, a perfect day for the Bombay film industry to shoot amidst this majestic location. The crew of the movie Amne Samne was shooting a romantic sequence with Shashi Kapoor and Sharmila Tagore, while Kamal Kapoor, Madan Puri, and a young Prem Chopra looked on intensely. We joined the other cast members of the movie as onlookers.

When the crew was done with the shot, they took a long break and we availed the opportunity to personally meet all the stars. They kindly obliged and were very intrigued to find that we had come all the way from Africa to visit Kashmir. I distinctly remember Kamal Kapoor asking us if we had tried any Kashmiri cuisine and suggesting a dhaba in Srinagar that served some great food. He insisted that we try the tabak maaz, a dish that I had never heard of before. That evening, upon our return to Srinagar, we found this gem of a dhaba situated in the back streets of Srinagar, and like true foodies we ordered rogan josh, tabak maaz, and daal tardka with some tandoori rotis for our evening feast.

My curiosity was killing me; I wanted to dive straight into the tabak maaz, and when I did—wow!—I was speechless. What aromas and unique flavours and tastes! I thoroughly enjoyed this lamb chop delicacy that must have been prepared painstakingly by some master chef at that eatery. I did not even bother to try the daal or the rogan josh, as the tabak maaz was so finger-licking and lip-smacking good. After the meal, I cleverly asked the chef behind the tandoor about the preparation of this unique dish. Reluctantly, he shared a quick recipe and I remembered enough to come back home and try my hand at this Wazwan delicacy. I have cooked it several times since then and have managed to improve my recipe enough to share it with you now.

INGREDIENTS:

1 kg spring lamb chops or ribs

½ cup clarified butter

1 onion, finely grated

1 tsp cumin powder

1 tsp ginger powder

1 tsp coriander powder

1 tsp fennel powder

2 small bay leaves

2 cinnamon stick pieces, about 1" long

1 black cardamom pod, crushed

4 cloves

1 tbs garlic paste

1 tbs ginger paste

1 cup hung yogurt

1 tbs deggi mirch

Salt to taste

1 onion, thinly sliced

2 green chilies, finely chopped

1 bunch green onions, finely chopped

Fresh coriander, chopped

1 fresh lemon, cut into 8 wedges

METHOD:

In large saucepan heat half of clarified butter and add finely grated onions and garlic and ginger pastes, and sauté mixture for a few minutes. Then add lamb chops or ribs, cumin, ginger, coriander, fennel, bay leaves, cinnamon sticks, black cardamom, cloves, deggi mirch, and salt and mix well. Continue to stir and cook for about 8 minutes.

Next, add hung yogurt and stir well with meat. Cover pan with lid and continue to cook on medium heat until meat is almost done, but not overcooked, and make sure to occasionally stir to avoid any scorching. If liquid dries up you may wish to add some hot water to pot. With slotted spoon carefully remove bay leaves, cinnamon sticks, black cardamom shells, and cloves and discard.

Next, remove all chops or ribs from pan with slotted spoon and keep aside. Save any sauce in pan.

In clean saucepan heat remaining butter and sauté sliced onions along with chopped green chilies until onions get lightly browned. Remove browned onions and add them to saved sauce. At this stage transfer cooked chops or ribs to pan with butter in which you fried onions and quickly fry meat to brown nicely.

Once chops or ribs are browned, add rich sauce and mix well, and cook for another few minutes to thoroughly heat and glaze meat. Immediately plate chops on serving platter and garnish with chopped spring onions, coriander, and lemon wedges. Serve hot with rice, naan, or lachedar parathas.

Stir-Fried Chicken Strips With Yu Choy Sum

YU CHOY SUM HAS BEEN USED AS A VEGETABLE IN ASIAN CUISINE SINCE ANCIENT TIMES. THIS VEGetable is a unique source of many essential vitamins, minerals, and trace elements. Used throughout northern China, yu choy sum is now commonly found in Chinese restaurants in North America as well.

Yu choy sum looks like gai lan (Chinese broccoli), but is skinnier and from the bok choy family. So much more tender and sweet than its larger cousin bok choy, yu choy sum tastes like a cross between broccoli and spinach. This amazing vegetable works well in stir-fries and soups.

The following is a fairly healthy veggie and chicken stir-fry preparation using this unique green that is easy to make and can be served with steamed rice or rice noodles. Please note that this delicacy can be prepared without meat for vegetarians. You may also want to use snow peas, green bell peppers, and green beans in this preparation.

INGREDIENTS:

½ lb chicken breast, skinless, boneless, and cut into ¼" strips

4 red chilies, dried

1 tbs ginger root, chopped

1 tsp garlic paste

1 tbs chili oil paste

2 tbs soy sauce

½ lb fresh yu choy sum, washed and cut in half

4 spring onions, washed and cut on a bias, about 1" long

2 stalks celery, sliced on a bias

4 large white mushrooms, sliced

1 medium zucchini, cut in half and sliced on a bias

3 tbs hoisin sauce

2 tbs peanut or corn oil

METHOD:

Heat large wok and add oil. As soon as oil gets hot gently add dried chilies and chicken strips. Stir well, then add ginger, and garlic and chili oil pastes. Stir-fry chicken until almost cooked. Next, add soy sauce, mix well, and cook for a few minutes. Then gently add all vegetables.

Mix well and cook on high heat for a few minutes. Then add hoisin sauce, stir well, and continue to cook for another 2 minutes. Make sure not to overcook, otherwise veggies will become soggy. Immediately plate delicacy on platter and serve hot with rice or noodles. Garnish with fresh coriander and chopped green onions.

Tip: Whenever adding veggies to any stir-fried delicacy, it is best to quickly blanch them in boiling water and immediately drain them.

Spicy Kung Pao Chicken

THIS IS A HEALTHIER VERSION OF TRADITIONAL KUNG PAO CHICKEN SERVED IN MOST CHINESE RES-taurants. The chicken in this preparation is stir-fried instead of being coated and deep-fried.

INGREDIENTS:

2 chicken breasts, boneless, skinless, and cut into 1" cubes

8 small red chili peppers, dried

2 cloves garlic, peeled and finely chopped

2 green onions (spring onions, scallions)

2 stalks celery, cut into ½" pieces

4 tbs oil for stir-frying, or as needed

½ cup peanuts, pan-roasted

3 tbs peanut oil

MARINADE:

2 tsp soy sauce

2 tsp Chinese rice wine or dry sherry

1 tsp sesame oil

1½ tsp cornstarch

SAUCE:

2 tbs dark soy sauce

2 tbs Chinese rice wine or dry sherry

1 tbs hoisin sauce

1 tbs sweet chili sauce

METHOD:

In mixing bowl combine chicken with marinade ingredients and add cornstarch last. Marinate chicken for about ½ hour.

Cut chilies in half so they are approximately the same size as chicken cubes. Cut green onions on a bias, about ½" apart.

Next, in small bowl mix all sauce ingredients and set aside.

Heat wok over medium-high to high heat. Add peanut oil. When oil is hot, add chicken. Stir-fry until almost cooked. Gently remove cooked chicken from wok with slotted spoon and keep aside.

Next, add remaining oil to wok, and as soon as it heats up add garlic and stir-fry for about 30 seconds. Immediately add red chili peppers and celery. Stir-fry briefly, then add sauce to wok and bring to a boil. Promptly add chicken to wok and stir well. Finally, add peanuts and green onions. Plate on serving platter and serve hot with steamed rice.

Peri Peri Chicken Livers

OVER A DECADE AGO WHEN I WAS IN DURBAN, SOUTH AFRICA, ATTENDING THE WORLD CONFERENCE on Racism, I stayed about twenty-five miles away from the main city in a small seaside resort called Umbshlotti. The tavern in the neighbourhood served some exciting and delicious hot and spicy foods. My favourite snacking foods were the peri peri chicken wings and wicked chicken livers served with lightly toasted buttered homemade biscuits and breads. The chilled beer was a great companion to these most succulent peppery hot livers and certainly helped cool off the palate. I think I have mastered this delicacy and am ready to share it with you here. Please note that the use of authentic peri peri peppers is a must—you may use an alternative red chili powder, but it will not impart an authentic taste.

INGREDIENTS:

1 lb fresh chicken livers, cleaned and any membrane removed and discarded

2 tbs clarified butter

½ small onion, sliced

1 tsp garlic paste

1 tsp ginger root, finely chopped

½ tsp cumin powder

½ tsp coriander powder

1 tbs peri peri pepper powder

2 tomatoes, peeled and finely chopped

1 tbs tomato paste

Salt and freshly ground black pepper to taste

Fresh lemon for garnish

Coriander for garnish

Onion for garnish

Hot chili peppers for garnish

METHOD:

In heated saucepan add clarified butter and sauté sliced onions for 1 minute. Then add garlic paste and chopped ginger root. Stir mixture well and add cumin, coriander, and peri peri pepper powders and continue to stir and cook for a few minutes. Next, add tomatoes and tomato paste to pan and cook sauce for about 10 minutes. As soon as sauce gets rich, add chicken liver, cut up into bite-sized pieces, and mix well. Add salt and pepper and continue to cook and stir liver for another 8 minutes on high heat, making sure sauce does not scorch. It does not take long to cook liver, so avoid overcooking, otherwise liver will turn tough. Immediately plate and serve piping hot with your favourite bread. Garnish liver with sliced onions and lemon, coriander, and chili peppers.

NYAMA CHOMA

Char Siu

IN ANY CHINATOWN AROUND THE GLOBE STRIPS OF RED CHAR SIU HANG FROM HOOKS IN THE windows of Chinese restaurants. "Char siu" means "fork burned," a reference to the traditional preparation, which is skewered and BBQ'd over a fire.

The origin of char siu is Cantonese. Skewers of pork meat are marinated in a honey hoisin sauce, and then char-roasted in an oven to a savoury and sticky-sweet perfection.

Perhaps you have tasted this BBQ pork in buns or Vietnamese phos. The meat prepared by this traditional method is moist and flavourful on the inside, and caramelized and slightly chewy on the outside, with a sweetness infused with a hint of garlic and five-spice.

Being a foodie I always wanted to make this delicacy at home, and after several attempts have succeeded in creating a char siu dish very similar to the one that I used to buy at Chinese food stores.

INGREDIENTS:

1 lb pork butt, skin removed, cut into 4 pieces lengthwise

1 tsp garlic paste

1 tsp sesame oil

2 tbs peanut oil

FIVE-SPICE POWDER:

1 tsp Sichuan pepper, ground

1 tsp star anise, ground

1¼ tsp fennel seeds, ground

½ tsp cloves, ground

½ tsp cinnamon, ground

CHAR SIU MARINADE:

2 tbs maltose

2 tbs honey

2 tbs hoisin sauce

2 tbs dark soy sauce

1 tbs Chinese rice wine

¼ tsp white pepper, ground

1 tbs Sriracha sauce

3 drops permitted food colour

½ tsp five-spice powder

METHOD:

Combine all five-spice powder ingredients in small airtight container. Store in cool, dry place.

Add all marinade ingredients into saucepan, heat up, and stir well until fully blended, slightly thickened, and sticky. Turn heat off and let sauce cool.

Once sauce has cooled marinate pork butt pieces with 2/3 of sauce, garlic paste, and sesame oil and refrigerate overnight.

Add peanut oil to remaining marinade sauce. Mix well and keep aside.

Pre-heat oven to 375°F and roast pork pieces placed on ovenproof dish for 15 minutes. After 15 minutes take pork out of oven, thread onto metal skewers, and grill over BBQ. Brush remaining sauce mixture on meat while grilling until char siu are perfectly charred. Slice meat into bite-sized pieces, drizzle with any remaining sauce, and serve immediately with steamed white rice.

I love to serve the sliced char siu garnished with slices of lemon, green chilies, and fresh coriander—it makes an excellent appetizer and perfect companion for chilled beer.

GRILLED VEGGIES

Vegetarian Delights

Basic Masala Chickpeas

CHICKPEAS ARE MADE IN VARIOUS WAYS IN MOST PUNJABI KITCHENS. PUNJABIS USUALLY USE THE dried beans and soak them overnight before cooking. The following is a quick basic recipe using canned chickpeas that are readily available in almost all food stores. The results are no doubt faster and almost equally as good.

INGREDIENTS:

1 19-oz can chickpeas, rinsed, washed, and drained

2 tbs cooking oil or butter

½ cup onions, diced

½ tsp garlic paste

1 tbs ginger root paste

1 tsp coriander, ground

1 tsp cumin powder, ground

1 tsp garam masala

2 tbs tomato paste

½ cup warm water

Salt and pepper to taste

Sliced onions for garnish

Sliced tomatoes for garnish

Fresh coriander, chopped, for garnish

METHOD:

In saucepan heat oil and add onions, garlic, and ginger root and sauté until golden brown. Add all spices and stir well. Then add tomato paste. Cook for about 2 minutes and then add drained chickpeas and water. Stir mixture well and add salt and pepper. Cover pan and cook for another 10 minutes on medium heat.

Garnish with sliced onions and tomatoes and fresh coriander leaves. Serve hot with rice or Indian bread. To make this dish even spicier, add 2 chopped finger hot green chilies.

Daal Makhani

AMONGST INDIANS ALL OVER THE GLOBE, DAAL MAKHANI HAS TO BE THE MOST FAVOURITE LENTIL delicacy. I recall eating this dish at a Dhaba near my college in Delhi. A couple of tandoori rotis and daal makhani used to hit the spot at lunchtime. Soon I learnt that whenever I over indulging eating this particular lentil, I used to cause quite a commotion in the class room in the afternoons. It is interesting to note that like many curries, this daal tastes much better after refrigerating it for a day.

This daal goes great with jeera rice or tandoori roti

INGREDIENTS:

1 cup whole urad daal

¼ cup red kidney beans

1 small onion, finely chopped

2 tbs ginger paste

1 tbs garlic paste

1 medium ripe tomato, finely diced

2 tbs tomato paste

2 finger hot green chilies, finely chopped

¼ cup fresh coriander stems, finely chopped

Salt to taste

½ cup butter

½ cup full cream

METHOD:

In flat dish spread lentils and beans. Pick and discard any stones or dirt. Thoroughly wash lentils in running water and soak them for about 3 hours. Put drained lentils into heavy-bottomed pot, add about 6 cups water, and bring to a boil. Remove any scum from surface, add chopped onion, cover pot, and simmer until lentils are almost cooked and two-thirds of liquid has dried up. Stir daal well and then add ginger and garlic pastes, green chilies, tomatoes, and tomato paste and stir. Now add coriander stems and butter. Stir daal and cook for another ¾ of an hour. Finally, stir cream into daal and cook on low heat for another 5 minutes. Taste and make any necessary adjustments.

Serve piping hot. You may wish to garnish with finely julienned fresh ginger root and fresh coriander leaves.

Stuffed Chili Potatoes

HERE IS ANOTHER DISH FOR THE VEGETARIANS THAT WILL ADD SOME FIRE TO YOUR COCKTAIL PARTY entertaining. This can be served as an appetizer or even as one of the main course dishes.

INGREDIENTS:

2 lb Parisian potatoes

½ tsp turmeric

Salt and pepper to taste

Cooking oil

3 tbs brown onion paste

2 tbs white vinegar

1 tbs garlic paste

1 tbs ginger root paste

2 tbs finger hot green chilies, chopped

2 tbs dark soy sauce

1 tbs tomato paste

1 tbs fresh coriander leaves, chopped

2 sprigs green onions, chopped

1 fresh lemon

METHOD:

For this particular dish, use Parisian potatoes. They are specific in the way they are cut into round balls, about ¾" in diameter, and are all the same size. If you cannot find these pre-cut potatoes, then make sure you buy new potatoes, which are small in size and handpicked so they are all the same size.

Wash potatoes and peel skin. In pot add potatoes with turmeric and some salt and cover with enough water to boil. Cook potatoes on high heat, making sure not to overcook. Potatoes must be cooked, but at the same time be firm and not break easily. Drain potatoes immediately and set aside. Do not leave cooked potatoes in hot water, otherwise they will get mushy.

Now in wok or frying pan add some oil, garlic, ginger, chilies, and brown onion paste. Stir-fry ingredients, making sure that garlic does not burn. Add vinegar and stir well. Add tomato paste and soy sauce and stir mixture well.

Taste for seasoning; you may need to add salt, and if you like it hot then add more chopped chilies.

Using a small apple corer gently bore holes in boiled potatoes, making sure they do not break, and fill each hole with cooked masala filling. Place stuffed potatoes on platter, brush lightly with oil or melted butter, and slide into pre-heated oven to heat them thoroughly. Serve piping hot, garnish with coriander, and squeeze lemon juice all over potatoes.

Palak Koftas

THIS IS A DELICIOUS PREPARATION OF SPINACH BALLS IN A CASHEW SAUCE.

INGREDIENTS:

200 gm fresh spinach

½ cup besan

3 tbs cashew paste

2 tbs fresh coriander, finely chopped

1 tsp cumin powder

1 small potato, boiled and mashed

2 finger hot chili peppers, finely chopped

Salt to taste

Cooking oil for deep-frying

SAUCE:

2 tbs clarified butter

1 medium onion, finely chopped

1 tsp garlic paste

1 tsp ginger paste

½ tsp cumin seeds

½ tsp garam masala

½ tsp turmeric powder

½ cup cashew paste

1 tbs white poppy seeds, ground

2 tbs almond paste

1 cup tomatoes, crushed

1 tbs tomato paste

1 tbs fresh coriander leaves, chopped

¼ cup full cream

Salt and pepper to taste

METHOD:

Clean and wash spinach leaves and parboil them. Let cool, squeeze out as much liquid as possible, and mash spinach. Add remaining ingredients except oil to spinach and mix well. Divide mixture into 10 portions and form balls by rolling each portion between palms. You may wet palms before rolling balls. Heat oil in wok and deep-fry balls until golden brown. Keep fried balls aside.

Heat butter in saucepan and brown onions. Then add turmeric, garlic and ginger pastes, cumin seeds, garam masala, cashew and almond pastes, and poppy seeds and stir-fry for a few minutes. Stir continuously to avoid any scorching and then add crushed tomatoes and tomato paste. Mix well, add ½ cup warm water, and simmer sauce for 5 minutes. Add salt and pepper.

Just before serving add fried koftas to sauce and simmer for another 5 minutes. Serve in shallow serving dish and garnish with fresh coriander leaves and full cream.

Tip: Kofta mixture may be shaped into oval kebabs and deep-fried. These kebabs may be served piping hot or cold as appetizers with your favourite chutney or relish.

Karelas Fit For The Maharajas

KARELAS ARE BITTER MELONS THAT MOSTLY GROW IN TROPICAL COUNTRIES. ASIAN COMMUNITIES around the globe enjoy this vegetable; it is very popular amongst Punjabis, and the Chinese use it in several preparations.

I must admit that when I tried karelas for the first time, I simply hated them, as I found them too bitter for my taste. It took me almost two decades before I started to cook them and developed a keen liking for them.

Many years ago when we were visiting the palace of the maharaja of Patiala, I remember my father suggesting that the maharaja must have been enjoying stuffed karelas for lunch as we spoke. Later that evening we were treated to sweet karelas stuffed with sweetened paneer blended with almonds and pistachios, a creation only available in Patiala, Punjab.

Punjabis prepare this delicacy in many different ways, and here I am sharing a recipe my dear father mastered many years ago. Please note that this is a tedious recipe—no wonder I call it "fit for the maharajas."

INGREDIENTS:

12 fresh small tender karelas

1 large onion, sliced

2 finger hot green chilies, sliced lengthwise

2 tbs fresh ginger root, julienned

2 tbs fresh coriander leaves, chopped

½ cup cooking oil

FILLING:

1 tbs homemade garam masala

1 tbs turmeric

1 tbs amchoor

1 tbs coriander powder

1 tbs pomegranate seeds, dried and ground

2 tbs onion flakes, dried and crushed

1 tsp fennel seeds, crushed

1 tbs tomato paste

1 tbs cooking oil

Salt and red chili powder to taste

METHOD:

First prepare karelas for filling. Lightly scrape surface of vegetable with serrated knife and save shavings. Using sharp knife slit karelas, remove seeds from opening, and save them along with shavings. Apply salt to karelas and place into deep bowl for a few hours until they release their moisture. Remove karelas from bowl and pat-dry with paper towel. Set aside and discard liquid.

Now prepare filling by mixing all filling ingredients well. You can make a larger batch of filling to use for stuffing potatoes, lady's-fingers, or baby eggplants. Filling can be stored in airtight jar in fridge for months.

Once filling is ready, using a teaspoon fill cavities of karelas with filling and tie thread around them to

hold filling in place. In shallow frying pan heat oil and fry stuffed karelas on medium heat until they turn dark brown. Remove karelas from pan, place into dish, and set aside.

In frying pan add enough oil to pan-fry shavings and seeds from karelas. Sauté these ingredients with a little leftover filling mixture and continue to sauté until seeds start to brown. Now add onions, chilies, and ginger. Mix well and cook for another few minutes.

Transfer onion mixture to serving dish that can be placed in oven and set aside. Gently remove threads from pan-fried karelas and arrange them neatly over onions. Cover dish with foil and store in fridge until serving time. This vegetable also has an excellent freezer life after being cooked. When ready to serve, pre-heat oven to 375°F and place serving dish on middle rack for about 20 minutes or until fully heated. If karelas are frozen, then thaw at room temperature before putting in oven. Remove foil from piping-hot dish and garnish with fresh coriander and julienned ginger root.

Serve with lachedar parathas cooked with clarified butter. For extra flavour add some melted butter over karelas just before serving, and you'll truly have a treat fit for the maharajas.

Tawa Masala Paneer

THIS DELICACY CAN ALSO BE PREPARED IN A WOK OR FRYING PAN. IT IS BEST WHEN FRESHLY COOKED just before serving. Paneer cooked in this fashion can be served as an accompaniment to a main course or used as a filling for sandwiches or wraps. It is an excellent delicacy for vegetarians, and a hit amongst non-vegetarians as well.

INGREDIENTS:

1 lb paneer, cubed into ½"

Vegetable oil for deep-frying paneer

4 tbs clarified butter

½ tsp cumin seeds, rubbed between palms

½ small onion, finely chopped

1 tbs garlic paste

1 tbs ginger paste

2 green chilies, chopped

1 tsp red chili powder

1 tsp coriander powder

½ tsp garam masala

¼ tsp ajwain, rubbed

Salt to taste

½ cup tomatoes, diced

½ cup green peppers, cubed

½ cup red peppers, cubed

1 onion, cut into half horizontally and then quartered

1 tbs ginger, julienned

2 tbs fresh coriander leaves, chopped

½ of fresh lime

METHOD:

Heat oil in wok and deep-fry paneer until golden brown. Drain on paper towel and keep fried paneer aside.

Heat butter on tawa and add cumin seeds. As soon as seeds start to sputter add chopped onions and brown them. Next, add garlic and ginger pastes, chilies, coriander powder, chili powder, garam masala, ajwain, and salt and stir-fry mixture on medium heat for a few minutes.

Then add tomatoes and julienned ginger root and continue to cook until a rich masala paste forms.

Turn heat to medium-high and add fried paneer, quartered onions, and cubed peppers and continue to stir-fry all ingredients for another few minutes, until well glazed with masala.

Finally, garnish with fresh coriander leaves and squeeze lime juice all over just before serving.

Shahi Badami Paneer

A DELICIOUS DELIGHT INTRODUCED TO MY FAMILY BY MY GRANDFATHER, THIS TRULY IS A DELICACY enjoyed by the rich and famous of northern India. The harmony of the nuts and cream, blend of spices, and paneer takes you back to the time of the Moghul Empire in India.

INGREDIENTS:

1 lb paneer, cubed and golden-fried

4 oz cashews

4 oz almonds, skinless

1 medium onion, finely chopped

1 tbs ginger root, finely chopped

1 tsp garlic paste

1 green chili, chopped

½ tsp turmeric

1 tsp cardamom powder

1 tsp Kasoori methi

1 tomato, diced

1 cup hung yogurt

½ tsp garam masala

3 tbs cooking oil

Salt and pepper to taste

¼ cup fresh cream

¼ cup fresh coriander leaves, chopped

METHOD:

Heat oil in pan and add onions, Kasoori methi, ginger root, garlic paste, green chili, chili powder, turmeric, and garam masala. Sauté mixture until golden brown. Add diced tomato and cook for 5 minutes, then add yogurt, salt, and pepper. Turn heat off. Once sauce has cooled, using hand blender puree mixture.

Grind cashews and almonds. For best results always slightly toast nuts before grinding. Add ground nuts and cardamom powder to sauce and mix well.

Just before serving, heat sauce well, add fried paneer and cream, and stir lightly. Garnish with fresh coriander. Serve hot with your favourite Indian bread or a rice pilaf.

Stir-Fried Asian Vegetables

THIS COLOURFUL SELECTION OF VEGETABLES ADDS FLAIR TO YOUR MAIN COURSE. THE BEAUTY OF this dish is in offering a limitless choice of your favourite greens and being extremely easy and quick to prepare.

INGREDIENTS:

4 tbs vegetable or peanut oil

½ tsp garlic paste

1 tbs chili paste

1 tbs fresh ginger root, julienned

1 cup Chinese cabbage, shredded

2 stems bok choy, washed and cut into 1" pieces

1 large carrot, washed, peeled, and cut into 1/8"-thick discs

8 whole baby corn

½ cup fresh snow peas

½ cup fresh green beans

½ cup small white mushrooms, cut in half

½ cup green pepper, cut into small pieces

2 stems green onions, chopped

½ cup vegetable stock

2 tbs light soy sauce

1 tbs cornstarch

Salt and pepper to taste

½ tsp granulated sugar

METHOD:

In wok heat oil, add garlic and chili pastes, and stir well. Immediately add all vegetables and stir-fry for a few minutes. Now add vegetable stock, stir, cover wok, and cook for another 2 minutes on high heat.

In small cup combine soy sauce, cornstarch, salt, and pepper with 2 tbs cold water. Mix well and set aside.

Gently remove vegetables from wok using slotted spoon and keep aside. Now add soy sauce mixture to wok and mix well. Bring to a boil, stirring constantly until mixture thickens slightly, and then stir in sugar.

Return vegetables to wok, toss gently in thickened sauce, and heat through. Transfer vegetables to platter and serve immediately. Steamed rice makes a good accompaniment to these succulent vegetables.

Bhindi Kurkuri

THESE CRUNCHY LADY'S-FINGERS WILL MAKE AN ELEGANT VEGETARIAN ACCOMPANIMENT TO YOUR dining table spread at your next gathering.

INGREDIENTS:

1 kg fresh tender okra

Salt to taste

1 tsp red chili powder

1 tsp garam masala

1 tsp amchoor

1 tsp anardana powder

3 tbs besan

Oil for deep-frying

1 tbs fresh ginger root, finely julienned

1 lemon, cut into 8 wedges

2 finger hot green chilies, slit lengthwise 4 times

METHOD:

Clean okra with dry cloth, snip off ends of each finger, and slice them lengthwise into halves. Spread cut okra on flat cookie sheet. In bowl mix all spices and besan and sprinkle evenly over okra, mixing well so all okra is evenly coated.

Heat oil in wok until it is smoking. Then gently add okra to hot oil without overcrowding. Using fork, separate

and turn okra pieces to keep them from sticking to each other. Remove okra when crispy and brown on both sides and place on paper towel.

Arrange neatly on serving platter and garnish with julienned ginger root, chili slices, and lemon wedges.

Punjabi Pakora Kadhi

JUST LIKE SARSON DA SAAG AND MAKI DI ROTI (CURRIED MUSTARD GREENS SERVED WITH CORN bread laced with butter) excites any Punjabi, kadhi is the other delicacy guaranteed to win any Punjabi's heart. Almost every state in India has its own kadhi specialty and Punjab boasts its very own that is flavourful, thick, creamy, and silky smooth. A preparation of yogurt, besan, onions, and masalas, this is a delicacy that can be prepared in a jiffy, unless one is making it with pakoras. Punjabi kadhi makes a scrumptious Sunday lunch and is often served with plain steamed or cumin rice. Many like it with buttered tandoori rotis or phulkas.

The following recipe is my mother's favourite, which she inherited from her mother. I am sure I will pass this on to my granddaughter and the legacy will live on for generations to come.

INGREDIENTS FOR SAUCE:

3 cups fresh homemade yogurt

1½ cups besan, well sifted

1 tsp red chili powder or deggi mirch

½ tsp turmeric

5 tbs vegetable oil

1 medium onion, thinly sliced

2 tbs ginger root, julienned

3 cups water

INGREDIENTS FOR PAKORA DUMPLINGS:

½ medium onion, diced into ¼"

1 medium potato, diced small

1 tbs coriander, finely chopped

4 green chilies, chopped

½ tsp ajwain

Salt to taste

¼ tsp baking soda

Oil for deep-frying

INGREDIENTS FOR TARKA (TEMPERING):

2 tbs cooking oil

¼ tsp hing (optional)

1 tbs ginger root, finely chopped

½ tsp cumin seeds

½ tsp coriander seeds, slightly crushed

¼ tsp fenugreek seeds

4 whole red chilies, dried

6 curry leaves

3 red chilies, dried

3 cloves

2 cinnamon stick pieces, 2" long

¼ tsp mustard seeds

2 tbs coriander, finely chopped, for garnish

METHOD:

In mixing bowl, whisk yogurt, half of besan, salt, red chili powder, and turmeric powder. Mix well and keep aside.

Sift other half of besan into bowl and add baking soda, onions, potatoes, green chilies, ajwain, and salt. Mix well and make into thick batter by adding water to mixture.

Heat enough oil in wok to fry pakoras. Gently drop tablespoons full of batter into hot oil to make 1½" puffed-up pakoras. Fry all pakoras until evenly golden brown. Remove fried pakoras, drain, and keep aside on paper towel.

Next heat 3 tbs oil in pot and sauté sliced onions along with ginger root for a few minutes. Then gently add whisked yogurt mixture and stir well. Add 3 cups water, bring to a boil, reduce heat to medium, and simmer for about 30 minutes, stirring constantly to keep yogurt from curdling. Gently add fried pakoras to pot and simmer for another 4 to 5 minutes.

In small frying pan heat remaining 2 tbs oil and add hing, ginger root, cumin, coriander seeds, mustard seeds, fenugreek seeds, curry leaves, cloves, whole red chilies, and cinnamon pieces and sauté until cumin and mustard seeds start to crackle. Stir and immediately pour this tarka over silky-smooth kadhi.

Transfer kadhi to serving dish and garnish with fresh coriander. Serve with steamed basmati rice or tandoori rotis. Fried ginger root slices in butter and fresh sliced daikon make good condiments for this delicacy. Ambarsari black pepper papads would complete the meal.

Dhaba-Style Daal Amritsari

THIS LENTIL DELICACY COMES FROM A DHABA, A ROADSIDE EATERY OUTSIDE THE GOLDEN TEMPLE IN Amritsar, the holy city of the Sikhs. Many years ago, I enjoyed this daal near the temple, and its taste and flavours have been tantalizing my taste buds ever since. Interestingly, this dish hardly has any spices.

INGREDIENTS:

1 cup urad daal

½ cup channa daal

2 tbs fresh ginger root, chopped

1 tbs garlic, chopped

3 finger hot green chilies, chopped

½ cup onions, diced

½ cup fresh tomatoes, diced

1 tsp Kasoori methi

¼ lb butter

¼ cup fresh coriander stems, chopped

½ cup whole milk

Salt to taste

METHOD:

Spread both types of daal on flat dish, pick out any stones, and discard. Thoroughly wash daal in running water and soak in warm water for about 1 hour. Place drained daal in heavy-bottomed pot and add about 1 tsp salt along with about 8 cups water. Bring water to a boil on high heat and then reduce heat to low. Remove and discard any scum that appears on surface. Now add half of ginger and garlic to daal and stir. Add coriander stems, cover pot, and let simmer until two-thirds of liquid has evaporated and daals are almost cooked.

In small frying pan, heat butter, onions, and remaining ginger and garlic and sauté until onions are slightly browned. Now add green chilies, Kasoori methi, and tomatoes and stir well. Cook mixture until tomatoes are fully mashed. Transfer mixture from frying pan to pot and stir well, adding milk and letting daal simmer for about 15 minutes. Taste daal and make any necessary adjustments. Just before serving, garnish daal with julienned ginger root and fresh coriander. Serve with tandoori rotis or phulkas. You may add extra butter or ghee just before serving.

Kashmiri Dum Aloo

KASHMIRI CUISINE IS USUALLY RICH, FLAVOURFUL, AND DELICATELY SPICED. ONE OF THE MOST popular vegetarian dishes from Kashmir is dum aloo.

This delicacy is often served in restaurants all over India with a creamy and slightly sweet sauce that has nut paste in the preparation. The authentic Kashmiri dum aloo is cooked with yogurt, fennel, ginger powder, and a few other spices, and these babies are served coated and infused with spices and hardly any sauce or gravy. Potatoes are usually pricked before deep-frying so they can absorb all the flavours.

Having eaten the real Kashmiri dum aloo in Srinagar a few decades back, I have tried to cook it many times. After several disasters, I think I finally have a good recipe to share with you here.

INGREDIENTS:

1 kg small new potatoes, peeled, all same size

¼ tsp asafoetida

1½ tsp coriander powder

1 tsp garam masala

1½ tsp red chili powder

1½ tsp cumin seeds

1 tsp turmeric powder

2 green cardamom pods, mashed

2 cloves

1 bay leaf

1 cinnamon stick, 1" long

1½ cups yogurt

Salt to taste

Oil for frying

2 tbs fresh coriander leaves, finely chopped

METHOD:

Heat oil in wok and prick potatoes with fork. Deep-fry potatoes until golden brown. Remove and drain them with slotted spoon and keep aside.

In saucepan heat 3 tbs vegetable oil and add all remaining spice powders and spices except coriander leaves. Mix well and stir-fry until golden brown. Add fried potatoes, beaten yogurt, and 1 cup water. Mix well, cover pot

with tight lid, and cook until potatoes are just tender but not overdone. Please do not allow sauce to dry out completely; you may sprinkle a little water occasionally if required.

Transfer potatoes into serving dish, garnish with coriander leaves, and serve immediately with pooris or rice.

Maharaja Shahi Paneer

THIS INDIAN COTTAGE CHEESE PREPARATION IS FIT FOR KINGS. IT'S A LITTLE RICH, BUT ONCE IN A while one should be able to indulge a bit without worrying about the battle with the bulge. Trust me—you won't regret experiencing this fabulous delicacy.

INGREDIENTS:

750 gm paneer

FILLING:

5 tbs khoya

2 tsp cashews, crushed

1 tbs tomato paste

1 tbs prepared hot lemon pickle masala

BATTER:

5 tbs corn flour

½ tsp salt

1 pinch yellow food colour

Water as required

SAUCE:

2 tbs clarified butter

1 tbs garlic paste

1 tbs ginger paste

2 cups tomatoes, crushed

1 tbs tomato paste

1 tsp red chili powder

1 pinch fenugreek leaves

1 tsp garam masala

1 tbs magaz, crushed

1 tbs cashews, crushed

Salt to taste

½ cup heavy cream

12 cashews, toasted

1 tbs fresh coriander leaves, finely chopped

Vegetable oil for deep-frying

METHOD:

Cut paneer into ¼"x1"-long strips. Using 1"-diameter round cookie cutter cut discs and keep aside. Try not to waste too much paneer when cutting discs, and save scraps and crumbles to use in sauce later.

For filling mix all filling ingredients and place small amount of stuffing between two paneer discs, pressing gently. Set aside.

For batter, mix all batter ingredients, making sure batter is not runny, but slightly thick.

Heat oil in wok and gently dip each disc into batter, coating evenly, and then drop it into oil carefully without letting stuffing escape while frying. Fry for about 3 minutes, then remove, drain excess oil, and keep fried discs aside.

Heat butter in saucepan, and add garlic and ginger pastes, red chili powder, garam masala, fenugreek leaves, crushed magaz, cashews, and salt. Sauté mixture for about 5 minutes on medium heat and continue stirring constantly. Next, add crushed tomatoes and paste to pan and cook for about 10 minutes until sauce thickens slightly. Gently whisk cream into sauce and turn heat off.

Arrange fried paneer sandwiches neatly in shallow platter and pour hot sauce over paneer. Garnish by placing 1 piece of cashew on each disc and sprinkling with coriander leaves. Serve hot with a rice pilaf or lachedar parathas.

Sarson Da Saag

THE WINTER IS PUNJAB'S GREATEST SEASON; THE WEATHER IS CLEMENT AND THE HARVEST IS IN. THE fields are full of mustard and spinach greens, and it is during this season of mellow mists that the Punjabis eat their regional delicacy: sarson da saag and makki di roti.

We often had this delicacy in Kenya and later in Canada, where we used rapini greens as a substitute for spinach. But this preparation was in no way close to what I enjoyed in a village in the Punjab a few years ago. The hot bowl of saag was laced with fresh homemade white butter and served with makki di roti, green chilies, and fried ginger root.

Several years ago we took our son to the village in the Punjab, where my in-laws hail from, and enjoyed this exquisite Punjabi meal. Our son fell in love with it too, and to this day recalls his dining experience. The following is my recipe, which comes fairly close to the village preparation.

INGREDIENTS:

1 kg mustard greens, washed and finely chopped

¼ kg spinach, washed and finely chopped

1 large onion, finely chopped

3 finger hot green chilies, chopped

½ cup clarified butter

3 tbs fresh ginger root, chopped

2 tbs garlic paste

4 whole small green chilies

TEMPERING:

2 tbs fresh ginger root, julienned

2 cloves garlic, finely chopped

2 tbs gram flour, sifted

Salt to taste

METHOD:

In large pot heat 4 tbs clarified butter and sauté onions lightly. Add chopped green chilies, chopped ginger root, and garlic paste and stir-fry for 1 minute. Then add greens and enough water to cook greens until soft. When greens are cooked, mash and reserve. Should there be excess water, carefully skim it and discard.

In small saucepan heat remaining butter and add whole slit chilies, julienned ginger, chopped garlic, and salt.

Sauté mixture until lightly browned, and immediately add to mashed saag. Next, add gram flour and mix well. Simmer saag for another 20 minutes. Serve hot with butter and makki di roti. You may also serve it with buttered tandoori rotis or parathas. Punjabis love sliced onions, daikon, and butter-fried slices of fresh ginger root. The icing on this meal is more home-churned butter and jaggery.

Fried Tofu With Peanut Sauce

THIS IS ANOTHER EXCITING APPETIZER FOR VEGETARIANS THAT CAN ADD A TOUCH OF CLASS TO YOUR dinner table at your next gathering. This is truly a delicacy for social gatherings, and your guests can help themselves with cocktail forks or fancy sticks.

INGREDIENTS:

1 lb firm plain tofu (bean curd)

5 tbs all-purpose flour

2 whole eggs

4 tbs milk

½ tsp baking powder

½ tsp chili powder

Oil for deep-frying

For peanut sauce see Malaysian Peanut Sauce recipe (page XX). Please note that to make dish totally vegetarian you may omit fish sauce and substitute soy sauce.

METHOD:

Cut tofu into 1" triangles and keep aside.

For batter sift flour into bowl and gently whisk in beaten eggs and milk. Stir in baking powder and chili powders and mix well to form a nice, creamy batter.

Heat oil in wok, dip tofu triangles in batter, and deep-fry until golden brown. Remove and drain fried tofu and place onto paper towel. Arrange tofu on platter and serve with peanut sauce.

Stir-Fried Asparagus, Cauliflower, And Carrots

THIS IS A VERY SIMPLE VEGETABLE DISH AND YOU MAY ADD TOFU, MUSHROOMS, ONIONS, BELL peppers, and string beans to make it more colourful. I enjoyed this dish in Penang with fish sauce in it. I have slightly modified the recipe to make it vegetarian and am using dark soy sauce instead of the nam pla.

INGREDIENTS:

8 oz tender asparagus

1 large carrot, peeled

½ head small cauliflower, cut into small florets

2 tsp fresh garlic, coarsely chopped

1 tsp fresh basil leaves, chopped

2 tsp dark soy sauce

1 tsp fresh ginger root, julienned

1 tsp palm sugar

4 tbs water

1 tsp chili oil

3 tbs cooking oil

METHOD:

Wash and drain asparagus, discard any tough portions, and cut into halves. Wash and drain florets of cauliflower and set aside in plate with asparagus. Cut carrot into small discs, about ¼" thick, cook in boiling water for a couple minutes, drain, and place onto plate with other vegetables.

In wok heat cooking oil, add garlic and sauté for 1 minute, then add cauliflower florets and stir. Add chili oil, ginger root, basil, palm sugar, soy sauce, and asparagus. Mix well and add water and carrots. Keep stirring until all liquid has dried. Transfer to serving dish and serve hot with steamed rice and other main course entrées.

Gobi Ka Keema

MY VEGETARIAN FRIENDS WOULD LOVE ME FOR THIS AMAZING RECIPE INSPIRED BY MY DEAR FRIEND Salman Sheikh Khan from Atlanta, Georgia, in the USA. After visiting us with his family, Salman said that he was inspired by me to whip up gobi keema, so he tried his hand in his kitchen and surprisingly came up with a winner! He texted me a picture of his precious dish, and I was so impressed and wanted to dig in so badly that I was compelled to recreate it with a twist. Remarkably, with the first mouthful of this delicacy I experienced a tsunami of flavours in my mouth—all thanks to up-and-coming chef Salman Sheikh.

INGREDIENTS:

1 head cauliflower

¾ cup green peas, fresh or frozen

1 medium onion, diced or finely chopped

1 tsp Kasoori methi

1 pinch hing

1 finger hot green chili, finely chopped

½ cup pureed tomatoes

1 tbs ginger paste

1 tsp turmeric powder

1 tsp garam masala

1 tsp deggi mirch

½ tsp coriander powder, coarsely ground

1 tsp cumin seeds

½ cup fresh coriander stems, finely chopped

2 tbs oil

1 tbs butter

Salt to taste

Fresh coriander for garnish

METHOD:

Clean cauliflower and discard stems. Cut and separate florets and coarsely chop them fairly small by hand or food processor.

In frying pan heat about 1 tbs oil, add grated cauliflower, and gently pan-fry on medium heat until it starts to turn light golden brown. With slotted spoon remove pan-fried cauliflower and keep aside.

Next, in same pan heat remaining oil and butter and add cumin seeds, hing, and Kasoori methi, and as soon as cumin starts to sizzle add onions, chopped chili, ginger, turmeric, and green peas (please note that I used frozen peas and defrosted them before adding to pan by cooking them for 1 minute in microwave). Mix well and sauté

for a few minutes, then gradually add tomato puree and garam masala. Stir well and let sauce simmer for another few minutes.

Next, add coriander stems, fried cauliflower, and salt. Mix well, cover pan, and let cook, stirring occasionally to avoid scorching. Once all liquid has dried up, gobi keema is ready to be served.

Garnish dish with fresh coriander. You may wish to squeeze it with fresh lemon or lime before serving. Serve with lachedar parathas, tandoori naan, or rotis. I think hot pooris would go great too. This delicacy would make an excellent filling for wraps or sandwiches as well.

Khatte Chaat Patte Tamatri Aloo

THIS IS A DELICACY THAT I HAVE ADAPTED FROM THE GUJARATI KITCHENS IN KENYA. IT IS AN EASY-peasy recipe that goes great with pooris or bhaturas for Saturday or Sunday lunch or brunch gatherings. In Kenya we used to enjoy these potatoes with tikki or jeera pooris and sometimes with thin Gujarati-style chapatis. Sweet lemon pickles or spicy-hot lemon and chili pickles were a must with this meal.

INGREDIENTS:

1 kg small red potatoes, boiled and peeled

3 tbs vegetable oil

3 red chilies, dried

8 curry leaves

1 tsp mustard seeds

½ tsp cumin seeds

1 small cinnamon piece

4 whole cloves

1 tsp ginger paste

½ tsp garlic paste

1 tsp coriander powder

½ tsp turmeric powder

1 tsp deggi mirch or paprika

Salt and pepper to taste

4 large ripe tomatoes, diced

Fresh coriander for garnish

½ cup warm water if needed

METHOD:

In large saucepan heat oil and add red chilies, curry leaves, mustard seeds, cinnamon stick, cloves, and cumin seeds and as soon as mustard seeds start to sputter, add ginger and garlic pastes and mix well. Immediately add coriander powder, turmeric powder, deggi mirch, salt, and pepper. Mix all ingredients well and sauté for a few minutes, ensuring that garlic and ginger pastes do not start to burn. Next, add diced tomatoes, mix well, and cook mixture for a few minutes on high heat, stirring occasionally. Turn heat down and let sauce simmer until all tomatoes are well blended into sauce and oil starts to separate.

Cut peeled potatoes into eighths and gently add to cooked sauce. Gently stir potatoes into sauce and if sauce is too dry add some more water. Simmer dish for another few minutes.

For best results, let dish stand for a few hours before serving. Just before serving, thoroughly heat dish, plate on serving bowl, and garnish with fresh coriander.

Khumb Mattar Korma Curry With Cashews

GREEN PEAS AND PANEER CURRY IS A COMMON DISH PREPARED IN MANY INDIAN KITCHENS. Replacing paneer with mushrooms and roasted cashews takes this delicacy a notch higher and adds elegance to your meal. The mushrooms and crunchy nuts in this dish prove to be an amazing combination.

INGREDIENTS:

1 lb fresh green peas, shelled

½ lb small-sized white mushrooms, cut into halves

2 tbs clarified butter

1 tbs vegetable oil

½ cup onions, diced

1 tsp garlic paste

1 tbs ginger root paste

2 green chilies, seeded and finely chopped

1 tsp turmeric powder

1 tsp deggi mirch

¼ tsp cinnamon powder

½ tsp garam masala

1 cup fresh ripe tomatoes, crushed

2 tbs fresh coriander stems, finely chopped

1 cup warm water as needed

½ cup half-and-half

½ cup cashews, roasted

Salt to taste

Fresh coriander for garnish

METHOD:

In saucepan heat butter and oil and add onions and garlic and ginger pastes and sauté until golden brown. Add green chilies, turmeric powder, deggi mirch, cinnamon powder, and garam masala and stir mixture well. Next, add crushed tomatoes and coriander stems. Cook for about 4 minutes and then add fresh peas, mushrooms, and water as needed. Stir mixture well and add salt. Cover pan and cook for another 10 minutes on medium heat, stirring occasionally.

Once peas seem fully cooked and fat starts to separate from sauce, add half of cashews, gently mix curry, and gradually add cream, simmering for a few minutes. Allow preparation to rest for at least 6 hours before serving to achieve best flavour.

Just before serving heat korma curry well and garnish with chopped coriander and remaining cashews. Serve with jeera rice, hot buttered naan, lachedar parathas, or garma garam buttered phulkas.

Manchurian Tofu

IN MANY PARTS OF INDIA, THE CHINESE HAVE MADE HAKKA AND MANCHURIAN STYLES OF COOKING very popular for a long time. This type of Chinese cooking is fairly hot and compatible with many Indian masala dishes.

This trend in Chinese cooking has inspired me to share some recipes from my own kitchen. For starters, I'll feature a tofu dish that can be easily adapted for chicken, shrimp, fish, or vegetables.

INGREDIENTS:

1 lb firm tofu, cubed

1 lemon

½ tsp garlic powder

Salt and pepper to taste

MANCHURIAN SAUCE:

2 whole bunches spring onions, washed, cleaned, and finely chopped

1 tbs ginger paste

1 tbs garlic paste

1 cup fresh tomatoes, chopped

3 finger hot green chilies

½ tsp turmeric

½ tsp red chili powder

½ cup fresh coriander stems, chopped

1 tbs soy sauce

2 tbs hoisin sauce

2 tbs tomato paste

2 tbs fresh coriander leaves, chopped

1 tbs fresh ginger root, julienned

1 tbs butter

3 tbs cooking oil

½ red bell pepper, cut into cubes

½ green bell pepper, cut into cubes

1 medium onion, cubed

Fresh coriander, chopped, for garnish

Ginger root, julienned, for garnish

Green chilies for garnish

METHOD:

In mixing bowl place tofu and add garlic powder, salt, and pepper and mix well. Now squeeze juice from 1 lemon onto tofu and mix well. Cover bowl and let tofu marinate for at least 1 hour or so.

In heated saucepan add cooking oil and butter. Add onions to pan. Make sure to chop up whole spring onions, including green parts. Sauté onions for about 5 minutes, then add garlic, ginger, and green chilies and keep stirring. Now add turmeric and chili powder and keep stirring for another minute. Then add tomatoes and coriander stems.

Cook sauce for another 5 minutes and then add soy sauce, hoisin sauce, and tomato paste. Sauce should be almost ready when fat starts to separate from masala. You may wish to discard any excess fat from sauce.

Pour juices from bowl with marinated tofu. Cook sauce for a minute or two. Check seasoning of sauce and make any necessary adjustments. Sauce should not be too dry and thick like a paste; it should have some fluid so it can easily coat tofu chunks. But make sure it is not runny. Next, add peppers and cubed onions and gently mix well.

Now in shallow ovenproof pan, spread half of sauce and gently lay tofu cubes on top. Then smother remainder of sauce on top of tofu, covering all pieces, and let sit.

When ready to serve, pre-heat oven to 500°F and place tofu onto middle rack. Cook for about 5 minutes, until tofu starts to sizzle. Immediately remove pan from oven and garnish with fresh coriander leaves, ginger root, and hot chilies.

You may wish to skip the oven step and quickly stir-fry everything in a big wok. Serve piping hot with steamed basmati rice or noodles.

Medley Of Sweet Baby Peppers With Mushrooms And Onions

THIS COLOURFUL VEGETARIAN DISH IS AN EXCELLENT ADDITION TO ANY LUNCH, BRUNCH, OR DINNER buffet, and a succulent, crunchy, and healthy dish for any gathering overall. I have served this simple and easy-to-prepare dish at many functions and it has always been a hit.

INGREDIENTS:

1 lb baby sweet peppers, different colours

½ lb medium-sized white mushrooms

1 medium onion, peeled and sliced

2 tbs olive oil

½ tsp garlic paste

1 tsp ginger paste

1 tbs Worcestershire sauce

1 tbs brown onion paste

1 tsp hot sauce

Salt to taste

½ fresh lemon

METHOD:

Wash and wipe peppers and slice and discard tops. Cut all peppers in half and deseed. Put peppers in bowl. Next, wipe mushrooms clean, cut into halves, and add to peppers. Then cut peeled <u>onion</u> in half, slice, and add to bowl.

In large frying pan or wok, heat olive oil, add garlic and ginger pastes, stir well, and cook for a few minutes. Then add onion paste and Worcestershire and hot sauces, and mix well. Add all cut-up ingredients and mix well.

Continue to stir-fry vegetables on high heat for a few minutes and do not overcook. Add salt, immediately plate dish, squeeze juice of 1 fresh lemon on veggies, and serve.

One may use cauliflower florets, sugar or snow peas, green beans, baby corn, baby carrots, celery, and asparagus spears in this vegetarian delight. For added heat please feel free to add finger hot green chilies. Garnishing with sliced spring onions also gives it a classy touch.

Pav Bhaaji

MY FORMER ROOMMATE IN SASKATOON WAS FROM MAHARASHTRA AND ALWAYS USED TO RAVE ABOUT pav bhaaji. On a few occasions he cooked this delicacy for us, but honestly, I did not like it. However, when I visited Mumbai for the first time, I had to try this street food. It was amazingly tasty and very different from what my roommate had prepared.

This is a spicy fast food that originated on the streets of Mumbai and over the years has become very popular all over India. Pav originates from the Portuguese word "pao" meaning "bread." Bhaaji in Marathi means "a vegetarian dish."

The origin of this dish can be traced to textile mill workers in Mumbai in the 1850s. The mill workers used to have lunch breaks too short for a full meal, and a light lunch was preferred to a heavy one, as employees had to return to performing strenuous physical labour after lunch. A vendor would create this dish using portions of other dishes available. Roti or rice was replaced with pav, and the curries that usually go with Indian bread or rice were amalgamated into just one spicy concoction, the bhaaji. Initially, it remained the food of the mill workers. But with time the dish found its way into some restaurants. Interestingly, the popularity of this dish has over the years led it to creep into many Indian restaurants serving fast food in Singapore, Hong Kong, New York, London, and Switzerland.

The recipe for pav bhaaji varies greatly, as it is essentially a fast-food dish prepared quickly using any available fresh vegetables. A special blend of spices, the pav bhaaji masala, is added to the pan-fried vegetable mush with loads of butter and then served on top of a buttered bun. The bun is buttered on both sides and slightly toasted, and the pav bhaaji filling is garnished with diced onions, green chilies, and cilantro.

The following is a recipe that I have often used for large gatherings.

INGREDIENTS FOR PAV BHAAJI MASALA POWDER:

1 tsp garlic powder

2 tbs ginger powder

2 tbs onion flakes, dried

2 whole black cardamoms

4 green cardamoms

¼ cup coriander seeds

4 tbs amchoor

¼ cup cumin seeds

1 tbs black peppercorns

2 cinnamon sticks

10 whole red chilies, dried

2 tbs fennel seeds

8 whole red chilies, dried

INGREDIENTS FOR PAV BHAAJI:

½ cup vegetable oil

½ tsp garlic, chopped

1 tsp green chili peppers, finely chopped

1 cup onions, chopped

2 tsp fresh ginger, grated

1 cup vine-ripe tomatoes, chopped

1 cup cauliflower, finely chopped

1 cup green peas

1 cup carrots, grated

4 potatoes, boiled and mashed

3 tbs pav bhaaji masala

Salt to taste

1 fresh lemon

4 tbs butter

8 dinner rolls, 2" squares

½ tbs butter

¼ cup onions, finely diced

1 tbs green chili peppers, finely chopped

¼ cup fresh cilantro, chopped

METHOD:

In a mini grinder add all masala ingredients and grind into coarse powder. Store in airtight container.

Heat oil in wok over medium heat and sauté garlic and green chili for 1 minute, and then stir in onions and ginger. Cook until onions are brown. Add tomatoes, and cook until tomatoes are well blended. Stir in cauliflower, cabbage, peas, carrots, and potatoes. Season mixture with pav bhaaji masala. Cover and cook for 15 to 20 minutes, until veggies are cooked, and make sure to stir occasionally. Add salt and squeeze juice of lemon all over bhaaji. Just before serving add butter, mix well, and garnish with chopped onions and coriander. Serve bhaaji hot on lightly toasted buttered buns.

Shahi Mattar Paneer Curry

MATTAR PANEER CURRY IS A FAIRLY COMMON DISH PREPARED IN INDIAN KITCHENS ALL OVER THE globe, and I am sure every household has its own recipe. In earlier times one could not buy readymade paneer like one can today and thus had to make this cheese from scratch.

This is a simple and delicious vegetarian curried preparation with paneer and fresh garden peas that I simply adore. I recall during my younger days growing up in Kenya, every wedding reception used to serve this delicacy and I always overindulged. I still remember the flavours and seasonings that made this such a special dish, and am pleased to share my childhood memories with you all through my recipe.

INGREDIENTS:

1 lb fresh green peas, shelled

½ lb fresh paneer, cut in ¾" cubes and lightly deep-fried

3 tbs clarified butter

1 tbs vegetable oil

¾ cup onions, diced

1 tsp garlic paste

1 tbs ginger root paste

2 green chilies, finely chopped

1 tsp turmeric powder

1 tsp deggi mirch

1 tsp Kasoori methi

1 tsp cinnamon powder

1 tsp garam masala (homemade)

1 cup fresh ripe tomatoes, crushed

2 tbs fresh coriander stems and roots, finely chopped

1 cup or more warm water

Salt to taste

Fresh coriander and green chilies for garnish

GARAM MASALA:

1 tbs coriander seeds

1 tbs cumin seeds

1 bay leaf

½ tsp fennel seeds

¼ tsp nutmeg

6 black peppercorns

4 cloves

6 green cardamom pods

2 small cinnamon sticks

METHOD:

Lightly roast all garam masala ingredients in pan. As soon as spices start to release their aromas, take pan off heat and allow to cool. When spices have cooled, coarsely grind masala and store for future use.

In saucepan heat butter and oil, add onions and garlic and ginger pastes, and sauté until golden brown. Add green chilies, coriander stems and roots, turmeric powder, deggi mirch, Kasoori methi, cinnamon powder, and homemade garam masala and stir mixture well. Next, add crushed tomatoes and cook for about 5 minutes, then add fresh peas and water (you may use frozen peas but make sure to thaw them before using).

Stir mixture well and add salt. Cover pan and simmer for another 10 to 15 minutes, stirring occasionally.

Once peas are fully cooked and fat starts to separate from gravy, add fried paneer, gently mix well, and let simmer for another few minutes. Let preparation rest for at least 6 hours before serving, as this will enhance taste and flavour.

Just before serving, heat well and garnish with chopped coriander. Serve with hot buttered naan, lachedar parathas, or garma garam buttered phulkas. This delicacy tastes great with plain pooris as well.

Spiced Bhindi With Piaz

MY MOTHER USED TO MAKE STUFFED BHINDIS WITH A BLEND OF SPICES AND THIS DELICACY WAS very popular with the family. These days we are always looking for easy and quicker ways of creating good food, without having to go through the tedious processes that our parents were accustomed to. So I have come up with a magic masala blend that I call "Mag's Sabzi Masala." It works amazingly well for bhindis, karelas, aloos, and baingans. You may have some other brilliant uses for this precious blend as well.

INGREDIENTS:

1 kg fresh bhindis

3 tbs cooking oil

2 tbs clarified butter

1 large onion, sliced

1 tbs ginger paste

2 green chilies, seeded and sliced

2 tbs Mag's Masala Blend*

Salt and pepper to taste

Fresh coriander for garnish

Ginger root, julienned, for garnish

*Mag's Sabzi Masala:

1 tbs coriander seeds, coarsely ground

1 tsp ajwain, coarsely ground

1 tbs cumin, toasted and ground

1 tbs homemade garam masala (see page 14)

½ tsp cardamom powder

½ tsp cinnamon powder

1 tbs amchoor

2 tbs pomegranate seeds, ground

1 tbs saunf

1 tbs garlic powder

1 tbs ginger powder

2 tbs onion flakes, dehydrated and ground

2 tbs turmeric powder

Salt and pepper to taste

METHOD:

In large bowl gently mix all masala ingredients. Taste blend with tip of finger and make any necessary taste adjustments to your liking. Store magic blend in airtight container and use as required. It is always best to make a small batch first to get the right combination of spices. Once you have achieved the required flavours and seasonings, then this could be your own signature blend and you may wish to make a larger batch and store it.

Wipe bhindis clean with paper towel and cut and discard tops. Using sharp paring knife make slits in all bhindis and set aside. Cut onion in half and peel. Slice onion and set aside. In large frying pan heat oil and sauté ginger paste and sliced chilies. Immediately add bhindis and gently stir them and cook for a few minutes. Add half of Mag's Masala Blend and stir bhindis well. Turn heat to medium and cover pan. Cook for another 5 minutes or until bhindis are almost done, being very careful not to overcook; bhindis should maintain a slight crunch. Taste and make any necessary adjustments seasoning.

Gently remove bhindis with slotted spoon and set aside. Next, add sliced onions to same pan along with remaining Mag's Masala Blend, and stir-fry onions for a few minutes, just enough to sweat them. Transfer fried onions to serving platter and neatly arrange bhindis on top. Garnish with fresh chopped coriander and julienned ginger root. Finally, the finishing touch: pour clarified butter over bhindis, then reheat platter and serve piping hot with tandoori rotis or lachedar parathas.

Note: If stuffing bhindis, baingans, aloos, or karelas, then make paste by adding some oil and tomato paste to Mag's Masala Blend. Mix well and use paste for stuffing.

SPICY SPINACH
– SAAG

Stuffed Baby Eggplants, Sweet Peppers, And Lady's-Fingers

BABY EGGPLANTS, SWEET PEPPERS, AND OKRAS ARE STUFFED WITH AN EXOTIC SPICE MIXTURE AND pan-fried to perfection in this recipe. This delicacy is indeed a treat for vegetarians and fit for royalty.

Stuffed vegetables, where vegetables take centre stage, are an easy way to make your dinner table elegant. If a vegetable can be stuffed, an Indian chef will stuff it, even potatoes. The stuffing can be traditional or more avant garde—feel free to play with the spices and herbs to suit your taste. Just be careful when stuffing, as softer veggies may have the tendency to ooze while cooking. When serving stuffed vegetables, either arrange whole vegetables on dinner plates with the sauce on the side, or split them lengthwise and drizzle the sauce over the top.

South Asian communities around the globe enjoy various stuffed vegetables and every household uses its own blend of spice mixtures for stuffing. I have cooked stuffed karelas, bhindis, squash, potatoes, and onions in the past and today I am preparing a unique combination of baby eggplants, sweet peppers, and okras. You may choose any other combination for an equally delicious outcome.

For the exotic stuffing, I am sharing a recipe that my dear father mastered many years ago.

INGREDIENTS:

10 fresh small eggplants

1 lb fresh tender okra

6 different-coloured baby sweet peppers

1 tbs fresh ginger root, julienned

2 tbs fresh coriander leaves, chopped

4 tbs cooking oil and 2 tbs clarified butter, mixed

STUFFING:

1 tbs homemade aromatic garam masala

1½ tbs turmeric powder

1 tbs amchoor

1 tbs coriander powder

1 tbs cumin powder

½ tsp green cardamom powder

1 tbs pomegranate seeds, dried and ground

3 tbs onion flakes, dried and crushed

1 tbs fennel seeds, crushed

½ tsp ajwain, coarsely ground

½ tsp garlic paste

1 tsp ginger paste

1 tbs tomato paste

1 tbs cooking oil or butter

Salt and red chili powder to taste

METHOD:

Prepare filling by mixing all stuffing ingredients in saucepan and sautéing for a few minutes on medium-high heat. You may wish to make a larger batch of this filling and use it for stuffing potatoes, onions, and karelas. Filling can be stored in airtight jar in fridge or can be frozen for months and used in the future.

After stuffing is prepared start to prep vegetables. Carefully slit all eggplants to make a little pocket; similarly, slit okra lengthwise, making sure cut forms just a pocket and does not cut through vegetable. Finally, cut slits in peppers lengthwise. Once all vegetables are prepped, stuff them gently in slit cavities with spice mixture.

In shallow frying pan, heat oil mixture and fry stuffed eggplants on medium heat, turning occasionally until evenly cooked. Cover pan to ensure eggplants are fully cooked. Remove eggplants with slotted spoon, place into dish, and set aside.

Add more oil mixture to pan and gently pan-fry okras until cooked. Transfer cooked okra to another dish and set aside. Finally, add remaining oil mixture to pan and cook stuffed peppers for a few minutes until lightly charred.

On serving platter place stuffed eggplants on one side and arrange fried okras around platter. Finally, place charred peppers in middle. Garnish and serve.

Tip: If not serving immediately, cover platter with saran wrap, seal with tin foil, and store in fridge or freezer until serving time. This preparation has an excellent freezer life after cooked. Once ready to serve, pre-heat oven to 375°F and place serving dish on middle rack for about 20 minutes or until fully heated, making sure to remove and discard saran wrap and cover platter with foil. For best results allow veggies to thaw before placing into oven. Once heated, remove foil from dish and garnish with fresh coriander and julienned ginger root. Serve with lachedar parathas or buttered tandoori rotis. For that extra-rich touch, drizzle some warm melted butter over veggies just before serving.

Ultimate Pep Curry

THIS IS A SIMPLE BUT DELICIOUS CURRIED PREPARATION THAT I CALL PEP—"PANEER, EGG, AND PEAS."

INGREDIENTS:

1 lb fresh green peas, shelled

½ lb fresh paneer, cut into ¾" cubes and lightly deep-fried

4 eggs, fully boiled and cut into halves

2 tbs clarified butter

1 tbs vegetable oil

¾ cup onions, diced

1 tsp garlic paste

1 tbs ginger root paste

2 green chilies, finely chopped

1 tsp turmeric powder

1 tsp deggi mirch

1 tsp Kasoori methi

½ tsp cinnamon powder

1 tsp garam masala

1 cup fresh ripe tomatoes, crushed

2 tbs fresh coriander stems, finely chopped

1 cup warm water

Salt to taste

Fresh coriander for garnish

METHOD:

In saucepan heat butter and oil, and add onions and garlic and ginger pastes and sauté until golden brown. Add green chilies, turmeric powder, deggi mirch, Kasoori methi, cinnamon powder, and garam masala and stir mixture well. Next, add crushed tomatoes and coriander stems. Cook for about 4 minutes and then add fresh peas and water. Stir mixture well and add salt. Cover pan and cook for another 10 minutes on medium heat, stirring ocassionally.

Once peas are fully cooked and fat starts to separate from sauce, add fried paneer and halved eggs to pan, gently mix well, and let simmer for a few minutes. Let preparation rest for at least 6 hours before serving, as it will taste better.

Just before serving, heat well and garnish with chopped coriander. Serve with hot buttered naan, lachedar parathas, or garma garam buttered phulkas.

Toor Daal

OTHER THAN THE DAAL SERVED IN THE LANGARS AT SIKH TEMPLES, THIS DAAL HAS TO BE MY FAVOU-rite that I can enjoy at any time of day or night. I have been enjoying this delicacy for decades and do not believe we have made any changes to the original recipe that may have been passed on to our ancestors by our neighbours in Kenya.

INGREDIENTS:

1 cup toor daal, oily or dry

3 cups warm water

1 tomato, finely chopped

1 tsp coriander powder

1 tsp red chili powder

½ tsp turmeric powder

1 tsp garlic, minced

1 tsp ginger, minced

2 tbs lemon juice

1 tbs sugar

Salt to taste

Fresh coriander leaves for garnish

TEMPERING:

2 tbs oil

1 tsp mustard seeds

4 cloves

1 cinnamon stick

6 curry leaves

3 red chilies, dried

1 tsp cumin

2 green chilies, finely chopped

METHOD:

Soak daal for about 30 minutes in warm water. Next, add soaked daal to water in pot and place on high heat, bringing mixture to a boil. Add tomatoes, coriander, chili and turmeric powders, and minced ginger and garlic. Next, add salt and let daal cook for about 30 minutes or until fully cooked and completely blended. Depending upon consistency of daal you prefer, you may add some more hot water to your liking.

Once daal has cooked the final step is tempering. Heat oil in small saucepan and add all tempering ingredients. Let mustard seeds and cumin crackle and cook for 1 minute or so, ensuring ingredients do not burn. Immediately add tempering mixture to cooked daal and combine well. Next, add lemon juice and sugar, check seasoning, and make any necessary adjustments. Let daal simmer for about 10 minutes. Finally, garnish with fresh coriander leaves and serve piping hot with plain boiled rice or enjoy as a soup.

Vegetarian Frittata

FRITTATA IS AN EGG-BASED DISH SIMILAR TO AN OMELETTE OR QUICHE, ENRICHED WITH ADDITIONAL ingredients such as meat, cheese, vegetables, or pasta. It may be flavoured with herbs. This preparation makes an excellent addition to your brunch or lunch.

INGREDIENTS:

1 tbs butter

1 cup mushrooms, sliced

1 cup green or red bell peppers, chopped

1 cup hash browns, partially cooked

1 cup onions, chopped

6 cherry tomatoes, halved

2 sprigs green onion, finely chopped

1 tbs Parmesan cheese

1 cup Swiss cheese, grated

½ cup Panko bread crumbs

8 eggs, well beaten

Salt and pepper to taste

Seasoning and herbs of choice

½ cup milk

1 green chili, finely chopped

Fresh coriander, chopped, for garnish

METHOD:

In frying pan over medium heat melt butter and add mushrooms, onions, peppers, chili, and hash browns and sauté mixture until tender.

Lightly butter large ovenproof dish for frittata, or butter individual dishes. Add vegetable mixture to dish(es) and place cherry tomatoes on top. In large bowl break eggs, beat them with hand mixer, and add Parmesan and Swiss cheeses and seasoning of your liking along with salt and pepper. If you like herbs you may add chopped basil, rosemary, or marjoram. Next, add Panko bread crumbs and gently mix. Fill dish three-quarters full with egg mixture and place into pre-heated oven at 350°F for about 20 minutes. Make sure egg is fully cooked but not overdone, otherwise it will become dry.

Once frittata is perfectly baked, garnish with chopped spring onions and coriander. Serve hot as wedges or in individual dishes.

VEGETARIAN FRITTATA

TIRAMISU

Desserts

Badami Mango Kulfi

JUST AS GELATO IS TO ITALIANS, KULFI IS TO INDIANS ALL OVER THE GLOBE. THIS ICE CREAM IS MADE in aluminum molds shaped like cones and each cone is served individually. The secret for a good kulfi is the milk reduction on slow heat with the right ingredients. The most common kinds are pistachio, almond, and saffron, but these days kulfi makers are being bold and creating all kinds of exotic flavours like fig, passion fruit, apple custard, kiwi, key lime, cappuccino, and margarita. The following recipe is my favourite and has always been a hit at our get-togethers.

INGREDIENTS:

9 cups whole milk

1 cup full cream

1 cup sweet mango pulp

1 tsp green cardamom powder

¼ cup blanched pistachios, finely sliced

¼ cup blanched almonds, finely sliced

1½ cups sugar

¼ tsp saffron strands

METHOD:

In heavy-bottomed pot add milk, cream, and sugar. Bring mixture to a boil, stir well, and let simmer on medium heat, stirring occasionally until mixture is reduced to one-third. It should be thick and creamy. Now add mango pulp, cardamom, pistachio, almonds, and saffron strands and stir well. Cook mixture for about 5 minutes. Remove pot from heat and allow to cool to room temperature. If you have kulfi moulds, spoon mixture into moulds. Tightly cover with caps or tin foil and freeze overnight. If you do not have moulds, you may freeze mixture in plastic container with airtight lid. Serve individually with scoop and garnish with sprinkling of crushed nuts. I usually serve this kulfi on a thin slice of sweet pineapple soaked in syrup infused with cardamom powder.

Gajrella

THIS IS A POPULAR DESSERT ALL OVER INDIA, OFTEN SERVED AT MOST FESTIVALS, AND IS FAIRLY well liked among both adults and children. Originally it contained carrots, milk, sugar, and ghee, but nowadays includes many other ingredients like almonds, pistachios, cardamom, khoya, paneer, and even rose water or kewda flavourings.

If my memory serves me, this was one of the first Indian desserts I tasted as a young lad in Kenya. Over the years, having tried gajrella at several festivals, in many homes, and in different cities across the globe, I am somewhat biased about this delicacy and very strongly believe my mother makes it best. I must stress, however, that if you want to master this recipe, please follow the sequence exactly and take no shortcuts. This is an excellent dessert to end any classic Indian meal.

INGREDIENTS:

1 kg carrots, grated

4 cups whole milk

1 tsp green cardamom seeds, coarsely ground

4 tbs almond flakes

3 tbs pistachios, chopped

200 gm clarified butter or ghee

100 gm khoya, grated

1 cup sugar

METHOD:

In heavy-bottomed pot bring milk with cardamom seeds to a boil and immediately add grated carrots. Cook mixture on medium heat, stirring constantly until milk has thickened and almost evaporated. Make sure to gently stir mixture constantly so it does not scorch. Once all milk has dried up, add clarified butter or ghee and continue to cook carrots in butter until all moisture is gone and carrots turn golden brown. Next, add sugar and mix well. Gently add nuts and mix. Finally, turn heat off and mix in khoya. Transfer gajrella to shallow serving dish and garnish with a few almond flakes and some chopped pistachios or blanched cashews.

Paneer Barfi

BARFI IS A POPULAR INDIAN DESSERT SERVED AT MOST AUSPICIOUS OCCASIONS. THIS FUDGE-LIKE sweetmeat is made with various ingredients and the results are always delicious. Long ago when I first tasted barfi, it was made with besan and nuts. Later I tried barfi made with coconut, lentils, khoya, and chocolate. Paneer barfi has always been my favourite and this particular recipe comes from my better half's collection.

INGREDIENTS:

1 lb paneer, grated

½ cup unsalted butter

¾ cup granulated sugar

½ tsp green cardamom seeds, crushed

3 cups powdered milk

¼ cup blanched almond flakes

¼ cup pistachio, finely chopped

1 pinch saffron

METHOD:

In saucepan melt butter and add grated paneer. Mix well and cook on medium heat for about 10 minutes, constantly stirring and ensuring that paneer does not get stuck to bottom of pan. Add sugar and cardamom seeds and mix well. Cook mixture for another 5 minutes until it starts to form a nice, silky paste. Gradually add powdered milk, almonds, and pistachios. Mix all ingredients well and cook for another 5 minutes. Finally, dissolve 1 pinch saffron in 1 tbs warm milk and add to mixture, mixing well. Pour mixture onto buttered 8"x10" cookie sheet. Let barfi cool at room temperature and cut it with sharp knife into desired shape and size. This barfi can be refrigerated for 1 month.

Thai-Style Bananas With Ice Cream

A GOOD THAI MEAL WARRANTS AN EXOTIC DESSERT TO FINISH THE FEAST. USUALLY, AN ARRAY OF fresh tropical fruits does great justice to finishing off any meal. The following dessert is an exception, a simple yet an elegant manner of serving bananas the Thai way. I have enjoyed this dessert in two different preparations, one where the bananas were deep-fried, coated in a light batter and served with coconut milk. Obviously, my preference is the following recipe and I'll let you be the judge.

INGREDIENTS:

¼ cup unsalted butter

1 tbs ginger root, grated

1 tbs orange rind, finely sliced

6 bananas

¼ cup orange-flavoured liqueur

3 tbs coconut, shredded, lightly toasted, and browned

Lime rounds, thinly sliced, for garnish

Vanilla, ginger, or coconut ice cream

METHOD:

In heated frying pan melt butter and add ginger and orange rind. Stir-fry for about 30 seconds. Peel bananas and slice lengthwise. If bananas are large you may wish to cut them into halves. Place bananas cut side down in butter sauce and cook for 2 minutes. Gently shake pan to allow sauce to coat bananas well. Carefully add orange liqueur to bananas and flambé until flame dies out. Immediately plate bananas and garnish with toasted coconut. Serve bananas with ice cream of choice.

Chiang Mai Pancakes

TRY THESE THAI PANCAKES FOR YOUR NEXT BRUNCH PARTY OR JUST FOR THE FAMILY. I TRIED THESE exotic pancakes filled with tropical fruits in Chiang Mai, a resort town in Thailand. This was very similar to the waffles that we used to eat in Kenya.

INGREDIENTS FOR BATTER:

1 cup plain all-purpose flour

1 whole egg, plus 1 yolk

1 pinch salt

½ pint coconut milk

3 tbs vegetable oil

Clarified butter or vegetable oil for frying

INGREDIENTS FOR FILLING:

1 cup fresh papaya, cut into bite-sized pieces

1 banana, peeled and cut

2 tbs lime juice

2 passion fruit pulps

6 lychees, peeled, pitted, and coarsely chopped

1 large mango, peeled and cut

2 tbs honey

2 cups whipped cream, chilled

Fresh mint leaves for garnish

METHOD:

Make pancake batter by sifting flour into bowl and adding salt, eggs, and a little coconut milk and gently mixing. Gradually add remaining milk and beat to make a smooth batter. Add oil and mix well. Cover bowl and chill for at least 30 minutes. For filling combine all fruits, juice, and honey in bowl, mix well, and set aside. Heat a little butter or oil in crepe maker or frying pan and add enough batter to cover a 6" base. Tilt pan to spread batter thinly and evenly to form a nice, round circle. Cook pancake until just set and underside has lightly browned. Flip pancake and briefly cook other side. Remove from pan and keep warm. Repeat process to use up remaining batter. You should be able to make a total of 8 pancakes. To serve, place each pancake onto dinner plate, spoon a little fruit mixture along centre of pancake, and using both hands roll into a cone shape. Have 2 cones per serving. Serve stuffed pancakes immediately garnished with a blob of whipped cream and a couple of fresh mint leaves.

Motichoor Ke Ladoo

THESE ARE SWEET BALLS PREPARED WITH FINE BOONDI, A SNACK FOOD MADE OF BESAN BATTER
fried in clarified butter or ghee and then soaked in sugar syrup and formed into ladoos.

INGREDIENTS FOR BOONDI:

2 cups besan, sifted

1 cup water

Clarified butter for frying

INGREDIENTS FOR SYRUP:

3 cups granulated sugar

2 cups water

1 tbs green cardamom seeds, coarsely ground

1 tsp kewda water

INGREDIENTS FOR GARNISH:

½ cup almonds, sliced

6 sheets silver leaves

METHOD:

To prepare syrup, in large pot bring 3 cups water to a boil and add sugar, ground cardamom seeds, and kewda water. Mix well and cook for about 10 minutes. Then turn heat down to low and let syrup simmer. It should not be too thick.

To prepare boondi batter, in large mixing bowl place sifted besan and slowly add water, mixing into a smooth, thick batter.

To fry boondi, depending on the kind of ladoos you want to make, use appropriate spatula with desired hole size. In wok add clarified butter and heat to medium. Next, place spatula over wok, gently pour batter on it, and let droplets fall into heated butter. These droplets form into boondi. Fry boondi until it stops sizzling and make sure not to overfry. Using a cleaner spatula remove cooked boondi from wok, drain well, and add to cooked syrup. Continue process until all boondi is fried and added to syrup. Mix gently. Now add almonds to mixture and combine well. Let mixture sit until warm but manageable enough to form balls. Do not allow to cool. Gently take enough boondi mixture in hands to make each ball the size of a golf ball, pressing it hard between palms and squeezing out any extra syrup. Roll gently to form neat balls. Place finished ladoos on serving platter and garnish with silver leaves. Let ladoos sit for a few hours before serving.

Shahi Kheer

THIS POPULAR RICE PUDDING IS OFTEN SERVED AS A DESSERT AT TEMPLES AND GURDWARAS. I remember my father used to cook gallons of this dessert for the congregation during festive occasions at the Sikh temples in Nairobi. I used to watch him cook and the following is an adaptation of his recipe.

INGREDIENTS:

1 cup long-grain rice, basmati recommended

6 cups whole milk

2 tbs blanched almond flakes

2 tbs pistachios, chopped

1 tsp cardamom powder

1 pinch saffron

2 tsp raisins

2 tbs fresh coconut, grated

1 cup granulated sugar

METHOD:

Wash rice and soak in hot water for 1 hour. In heavy-bottomed pot bring milk to a boil and then add drained rice with cardamom powder. Reduce heat and simmer until rice is cooked, constantly stirring to keep rice from sticking to bottom of pot. Add nuts, raisins, and saffron and stir well. Add sugar and simmer, stirring constantly until milk thickens and rice is fully cooked. If rice is not fully cooked and blended with milk you may add more milk. For best rich and creamy results add some full cream or whipping cream. Serve rice pudding warm or chilled.

Gulab Jamun

A DELICATE ROSE-FLAVOURED DEEP-FRIED MILK BALL DELIGHT IN SUGAR SYRUP, GULAB JAMUN IS one of the most popular Indian desserts enjoyed by all ages. Every Indian restaurant worldwide has this dessert on the menu. It is served either warm or cold, has a fairly long fridge life, and can be easily frozen in an airtight container without the syrup.

INGREDIENTS:

1½ cups khoya

½ cup full cream

4 tbs all-purpose flour

½ tsp green cardamom seeds

3 drops rose water

¼ tsp sodium bicarbonate

4 cups sugar

2 cups water

1 pinch orange colour

Clarified butter for deep-frying

METHOD:

In wide mixing bowl add khoya and cream and mix well. Dissolve soda in 1 tsp water. Add mixture along with flour to khoya and knead mixture into smooth, soft, dough-like consistency. Divide dough into 24 balls and smoothen balls by rolling gently between palms. Place balls in shallow dish and cover with moist cheesecloth. In saucepan add sugar and water and mix well. Bring mixture to a boil and then add cardamom and colour. Cook syrup for about 10 minutes on medium-high heat until syrup thickens a little and turns golden brown.

Add rose water to syrup and leave on low heat, covering pan. In the meantime heat butter in wok to medium and gently slide balls, a few at a time, into butter, stirring gently until they rise to the surface and float freely. As soon as balls evenly turn golden brown, remove with slotted spoon, drain fat, and immediately immerse in syrup. Balls should remain immersed in syrup for at least 1 hour before serving. Serve in individual dishes along with some syrup. Often this dessert is garnished with silver leaves.

Tropical Fruit In Ginger Sauce

THIS SALAD BRINGS BACK FOND MEMORIES OF THE SEA ALONG THE COASTAL CITIES OF KENYA. I recall enjoying raahra meat luncheons after spending hours swimming in the white sand beaches of Bamburi, near Mombasa. This fruit salad was always served as a dessert to finish off the picnic meal.

INGREDIENTS FOR SAUCE:

3 tbs fresh ginger root, peeled and finely chopped

¼ cup granulated sugar

1 cup water

1 tbs lime rind

2 tbs lime juice

4 tbs ginger wine or marmalade, whisked

INGREDIENTS FOR SALAD:

1 fresh ripe pineapple, cored, peeled, and cut into bite-sized pieces

1 papaya, peeled, deseeded, and cut into bite-sized pieces

1 can lychees, drained

2 passion fruits, halved and pulp removed

4 kiwi fruits, peeled and sliced

2 large mangoes, peeled, destoned, and diced

2 bananas, peeled and sliced

1 litre ginger or vanilla ice cream

½ cup fresh coconut, grated

METHOD:

Place all sauce ingredients except wine in small saucepan and bring to a boil. Turn heat down and simmer mixture for a few minutes. Remove pan from heat and let cool. Strain cooled sauce in large glass serving bowl and add ginger wine or marmalade. Now add all salad fruits into

bowl and mix well with ginger sauce. Cover with plastic wrap and chill for a few hours. Into individual fruit cups, scoop 1 small ball ice cream. Spoon chilled fruit over ice cream and garnish with fresh grated coconut.

Mango Ice Cream Parfait

THIS IS A SUCCULENT, SILKY-SMOOTH PARFAIT THAT IS SERVED STRAIGHT FROM THE FREEZER WITH freshly sliced sweet mangoes. You may want to serve crisp biscuits or glaze the parfait top with passion fruit liqueur to add additional colour and flair.

INGREDIENTS:

2 large ripe mangoes

2 tbs fresh lime juice

2 tbs granulated sugar

¼ tsp green cardamom seed powder

4 egg yolks

4 oz icing sugar

½ litre whipping cream

¼ cup almond flakes, toasted

Fresh sweet mango slices

Ripe pomegranate seeds

Crisp biscuits for garnish (optional)

Passion fruit sauce for garnish (optional)

METHOD:

Peel mangoes and slice flesh away from stones. Put flesh into food processor and puree with lime juice and granulated sugar. Beat egg yolks with icing sugar until mixture is pale and thick. Then gently fold it into mango puree. Add cardamom powder and mix well. In chilled bowl beat whipped cream until it thickens and stands with soft peaks. Do not overbeat cream, otherwise you'll end up with butter. Now gently fold whipped cream into mango mixture with chilled metal spoon. Add toasted almonds and mix well. Pour mixture into freezerproof dessert or parfait cups and place in freezer for at least 5 hours. Serve parfait straight from freezer, and garnish with fresh mango slices and pomegranate seeds.

Tiramisu

TIRAMISU IS A FAIRLY POPULAR DESSERT THAT IS ENJOYED BY MANY ALL OVER THE WORLD. Interestingly, however, few are aware of its origin. It only started to appear in books from 1980 on.

I had this dessert about two decades ago and found it too rich for my palate. When a few years back I was challenged to prepare it, my efforts resulted in a total disaster. My stubbornness took over, though, and I continued my attempts until I was fully satisfied with the results, which I share here. Please be forewarned that this dessert is very rich, so if you are counting calories it is not for you. Nevertheless, once in a while a little indulgence can't hurt.

INGREDIENTS:

10 egg yolks

1 cup white sugar

½ cup milk

½ tsp vanilla extract

1 lb mascarpone cheese

2 cups whipping cream

1 cup strong brewed coffee, cooled

2 tbs rum

2 tbs coffee liqueur of choice

48 ladyfinger cookies

36 Ferrero Rocher chocolates

½ cup bittersweet chocolate shavings for garnish

METHOD:

In medium saucepan, whisk together egg yolks and sugar until well blended. Whisk in milk and cook in double boiler over low heat, stirring constantly until mixture turns a silky-smooth pale colour. Remove pan from heat and let cool. In chilled medium bowl, beat whipping cream with vanilla until stiff peaks form. Next, gently whisk mascarpone cheese into yolk mixture until smooth. Fold whipped cream into cheese and egg yolk mixture. In small bowl, combine coffee, rum, and coffee liqueur. Gently soak ladyfingers individually in coffee mixture for a few seconds. Letting ladyfingers soak too long will cause them to fall apart. Place soaked ladyfinger layer on bottom of glass dessert bowl, breaking them in half if necessary to fit on bottom. Then line side of dish with soaked ladyfingers all around bowl.

Spread one-third of mascarpone mixture over bottom ladyfinger layer. Next, crumble half of Rocher chocolates evenly over cheese mixture and then spread another one-third of cheese mixture over chocolate. You may wish to use fruit of choice instead of chocolate. Repeat laying remaining soaked ladyfingers and spreading remaining cheese mixture. Finally, cut Rochers carefully into halves and garnish edge of dessert with them all around. To finish off preparation, sprinkle top with chocolate shavings. Cover tiramisu with plastic wrap and refrigerate for at least 3 to 8 hours before serving.

Trifle

TRIFLE IS A DESSERT DISH MADE FROM THICK CUSTARD, FRUIT, SPONGE CAKE, FRUIT JUICE OR JELLY, and whipped cream. These ingredients are usually arranged in layers.

While some people consider the inclusion of jelly to be a recent variation, the earliest known recipe to include jelly dates as far back as 1747. Some trifles contain a small amount of alcohol such as port, or, most commonly, sweet sherry or Madeira wine. Non-alcoholic versions may use sweet juices or soft drinks such as ginger ale instead, as the liquid is necessary to moisten the dry cake layers. One popular trifle variant has the sponge soaked in jelly when the trifle is made, which sets when refrigerated. The egg and jelly bind together and produce a pleasant texture if made in the correct proportions.

The following is a version that our family has always used and is a hit.

INGREDIENTS:

1 pkg raspberry or strawberry Swiss cake roll

1 large pkg Jell-O, any flavour of choice

1 can ambrosia or Devonshire custard

1 large can chunky mixed tropical fruit, drained

1 small tub whipping cream

1 pkt Whip it Cream Stabilizer

1 large can peaches, sliced and drained

1 cup fresh strawberries, halved

1 cup blackberries

2 large kiwi fruit, peeled and sliced

¼ cup almond slices, toasted (optional)

METHOD:

Make Jell-O as per instructions and chill. In colander drain tropical fruits and separately drain sliced peaches. Wash berries and slice kiwi fruit.

Whip cream in chilled bowl with stabilizer and refrigerate. Now cut Swiss rolls about ¼" thick and start lining a large, deep bowl, starting with base layer and going around bowl all the way up to the top. Leave about ¾" clear around rim at the top. You may want to moisten cake with drained juice from fruit to make it stick around bowl. You may also use alcohol of choice to lightly soak bottom layer of cake. Now add half of fruit on top of bottom layer. Next, add Jell-O, cut into cubes.

On top of Jell-O, pour custard and then top it with remaining fruit. Neatly cover fruit with chilled whipped cream. Place 1 layer of halved strawberries neatly around the rim on top. In the middle garnish trifle with sliced peaches and kiwi fruit or any other attractive fresh fruit of choice; mango slices are amazing. Finally, place blackberries around rim of bowl.

Trifle should be placed in fridge to chill for at least 4 hours before serving. Garnish with toasted almonds just before serving. Fresh pineapple is another option to substitute for garnish and add colour. Pomegranate seeds or fresh passion fruit are additional exotic alternatives.

Viking Lychees

THIS EXQUISITE SWEET AND SHARP DELIGHT IS AN EXCELLENT WAY TO FINISH OFF A THAI OR AN Indian dinner. The ingredients in this creation cool and soothe the taste buds after a good spicy meal. By blending the fruit from Thailand, ginger from Kenya, cream from Europe, and nuts from India, this is an excellent example of a fusion creation, thus the name "Viking Lychees."

INGREDIENTS:

1 500-gm can lychees, fully drained

Filling:

125 gm cream cheese

2 tbs ginger syrup

1 tbs crystallized ginger, finely chopped

½ tsp fresh ginger root, ground

2 tbs almonds, toasted and julienned

METHOD:

Drain lychees thoroughly and chill them until firm while you prepare filling. With fork mash cream cheese until soft and then add ginger syrup, crystallized ginger, and fresh ginger. Mix well. With small teaspoon fill centre of lychees to top and place back into fridge to chill. It is extremely important that lychees be chilled well; they

must be served fairly cold. Just before serving, arrange fruit on serving platter and garnish by sticking 2 toasted almond sticks into each lychee to make it look like a Viking head. Do not place fruit in fridge with almond sticks, as almonds will lose crispness. Please note that 500 gm of lychees yields about 25 pieces.

Sharife Ki Kulfi

THIS IS A CUSTARD APPLE KULFI DELIGHT.

INGREDIENTS:

3 cups whole milk

1 cup whipping cream

½ cup canned condensed milk, sweetened

½ tsp green cardamom seed powder

2 tbs corn flour

2 cups fresh custard apple pulp, seedless

Sugar to taste

METHOD:

In heavy-bottomed pot boil milk, stirring constantly until thick and creamy. Remove pot from heat and cool completely. Whisk in whipping cream and condensed milk. In small cup combine cardamom powder with corn flour and 2 tbs cold milk and mix well. Add mixture to pot and mix in custard apple pulp. Taste mixture for sugar and make any necessary adjustments. Chill for about 30 minutes. Pour mixture into mould and freeze. When mixture is half frozen, pull out of freezer and churn mixture fully to break up any icicles. Place mould back into freezer until fully frozen. Serve as desired.

Badami Halwa

THIS IS A RICH ALMOND DELIGHT GARNISHED WITH SAFFRON AND PISTACHIOS.

INGREDIENTS:

2½ cups blanched almonds, skinless

1 cup clarified butter

1 cup milk

½ tsp green cardamom seed powder

¾ cup fine sugar powder

1 pinch saffron

2 tbs blanched pistachios, chopped

METHOD:

Blend skinless blanched almonds coarsely. Heat butter in shallow pan and add almonds and cardamom powder. Mix all ingredients well and stir-fry on low heat until golden brown. Stir in milk and sugar. Bring milk to a quick boil, constantly stirring, then reduce heat to medium and cook until milk has reduced to half. Remove pan from heat and pour halwa into serving platter. Garnish with chopped pistachios and saffron strands. Serve piping hot as a sweet snack with afternoon tea or as dessert.

Kesari Balushahis

BALUSHAHI IS A SWEET INDIAN DELICACY, FAIRLY POPULAR NOT ONLY IN INDIA, NEPAL, AND Pakistan but also very common in the UK, Africa, and the Americas. This delicacy is often compared to Western doughnuts. It is soft on the inside and slightly crispy on the outside, and is a preferred South Indian sweet served during marriages and other important festivals, especially Diwali.

INGREDIENTS:

250 gm maida flour

¼ tsp baking powder

1 pinch sodium bicarbonate

125 gm curd

150 gm water

¼ tsp green cardamom powder

250 gm sugar

¼ tsp saffron

50 gm butter

Vegetable oil for frying

Nuts of choice for garnish

METHOD:

In bowl, mix flour, baking powder, and sodium bicarbonate, and then slowly start adding butter. Using hands mix well. Next, add curds and mix dough well. Set aside and cover bowl with moist cloth for about 15 minutes. After 15 minutes take dough and form small round balls the size of a golf ball and punch a hole into middle with finger. Place balls in dish and cover with moist cloth. In saucepan add sugar, cardamom powder, and water and bring to a boil. Let simmer until it reaches a one-string consistency. Next, mix saffron in small quantity of water and add to syrup. Keep syrup warm. In wok heat oil and gently add balls, slightly flattened. Deep-fry them on slow or medium flame until golden brown. Add fried balls to sugar syrup and let soak for about 5 to 8 minutes. Drain balushahis and place onto serving dish. Garnish with coarsely ground nuts of choice and serve.

MOTICHOOR KE LADOO

CPSIA information can be obtained
at www.ICGtesting.com
Printed in the USA
LVOW05s2135300116

472933LV00019B/154/P